THE  TIMES

T0364485

LIVES LESS ORDINARY

Published by Times Books
An imprint of HarperCollins Publishers
Westerhill Road
Bishopbriggs
Glasgow G64 2QT

HarperCollins Publishers
Macken House
39/40 Mayor Street Upper
Dublin 1, D01 C9W8, Ireland

Hardback edition 2022
Paperback edition 2023

ISBN 978-0-00-863707-1

10 9 8 7 6 5 4 3 2

© This compilation Times Media Ltd 2023

The Times® is a registered trademark of Times Media Ltd

The Publishers acknowledge that views around what is acceptable language are continually changing. However the language, style and format of the obituaries in this book have not been amended from when they originally appeared in the newspaper and should be read in that context.

A catalogue record for this book is available from the British Library.

Typeset by Davidson Publishing Solutions

Printed in the UK using 100% Renewable Electricity at CPI Group (UK) Ltd

Our thanks and acknowledgements go to Robin Ashton and Joanne Lovey at News Licensing and, in particular, at The Times, Ian Brunskill and, at HarperCollins, Harley Griffiths, Evangeline Sellers, Kevin Robbins, Rachel Weaver and Evelyn Sword.

If you would like to comment on any aspect of this book, please contact us at the above address or online.
e-mail: times.books@harpercollins.co.uk
www.timesbooks.co.uk

THE ✦ TIMES

LIVES LESS ORDINARY

OBITUARIES OF THE ECCENTRIC,
UNIQUE AND UNDEFINABLE

EDITED BY NIGEL FARNDALE

TIMES BOOKS

CONTENTS

INTRODUCTION

If you are one of those peculiar people who like to turn to the obituaries first, take comfort in the thought that you are not alone. Newspaper readership surveys and focus groups suggest you may even be in a majority. And perhaps wanting to start your day by reading the obits first is not so strange, when you think about it. They are, after all, portraits of extraordinary lives – short biographies of people who made an impact, one way or another.

Far from being gloomy or morbid they are often life affirming and entertaining, too, full of colour, felicities and, more often than you would imagine, kindly humour. And in a world of social media snippets, they are not only "long-form", as we nowadays like to say when we mean "long", but they also have a satisfying narrative arc, with pleasing cadences and a natural, cradle-to-grave, beginning, middle and end.

As the obituaries editor of *The Times*, I encourage our team of writers to weave a spell and draw upon anecdote and illuminating personal detail to tell the story of a life, give insight into character and assess whether the subject of the obituary was right or wrong in the handling of their public affairs. We try to make our obits not only a cool mixture of fact and assessment but also deadpan in style and gently subversive. They should also be detached – hence they are not signed – and written with a certain literary swagger, but also alive to human frailty, conveying a mood in prose that is attractive and dispassionate, sympathetic rather than sentimental.

Although most *Times* obits are of the great and the good – the First Sea Lords, the Nobel Prize winners, the archbishops – they do not have to be. Sometimes they are of the bad, such as a mafia boss or City fraudster, or at least the wayward – a philandering footballer or a drug-fuelled, hedonistic rock star. You will meet some of them in this collection.

When we have a big name, such as a Stephen Hawking, David Bowie or Muhammad Ali, we will run only one obit, weighing in at around 3,000 words. But most days we have three, at shorter lengths, and because over the course of a year that adds up to more than a thousand obits, it is easy to lose track and forget some of the quirky, less well-known ones who ought not to be forgotten.

The eighty "lives less ordinary" here are mostly of them. And they date back to 2016, the slightly random time frame chosen because that was when I joined *The Times* and started, as an aide-memoire, keeping a list of the obit subjects who made me smile, or gasp. These were usually the eccentrics, rogues and mavericks who saw the world in different colours and marched to the beat of their own drum – the ones, in other words, who made the readers' eyes light up.

The term eccentric is often used as a synonym for charismatic or whimsical, which is why no one really minds being called it. The English especially pride themselves on their eccentricity, even though, almost by definition, anyone who calls themself an eccentric cannot be one. That is the curious thing: true eccentrics never think that their behaviour is eccentric.

The dictionary tells us that an eccentric is someone who deviates from the conventional or established norm. Literally, the word means off-centre, or outside the circle. Clearly though, there is more to it than that. According to Dr David Weeks, a clinical neuropsychologist who wrote a definitive study on this subject, eccentrics tend to be unembarrassable and have the sort of buoyant positivism that comes from being comfortable in their own skin. They are often possessed of a mischievous sense of humour, are opinionated, quixotic and impulsive – and they are wont to find unconventional solutions to problems. They tend to be gifted, intelligent and capable of extreme creativity, too, thanks to what Freud called their looseness of repression. Simon Norton, a maths genius with a passion for bus timetables, was a good example of this. He appears in these pages, chuckling not at the world but with it.

Eccentrics, being unconcerned with conformity and generally happier than most people, are naturally much less prone to stress and, so, tend to live longer. They also often have healthy libidos, such as James Wharram, also featured here, who spent his days sailing around the world with a harem of women, or the bohemian Eve Babitz, who wrote an insouciant and impish memoir about her many sexual conquests. There is also Zsa Zsa Gábor, she of the nine husbands. As we say in the opening line of her obit: "Provided that you were not married to Zsa Zsa Gábor – and many people were – she could be a lot of fun."

Among my other favourites are Baroness Trumpington, the codebreaking, chainsmoking, two-finger-flicking grande dame of British politics, Rod Temperton, the former fish filleter from Cleethorpes who made millions from writing hits such as *Thriller* for Michael Jackson, but eschewed fame, and Professor James Campbell, the Oxford don who was so absent-minded he nearly set himself on fire one day when he put a lit pipe in his jacket pocket. And let us not forget the wonderfully singular Earl of St Germans, who ran the Port Eliot rock festival, delighted in idleness and claimed he could barely read or write.

Some of the obit subjects featured here I knew personally – the reliably controversial philosopher Sir Roger Scruton, the bloody-minded co-founder of *Private Eye* Christopher Booker, and the socialite and gender reassignment pioneer April Ashley. Usually though, our first "encounter" with the subject we are writing about is when we talk to their family and friends – and sometimes their enemies – or when we are given access to their often unpublished memoirs, diaries and letters. In one strange case reprinted here I felt the subject, Clive Nicholls QC, was helping me with his own obit from beyond the grave. I talked to his identical twin Colin, who was also a QC, and asked him what his brother was like. "Well," he said, "he was just like me. We even sounded the same on the phone."

Most of the obits collected here are affectionate in tone, but not all. It is tempting to confer sainthoods on the recently departed, out of respect, but obituaries should be balanced accounts that are lively and irreverent, not bland hagiographies that only serve to diminish the memory of the subject. They should include character flaws as well as strengths, professional failures as well as successes. If someone was pompous, vain or prickly (or for that matter a spiv, pseud or charlatan) we like to reflect that. A little scuttlebutt can add to the flavour too.

One obit that stands out in this regard is the one of Sir Jeremiah Harman, the "rude, lazy, short-tempered, unpredictable" judge known in legal circles as "Harman the Horrible". If his notoriety bothered him, Harman never showed it. Indeed, he seemed to relish his waspish reputation. A member of his family got in touch after our obit appeared to say she thought we got him spot on.

What I enjoy about the obituary as a genre is that the casting is so unpredictable, with people from all walks of life rubbing shoulders on the page – a dotty dowager sharing column inches with a war veteran, a cross-dressing Venezuelan cabaret artist with a cabinet minister. I also like that it combines two of my favourite subjects, modern history – our job as recording angels is to deposit into the cultural memory three remarkable lives each day – and philosophy. For obits, by their nature, have meaning and profundity. They mark the moment where life comes full circle. And even though the general cause of death is always the same – birth – we try and give the specific cause. On one occasion I heard a colleague who had been struggling to find it out all afternoon, exclaim to a caller on the phone: "Arterial aneurism, that's brilliant!"

Long-form obituaries are unique to the quality press – social media platforms, TV news channels and tabloids don't seem to get the conceit. In the case of *The Times*, they date back to the mid 19th century. Other newspaper departments may come and go, as fashion dictates, but obituaries remain an enigmatic constant. Perhaps it is to do with their poignancy and what they reveal about the human condition. In a thousand words or so they encapsulate the tragedy and comedy of fully lived lives, as well as the array of ambitions, self-deceptions, vices, prejudices, loves and fears, that we all manage to cram into our allotted and decidedly finite time.

A story that has entered Fleet Street folklore may help explain this state of affairs. Back in the days of hot metal typesetting and inky fingers, a recruit was being given a tour of *The Times* editorial floor. The party came to a curious door which was opened with the words "And this is obituaries". There, before a blazing fire, were two men smoking pipes and playing chess, but since no one seemed to know what else to say, the door was simply closed on the mystery.

Nigel Farndale

LIVES LESS ORDINARY

SPLIT WATERMAN

———————————— ● ————————————

Glamorous if roguish speedway racer whose daredevil lifestyle led to
him mixing with the Krays and serving time for smuggling gold

Few opponents could catch Split Waterman, one of the finest motorcycle speedway racers of his generation, on two wheels. He later made headlines for a ride to East Sussex in a Triumph Herald car when he was stopped from boarding a ferry to France and customs officials made a dramatic discovery.

The daredevil streak that had served Waterman so well on the track was put to more dubious use after his retirement from speedway, as a judge at the Old Bailey observed when Waterman was sentenced to four years' imprisonment for smuggling gold and guns.

"You were a man by character prepared to face danger and to take risks, a gun-runner in Africa, and a man with the quick, decisive mind of the speedway rider," Sir Carl Aarvold, recorder of London, told him at the conclusion of the trial in 1968.

Waterman and his fiancée, Avril Priston, had sought to travel from Newhaven to Dieppe, but were under observation by police. Forensics officers found almost 790 ounces of gold, then worth about £10,000, expertly concealed in the chassis of the car.

The prosecution contended that the gold was part of a haul worth £711,000 that was snatched in east London the previous year during the robbery of a bullion van belonging to NM Rothschild & Sons that contained 140 gold bars. The court heard that Waterman, described by police as "a freelance arms dealer between Belgium and Africa", had bought two furnaces to smelt the gold.

Waterman pleaded guilty to receiving the stolen gold and unlawfully attempting to export it, and admitted illegally possessing two sub-machineguns, two rifles, three pistols and ammunition, as well as dies that could be used to make coins. Priston, a dressmaker from Bedfordshire, was sentenced to six months in prison for her part in the scheme.

Waterman's name cropped up in a sensational trial later in 1968, when Ronald and Reginald Kray and two others appeared at Bow Street magistrates' court, charged with conspiracy to murder.

Paul Elvey, a would-be hitman for the twins who became a witness for the prosecution after he was arrested at Glasgow airport carrying sticks of gelignite, claimed that Waterman made an attaché case that was fitted with a hypodermic syringe loaded with hydrogen cyanide. This was so that Elvey might inconspicuously murder a nightclub owner named George Caruana – inside the Old Bailey, of all places – by swinging the case against his legs to inject the poison.

"He claimed that in a hotel room Mr Waterman demonstrated the effectiveness of the device by first jabbing it into a soft armchair and then into his own legs several times," *The Times* reported. Another witness alleged that he saw Waterman sell three machineguns to the Krays outside a cinema.

Squire Francis Waterman was born in 1923 in New Malden, southwest London. His father was a printer; an uncle raced a motorcycle at the now-defunct Crystal Palace circuit in the 1920s. Waterman was a toolmaker's apprentice before his wartime service in the Royal Fusiliers. In 1944 he took part in one of the bloodiest episodes in the Italian campaign, the Battle of Monte Cassino, and killed a German paratrooper. After suffering shrapnel wounds, he was transferred away from the front line to the Royal Electrical and Mechanical Engineers.

"They put up a notice asking for people who could ride motorcycles, so I put my name down," he said, according to *Speedway Star* magazine. "We did a hundred-mile road race from Naples and I won it, more by luck than judgment, then we started speedway in a running stadium. And I started winning things there."

He became known as Split after a set of poorly stitched leathers came apart during a race, earning him the nickname "split arse". He was later posted to Germany, where his commanding officer had served with Major Alec Jackson, the manager of the Wembley Lions club, and arranged an introduction.

After the war, Waterman became a star on the all-conquering Wembley team, despite accidentally writing off Jackson's new Vauxhall car in a crash while driving a Hudson Terraplane coupé. In 1948 he won the prestigious London Riders' Championship and was described in a report in *Speedway Express* as a "cheeky, cheery, devil-may-care" character who raced "like a bolt out of the blue". A documentary film about the Lions dubbed him a "genial gagster".

Speedway was hugely popular in postwar Britain, with the Lions capable of attracting crowds in excess of 60,000 and London having five top-level tracks. In 1950 he switched to the Harringay Racers for a then-record transfer fee of £3,000 (the equivalent today of more than £100,000).

He was unfortunate not to win an individual world title, finishing as a runner-up in 1951 and 1953, and appeared for England in 30 test matches, captaining his country in a series against Australia in 1953.

He met his future wife in 1949 at the ice rink at what became known as Wembley Arena. Her father was a friend of Sir Arthur Elvin, the businessman who bought Wembley Stadium in 1927 and added a speedway track two years later. After his release from prison, Waterman and Avril, who survives him, married in 1970 at Caxton Hall register office, Westminster, and emigrated to the Costa del Sol later that decade.

Waterman had the looks and magnetism of a Hollywood star and the couple moved in glamorous circles in their heyday; among their friends was the actor Stewart Granger, who married the actress Jean Simmons, and was one of the most recognizable British leading men of the 1940s and 1950s.

Waterman was well known enough to be the face of a cigarette advertisement in 1952 that riffed on his fearless approach: "But when I smoke – I'm careful." His popularity with the public, if not the authorities, was underlined during an inquiry held by the sport's governing body after he walked out of a meeting (for which he was handed a severe reprimand) at West Ham that year in protest at the controversial award of a race to a rival whose tactics forced Waterman off his machine.

A half-dozen fans protested outside the venue, the Royal Automobile Club on Pall Mall, wearing sandwich boards that demanded "Fair Play for Split Waterman".

Unsurprisingly, given his riding style and the inherent dangers of the sport, Waterman was no stranger to injuries. In 1952 a crash at Odsal Stadium in Bradford, West Yorkshire, fractured a knee so severely that surgeons considered amputating his leg. He recovered and raced for a number of clubs after Harringay folded in 1954. After he retired in 1962, he went into the fabrication business: sheet metal-working and making plastic injection moulds for companies including Airfix.

In the 1970s he spent time in an Italian prison for possession of counterfeit Spanish pesetas worth nearly half a million pounds. This came to light during a 1978 trial at the Old Bailey of two alleged forgers, one of whom reportedly told British police that Waterman "said he wanted enough forged pesetas to bring down the Franco government".

On a visit from Spain for the annual dinner dance of the Veteran (now World) Speedway Riders' Association in Coventry in 2002, *The Guardian* found Waterman "second in the toasts only to the Queen" and noted that "his charisma at 79, in tinted aviators and royal-blue cummerbund, was still enough to send multitudes of septuagenarians sprinting to the top table, autograph books in hand". His racing prowess was not the only topic of conversation. "I smuggled gold! smuggled guns! Zambia, Rhodesia, the jungle," he declared.

Waterman reflected that when his speedway career faded, so did his prospects of escaping the attention of the police. "The people who worked at Wembley were ex-Old Bill," he said in a book, *Speedway:*

The Greatest Moments. "And that's how I used to get out of trouble. What sort of trouble? You name it, I've done it."

Split Waterman, speedway racer and smuggler, was born on July 27, 1923. He died on October 8, 2019, aged 96

THE EARL OF ST GERMANS

———————•———————

Aristocrat by birth and hippy by temperament who established the
eclectic Port Eliot festival but was beset by family tragedy

The 10th Earl of St Germans claimed to delight in idleness, recording his recreational interests in *Who's Who* as "mucking about" – more economical, perhaps, than his father's "huntin' the slipper, shootin' a line and fishin' for compliments".

Rude remarks seemed to trip off his tongue, such as in 1996 when he declined a request for an interview from Jane Procter, then editor of *Tatler*, saying: "I would rather spend the time of day with suppurating scum-sucking plague-pit ghouls than pass a single instant with a member of your staff." The piece appeared anyway. Other times he was merely politically incorrect, declaring that his preferred choice of music albums were those "that feature Black girls and violins".

Behind the laid-back approach, Peregrine Eliot – aristocrat by birth, hippy by temperament – was also a shrewd entrepreneur. He presided over the 6,000-acre Port Eliot estate on the Tamar estuary in Cornwall "like Aslan after an acid trip", according to *The Sunday Times*, and it was there that he hosted the counterculture Elephant Fayre of the 1980s.

After a locals' revolt and a long hiatus, he remodelled it as the more hipster Port Eliot festival, an eclectic celebration of literature, film, music and outdoor activities.

He described how the Elephant Fayre, which took its name from the pachyderm on the family crest, was first "cobbled together by some enthusiastic amateurs" in 1981 with the intention that it "was not going to be another rock show". The first one lost money, but the next two years featured bands such as Siouxsie and the Banshees and the Cure alongside the jugglers, magicians and storytellers, drawing huge crowds.

No one had heard of health and safety, he claimed. "We built a rickety pier into the middle of the wide river with a wobbly café at the end. Nobody fell in and nothing collapsed." Among the acts were "two jugglers called Boris and Norris dressed as medieval serfs who juggled with livers and hearts and live rats". An officious security guard patrolled the site ordering people to put out joints: "What stopped him from being taken seriously was that the dog at the end of the lead was dead." A giant wooden elephant gazed silently over the proceedings.

Soon the fayre was attracting unwelcome hippy "peace convoys", culminating in 1986 with the arrival of 100 vehicles and leading to open drug use, a mass of litter, burglaries and graffiti sprayed across the walls of Port Eliot. The earl was forced to let the fayre go.

He tried to get a permit for a rave in 1993 but was opposed by villagers and a district council still haunted by memories of plundered allotments. Instead, in 2003 the Port Eliot festival emerged. *The Times* awarded last year's a five-star review, citing its "fashion shows, literary readings, beekeeping courses, a branch of Fortnum & Mason and even that triumph of bourgeois life: clean toilets" – a far cry from the infamous "long drop" facilities of Elephant Fayre days.

The earl described his love for festivals as "a bit like herpes", adding: "Once you've done it ... there's an 18-year gap and the itch starts again." Yet he was anxious that Port Eliot should not be too highbrow, soon removing its literary tag. "I mean, I can barely read or write," he told *The Sunday Times* in 2009. "And 20 minutes of a guy reading from a book, then taking dumb questions from the floor, ain't rock'n'roll baby."

Peregrine Nicholas Eliot was born in 1941 into a family that, riddled as it was with lunacy, suicide and internecine division, did little to advance the cause of the hereditary principle. The 5th Earl's heir, Edward, killed himself during a village cricket match and was only found when he failed to come on to bowl; the 6th Earl, John, fell during a point-to-point race near Totnes and died soon afterwards; and the 7th Earl, Graville, ended his days in a mental hospital drawing rude appendages on to pictures of public figures in magazines.

Eliot's father, a tall, cadaverous and hedonistic dandy, was referred to as Old Nic; after moving to Tangier as a tax exile in 1962 he became known as the Tangerine Earl, taking as his telegraphic address Earls Court. He had divorced Eliot's mother Helen (née Villiers) shortly before his departure.

The young "Perry" and his sister Frances (later Countess of Shelburne) were entrusted to the care of their grandfather – the 8th

Earl, Montagu, a barrister once described as having "all the stiffness of a poker but none of its occasional warmth" and whose approach to child raising was to treat the youngsters as dogs, patting them on the head and whistling at them. His grandmother, to whom he was particularly close, killed herself in 1962. He was educated at Eton where, he recalled, "I failed quite spectacularly, even with the assistance of the birch, to take advantage of some of the best teachers in the land." He left early and spent time in Paris, New York and London.

At the start of the sixties, he was fêted as one of Britain's most eligible bachelors. He rode to Tangier on a souped-up 21-year-old Harley-Davidson named Veronique to visit his father and took part in an expedition to the Atlas Mountains in search of a Cornish chough, a bird that had been wiped out in Britain. He drove the hippy trail to Afghanistan and India in a VW Beetle, claimed to have traversed the Himalayas barefoot and walked from Port Eliot to London on a whim. "We were carefree adolescent boys and girls scampering about like rabbits and young lions," he reflected.

An astute conjurer, he toured America with his magic show but ended up in hospital in Vancouver with respiratory problems, where he was kept awake by chanting squaws entertaining a Native American chief.

For a time he lent his name to a company called Seltaeb (Beatles spelt backwards), which held the merchandising rights to Fab Four memorabilia, but the venture ended in the courts, leaving him out of pocket. He inherited the earldom in 1988 and seven years later caused a stir by selling the family's prized Rembrandt (*Daniel and Cyrus Before the Idol Bel*), the last in private hands, to the Getty Museum for £5 million.

He had an energetic private life and would present all his female companions with bottles of Fracas perfume. In 1964 he married Jacquetta Lampson, a raven-haired nude muse to Lucian Freud and daughter of Lord Killearn, who was British ambassador to Egypt from 1936 to 1946.

They had two sons: Jago became a Spanish surfing champion but he had a history of drug abuse and died in 2006 after suffering an epileptic fit in the bath; Louis is a musician who has played with bands such as Kinky Machine and Rialto and has also curated the Port Eliot festival. While they were married Jacquetta had another son, who now styles himself Freddie Freud and who trained as a whirling dervish. The earldom passes to Jago's son, Albie, aged 11.

The marriage was dissolved and in 1992 he married Elizabeth "Dizzy Lizzy" Williams, a photographic student who had once lived in a squat. His sister acerbically described her as "not good enough", while the first Countess of St Germans said of her successor: "It's not fair to describe her as working class because as far as I know she has never worked." Villagers wore T-shirts bearing the slogan: "It was better with Jacquetta." The couple separated after 18 months.

He was dating Emma Hope, a shoe designer, when Cathy Wilson, a journalist some 30 years his junior, visited as a guest of his son. They were married in 2005 and she soon became the driving force behind the Port Eliot festival, smoothing out his rougher edges. She survives him. Despite her best efforts, her husband could still be blunt to the point of being rude. He once told photographers he could not understand why they needed 45 minutes when the camera shutter would click in a 100th of a second. On another occasion he was taken to an industrial tribunal by Teresa Triscott, a housekeeper who had been sacked after rows over the distance she had to carry heavy trays and the amount of polishing the silverware required. She won a token payment in compensation.

He professed to have little idea about the domestic workings of the house, claiming to visit the kitchen no more than two or three times a year. "In it, and in the interests of household economy, I would hope to find the leftovers from several previous meals," he said. His principal source of entertainment was the internet: "I like trawling obscure radio stations, reading the rantings of bloggers and watching YouTube."

The earl's lifelong love was his estate, part of which dates from the tenth century and was acquired by the family after the dissolution of the monasteries by Henry VIII; the family had lived there in what *Tatler* described as "splendid and bizarre isolation" since 1564. The vast pile was once described as "having 11 staircases, 82 chimneys and a dining room 110 yards from the kitchen, which accommodates … a steam-driven cherry stoner".

He also enjoyed his motorcycles, scooters and quad bikes – the latter exaggerated, some said, by an equally abiding hatred of horses, which he referred to as "dangerous at both ends".

He also maintained a web page purporting to be written by his pet whippet, Roo, who slept every night on the end of the earl's bed. "The other day, the hunt came for a lawn meet," wrote Roo. "Can you believe it, there were 38 other dogs."

Heathcote Williams, the poet, actor and playwright, once turned up at Port Eliot for a weekend but stayed for eight years. The earl would send him memos along the lines of: "Time for your yearly bath, we can smell you in the front hall." Another long-time retainer was Robert Lenkiewicz, the artist who had faked his own death in 1981 and for a decade worked on a mural at the house; he died in 2002, leaving an embalmed tramp among his possessions.

Despite his unconventional and chaotic household, Eliot – who would style himself in letters to his local newspaper as "The Village Eliot" – could be relied upon to lunch at exactly 1pm and dine, with equal punctuality, at 8pm.

The 10th Earl of St Germans, landowner, was born on January 2, 1941. He died of cancer on July 15, 2016, aged 75

BARONESS TRUMPINGTON

●

Codebreaking, chainsmoking, two-finger-flicking grande dame of British politics whose sense of mischief coloured everything in her long and distinguished career

Baroness Trumpington was more than just a junior minister in the governments of Margaret Thatcher and John Major from 1983 to 1997. She was also a record-breaker and a character. By 1992, at 70, she was already the oldest female minister to have served. As a female peer she was an imposing figure: 6ft tall and with a deep stentorian voice – interlocutors on the phone thought it was a man on the other end – she spoke with authority and wit at the dispatch box.

In her eighties she became a minor celebrity and loved it. She was named "Oldie of the Year" in 2012 by *The Oldie* magazine and she played up to her caricature as a plain-speaking woman, who, in her own words, did "not give a damn". At the age of 89 she was caught on camera giving a two-fingered reproof to Lord (Tom) King of Bridgwater who had remarked on old-looking survivors of the Second World War and, turning in her direction, said: "… as my noble friend, the baroness, reminds me." The film went viral. "His family say he is famous now," she reflected drily when asked about the incident.

On an official visit to Outer Mongolia she was photographed riding a camel. Her aides, who treasured her, had the picture doctored so that she had a cigarette in one hand and a bottle of whisky in the other. She resembled a huge Margaret Rutherford playing the female head in *The Happiest Days of Your Life*. As a minister in Major's beleaguered government, she once emerged from her office and danced along the corridor singing, "There may be trouble ahead."

When she appeared on the BBC panel show *Have I Got News for You* she was the oldest guest to have been on the programme. Shown a film clip of Boris Johnson, she grimaced at the suggestion that she was looking at the next Tory leader and exclaimed: "God!" On *Desert Island Discs* she chose as her luxury item the Crown Jewels, "because somebody would come to look for me".

She was born Jean Alys Campbell-Harris in 1922, the daughter of Arthur Edward Campbell-Harris, MC, and his American wife, Doris (née Robson). Her father served with the Bengal Lancers and was aide de camp to the viceroy of India. The Robson wealth meant that she |was brought up in some affluence, with nannies and servants and meals at the Ritz or the Dorchester. Educated privately in England and France, she left school having never sat an exam. Her two brothers went to Eton.

For the first two years of the war, she was employed as a cheerful, hard-working and elegant land girl on the Sussex farm of the former prime minister David Lloyd George, who was also a family friend. Helped by her command of French and German and her family connections, she was recruited to work on naval intelligence for the Foreign Office at Bletchley Park. There she worked for Alan Turing, the father of computer science, who killed himself in 1954. In 2013 she added her signature to an appeal to David Cameron calling on him to overturn Turing's 1952 conviction for homosexuality.

After the war ended, she worked for three years for the European Central Inland Transport Organisation in London and Paris, and was later the secretary for two years to Viscount Hinchingbrooke, the Conservative MP for Southeast Dorset. In 1954 she married a schoolmaster, William Alan Barker. He was successively a teacher at Eton, a don at Queens' College, Cambridge, and a headmaster, first of the Leys School, Cambridge, then of University College School, Hampstead. At her husband's final speech day at the Leys she failed to curb her sense of fun and desire to be noticed and jumped fully clothed into the swimming pool in front of pupils and parents. Her outraged spouse (she always called him "Barker") did not speak to her for three weeks.

She suffered from the fairly blatant prejudice against women shown by certain local Conservative party selection committees and was never selected as a parliamentary candidate, despite being interviewed for a shortlisting in two seats. When asked by a selector in the Isle of Ely ("a godforsaken part of the world") why there were so few women MPs – and aware that she would not be chosen – she replied: "Because of selection committees like you."

Yet she was not lost to politics. She became a city councillor in Cambridge in 1963 and a county councillor for the Trumpington ward in Cambridge ten years later. When she was ennobled, Major asked why she had chosen the title Trumpington. She replied that she had known only two places well: "One was called Trumpington and the other was called Six Mile Bottom. Which one would you have chosen?"

Trumpington was the mayor of Cambridge in 1971, as well as serving as a JP, on the board of visitors of Pentonville Prison and a member of the air transport users' committee. When she was elected to an honorary fellowship by Lucy Cavendish College, Cambridge, she was already a significant figure in the politics and life of the city.

In 1980 she became a life peer and quickly made a mark in the House of Lords, successfully sponsoring a bill for relaxing the restrictions on shop opening hours. She thought that shopkeepers should have the right to decide for themselves when to open. She became a government whip in 1983, with remits for the Home Office, the Department of Health and Social Security, and the Foreign and Commonwealth Office. In 1985 she was appointed as a junior minister in Health and Social Security and two years later moved to the Ministry of Agriculture, Fisheries and Food.

When she went to a health farm with friends, more for the company than the regime, officials visited with her red box and an important document on top. Underneath were cakes, biscuits, chocolates and miniatures. She kept the last, but returned the rest "to resist temptation". Although a health minister she continued to smoke until she was 79.

Trumpington was not an expert in technicalities of the sometimes dry and complicated subjects for which her departments had responsibility. She therefore generally relied on briefings from officials. Yet the factual information she received from civil servants, often on subjects that appeared stodgy and indigestible, was presented to the House of Lords spiced with her own rare blend of humour, common sense and occasional cock-ups.

When opening the second reading debate on a seemingly dreary piece of legislation, Trumpington provoked laughter by inviting their lordships to fasten their seatbelts while she took them on a magical mystery tour of the Social Security Bill. Few could have matched her comic timing in announcing that a pilot scheme to prevent the fouling of pavements by dogs was to be tested in the borough of Barking. Even in exchanges on inherently serious subjects such as the prevention of the spread of AIDS she managed to introduce humour, without seeming merely flippant. She defended explicit adverts in the campaign against the disease.

She was well liked for her sense of fun and plain speaking, always gilded with an upper-class accent. In her 90th year she was still active in the Lords, regarding it as "family". Members listened to her interventions respectfully, recognizing her age, experience and commitment to public service. Colleagues forgave her publicity-seeking and journalists loved her for providing copy. Of the fuss being made of her memoir, *Coming Up Trumps*, in 2014, she said: "I don't understand all this excitement. I didn't write the damn book, and I haven't read it either."

By the time she retired in 2017 Trumpington was an institution, but her "retirement" did not last long. On December 29, 2017 she was a guest editor of the *Today* programme on Radio 4. One of her chosen topics was: should brothels be legalised?

She had a wide range of interests outside politics. She followed horse racing and was a local steward of Folkestone Racecourse. Other recreations included bridge, collecting antiques, and needlepoint. Her husband had died in 1988. She is survived by her son, Adam, a lawyer who became her political secretary.

Former colleagues will miss such "Trumpington"-like interventions as her interruption of a boring speech by a lord of appeal when she declared that if anyone wanted "a pee you should go now". On another occasion she was invited by a magazine editor to a lunch where Nicholas Soames praised Virginia Bottomley as "one of the chaps". The editor found this offensive and said that a woman cannot be a chap. Trumpington took the cigarette out of her mouth, put down her gin and simply said: "Balls."

Baroness Trumpington, politician, was born on October 23, 1922. She died on November 26, 2018, aged 96

STUART CHRISTIE

———————— • ————————

Scottish anarchist who set off on a mission to assassinate General
Franco after being made politically active by his grandmother

The only way that Stuart Christie was able to carry plastic explosives into Spain was beneath the thick woolly jumper that his grandmother had knitted to protect him from the biting Clydeside winds. "My body was improbably misshapen," he explained of his mission to assassinate the Spanish dictator General Franco. "At the risk of understatement, I looked out of place on the Mediterranean coast in August."

The kilt he was also wearing did not help, though he denied the subsequent reports that he had been hiding the explosives under it, rather than the jumper. One Argentinian newspaper described him as a "Scottish transvestite".

Christie was 18 and a committed anarchist when in 1964 he set off from the Scottish mining village of Blantyre, part of Red Clydeside, whose men had fought against fascism in the Spanish Civil War of 1936 to 1939. He claimed to have been inspired by reports of striking Spanish miners who were trying to organise themselves into trade unions.

Bizarrely, en route to Spain, he stopped off in London to be interviewed by Malcolm Muggeridge, a former MI6 officer, for the BBC Two programme *Let Me Speak*. When asked if he thought it would be morally right for Franco to be assassinated, Christie answered that it would, although those words were edited out when the programme was broadcast.

From Paris, where he used the only French he knew – "zut alors!" – as he collected a package containing explosives from an anarchist contact, Christie hitchhiked to Madrid to meet another contact at an American Express office. He planned to detonate his device when Franco visited the Real Madrid football stadium. There he was arrested at gunpoint by police, who had been lying in wait. He told them that he thought he was carrying leaflets.

While awaiting trial he was shown photographs of himself at Hyde Park Corner in London, which convinced him that the British authorities were collaborating with the Spanish. He was convicted in a military court of "banditry and terrorism" and, according to some reports, faced execution by garrotte. In the event he was jailed for 20 years.

After three years at the notorious Carabanchel Prison in Madrid, during which he passed A levels in Spanish and English, he was freed by the Franco regime, which had ceded to public and political protests led by Bertrand Russell and Jean-Paul Sartre. The Spanish authorities claimed it was his mother's "dignified" letters to Franco, in which she asked for clemency, that swung it.

He had been well treated, he said. "I had expected to be buried in a subterranean tunnel with water up to my neck, but it was nothing like that," he told Reuters as he left the British embassy in Madrid.

Stuart Christie was born in Partick, Glasgow, in 1946, the son of a hard-drinking trawlerman who quickly disappeared. He was raised in Blantyre by Olive, his hairdresser mother, and his grandmother, who had been in service all her life and to whom he attributed his political awareness, naming his wry autobiography *Granny Made Me an Anarchist* (2004). "She gave me a clear moral map and inculcated in me an inerasable ethical code – a sort of secular Calvinism – which led me directly and inexorably through the political and ethical quagmire to anarchism."

He was educated at Calder Street School, Blantyre, and became an apprentice dental technician. His social education in the Scouts came to an end when he accidentally lobbed a stone at the car of a magistrate, who denounced him as a "young anarchist". Keen to find out what this meant, he became involved in groups such as the Young Socialists, the Campaign for Nuclear Disarmament and the Anarchist Federation. In February 1963 he joined a protest outside Faslane naval base. The following year he set off on his fateful trip to Spain because, he said, "like George Orwell in 1936, it seemed the only conceivable thing to do".

After being freed in 1967, Christie settled in Camden, north London, working as a gas board foreman. He remained involved in anarchist groups, helping to form the Notting Hill branch of the Anarchist Black Cross movement and founded the *Black Flag* newspaper. In September 1968 he represented the British federation at the International Congress of Anarchists at Massa Carrara, Italy.

Before long Christie had been visited by police looking for explosive substances. Instead they found imitation dollar bills, for which he received a two-year suspended sentence.

On Bastille Day 1968 he met Brenda Earl, a teacher who had been involved in the student occupation of Hornsey College of Art. They had a daughter, Branwen, who became an actress. He wrote that she was also committed to the anti-Francoist cause, which brought her to the attention of the intelligence services, "as did her role as a co-founder, with me, of the anarchist publishing house Cienfuegos Press".

Christie was arrested again in 1971 as one of the Stoke Newington Eight, suspected of being involved with the Angry Brigade, a far-left group behind a series of bomb attacks targeting Edward Heath's government. For 18 months he was held in Brixton prison, where Brenda visited almost daily. Eventually a jury at the Old Bailey cleared him of possessing guns and explosives after he insisted that they had been planted by the police.

After the kidnapping of a Francoist banker in Paris in 1974 he and Brenda were visited at their flat in Wimbledon by a Special Branch officer who advised them to leave London. They moved to Honley, West Yorkshire, before settling on Sanday in Orkney. During this time he was involved in left-wing publishing enterprises, many of which ran out of money.

Stuart Christie, anarchist, was born on July 10, 1946. He died of undisclosed causes on August 15, 2020, aged 74

GREG LAKE

Virtuoso guitarist, songwriter and epitome of 1970s prog-rock excess who could only play when standing on his own £6,000 Persian rug

Greg Lake (middle) with bandmates, Emerson and Palmer at Heathrow airport in 1974.

When Emerson, Lake & Palmer toured America in 1977, it took 11 trailers to transport their gear from show to show. Their entourage included a 70-strong orchestra, two accountants, a doctor, a hairdresser, the drummer Carl Palmer's personal karate trainer and a crew of 63 roadies, one of whom was employed solely to transport, maintain, clean and sweep the £6,000 Persian rug that the group's singer and bass player, Greg Lake, insisted on standing upon during performances.

In fairness, the carpet, which had been imported from the holy city of Qum in Iran, had some practical purpose in reducing the risk of on-stage electrocution. However, the rug and Lake's employment of his own "carpet roadie" came to symbolise the worst excesses of "prog rock" and helped to make ELP the most deplored of the "dinosaur" bands excoriated by the nascent punk movement for their pomposity.

At the time ELP were one of the most commercially successful bands of the decade, tax exiles who were selling millions of copies of albums with titles such as *Tarkus* and *Brain Salad Surgery*, full of technically dazzling music and symphonic ambition. In total the group sold almost 50 million records, but the overweening extravagance of that 1977 tour turned into a disaster that hastened the end of the band's career. "We're risking everything we ever made and everything we're ever likely to make on this tour," Lake said before they set out. "I'm talking about our families, our possessions, everything. We'll have to sell our houses in England if it flops."

As the self-indulgence and the costs escalated, the orchestra was sacked and a set of stripped-down concerts were hastily arranged to recoup some of the losses. In the end, Lake didn't have to sell his house, but after a rock folly of such gargantuan proportions there was no way back into the hearts of increasingly cynical fans.

Amid howls of derision from the punk hordes, ELP made one more album and broke up. The infamous rug was retired to Lake's living room. In the eyes of the critics and the scene, "progressive" had become a dirty word synonymous with pretension – and ELP were almost universally regarded as the worst offenders. "I suppose it was a kind of rolling madhouse," Lake admitted many years later.

If prog rock brought about its own fall from grace through hubris, the backlash was also rather unfair. A powerful singer and an intelligent and gifted songwriter, much of the music Lake made first with the prog-rock pioneers King Crimson and then with ELP was imaginative and groundbreaking.

He was blessed with a felicitous pop touch, heard to best effect on his solo hit single *I Believe in Father Christmas*, which made number two in the charts in 1975 and has, along with offerings from Slade and Cliff Richard, become something of a seasonal blight in every shopping centre in the land ever since. Ironically Lake wrote the song as a protest against the commercialisation of Christmas. "It was quite bewildering to see it going up the charts," he said. "It's a bit like Blake's *Jerusalem*. It attaches itself somehow to this English spirit of restrained joy."

Amiable and articulate, his appetite for rock stardom declined markedly in later years. "To be honest I've not felt inspired for a very long time. How can you follow playing Madison Square Garden six times in a row? You can't," he admitted in 2012.

Never one of rock's wild men – "we weren't one of those bands

44

hurling TVs out the window", he once noted – he survived most of the pitfalls of the rock lifestyle and sought his kicks via more refined pursuits. He cited Copland and Prokofiev among his musical influences and was an avid collector of antiquarian books. His private library included numerous valuable first editions and two volumes that once belonged to Marie Antoinette.

He was married to Regina, who is a sculptor, for more than 40 years. She survives him along with their daughter, Natasha. The family remained close, Natasha and her husband living in Kew and Lake and his wife in nearby Richmond Hill, where the presence of Mick Jagger and Pete Townshend as neighbours led him to muse that the area had become "a rock'n'roll graveyard".

He was born Gregory Stuart Lake in 1947 in Poole, Dorset and spent his early years living in what he described as an "asbestos prefab". His father was an engineer, his mother a housewife. His grandfather had been a jockey who once rode in the Grand National.

Falling under the spell of the first rock'n'roll records in the mid-1950s, he learnt to play the guitar at the age of 12, sharing a teacher with two other Dorset boys who would become celebrated guitarists, Robert Fripp, with whom he would form King Crimson, and Andy Summers of the Police.

By his teens he was playing in bands at local clubs and pubs while studying at college to become a draughtsman. Late-night gigs led to him falling asleep at the drawing board: "Eventually they asked, 'What do you want to be, a draughtsman or a musician?' It wasn't a hard choice."

In late 1968 Fripp summoned him to London and asked him to join a new band he was assembling called King Crimson. The group's impact on the emerging "underground" scene was immediate – within months of their first gig they were playing for 500,000 people supporting the Rolling Stones at a free concert in Hyde Park.

The group's debut album, *In the Court of the Crimson King*, took rock experimentation to a level of invention rivalled at the time only by Pink Floyd. "The music was very fast and syncopated or it could be beautiful and symphonic," he recalled. The album made number five in the British charts and is regarded to this day as one of prog rock's defining masterpieces.

However, within a year Lake had left to team up with the keyboard virtuoso Keith Emerson from the Nice and the drummer Carl Palmer from Atomic Rooster in one of the first "supergroups". The band's name consisted of the surnames of its three members, but the cumbersome construction was soon widely initialised as ELP – and might have become HELP had putative talks for Jimi Hendrix to join the group come to fruition.

Greg Lake, rock musician, was born on November 10, 1947. He died from cancer on December 7, 2016, aged 69

THE REV DAVID JOHNSON

Colourful and quixotic rector who liked to write spoof letters, chastise American tourists and make mischief wherever he roamed

The Rev David Johnson was a uniquely troublesome "whisky priest" such as Graham Greene could have conjured, only without the illegitimate child.

Often quite exasperating to know, at times he was as if possessed by a talent that could not be properly channelled and so had fallen into the habit of mischief. The result was that apart from his many speeches, squibs, sketches and skits, his main contribution to literature was *The Spiritual Quest of Francis Wagstaffe* (1994), a funny iteration of the Henry Root letters to a variety of dignitaries in the Church. These lampooned various ecclesiastical trends, as well as individuals and their pretensions.

His personal style resembled that of a 1920s "high and dry churchman" who regularly "went to town". He was, in fact, often high, but almost never dry. The appurtenances of his lifetime of performance art included theatrical pipe-smoking, silk stocks, high starched ("Roman") collars and an array of garments for events requiring clerical morning and evening dress, including stockings ("I have good legs"), buckled shoes, frock coats, shovel hats and straw boaters.

His actual beliefs tended to the Anglo-Catholic, even through the troubled years when the ordination of women was being debated, and he would often warn of the dangers of succumbing to "Roman fever". However, he was thrilled to meet Cardinal Ratzinger, whom he interviewed and thought "really very good news". A convinced Eurosceptic, he would even send out signed copies of Ratzinger's book on the future of Europe with approval.

An inveterate attention-seeker and exhibitionist, as well as a compulsive dresser-up, he was profoundly interested in the superficial, but would say that "the little things would illumine the big".

David William Johnson was born in Ponteland, Newcastle, in 1953, to a civil servant father and Scottish mother, and with a sister to whom he was never close. After attending Dame Allan's School, he went up to Selwyn College, Cambridge, to read divinity. He seemed to think that taking the cloth could open interesting possibilities where vocation rather than background might provide the key to unlock what Evelyn Waugh called "that low door in the wall". He was both ashamed and proud of his northern background, and oblivious of the effect his diminutive stature and stratospherically strangulated way of speaking had on others. He attempted to ascribe the latter to his mother having taught elocution.

His Cambridge years were for him a finishing school, though he never really grew up there. When Archbishop Donald Coggan visited his college, he hung the organ scholar's underwear on a washing line between the chapel towers by way of a greeting. His election to the presidency of the Cambridge Union in 1976 was, nevertheless, his crowning moment. He quickly adapted to the union style and became a scintillating speaker in his own right (though, in truth, a less than rapier-sharp debater). It was for his speaking and his words that he rightly became known.

He would arrest attention, beginning with thunderous countenance and haughty, shatter-glass tones: "Mr President, it is not only a great privilege to be here ... but also ... highly inconvenient."

Another gambit was apparently to read out a portentous message of greeting and sermonising from a foreign potentate in an impenetrable and totally fabricated tongue: "And Madam President, I think we can all agree that those words are as true today as they ever were!"

Women were regarded as generally getting in the way of his male friendships, with occasional exceptions such as Christine Hamilton and Benazir Bhutto (who would always be breathing "*Ah, Daaaaavid ...*" to him, at least in his fond recollection). He later married not Christine Hamilton, as he claimed to have wished, but Neil and Christine Hamilton.

As an undergraduate he assiduously acquired the habits of intemperance – and his alcohol consumption began an ultimately sad, exponential trajectory that, in the absence of family, career demands or anything else to anchor him, never looked back.

From Cambridge he went to Cuddesdon Theological College to train for the priesthood. On ordination, he moved to London as a curate at St Etheldreda's, Fulham. It was during this time that he produced a satirical edition of *The Church Times*. Coming only months after the excitement of the royal wedding of Prince Charles and Lady Diana Spencer at St Paul's Cathedral, the frontpage of his *Not the Church Times* breathlessly proclaimed the arrival of Graham Leonard to the capital's see and adorned it with a picture of Heinrich Himmler, captioned "London's new Bishop". It amused many but did not go down well in all quarters.

In 1982 he took up a post at Church House as communications secretary to the Church of England board of mission and unity, officially on ecumenical relations. This period, too, soon dissolved into high jinks, which were also indulged at the bohemian Chelsea Arts Club, which he had joined.

During this period he also became a priest-vicar of Westminster Abbey, an honorary position. In this role he would make a point of marching up to unsuspecting American tourists in baseball caps and barking, "Hats off in church!"

He was encouraged in some ways by Sir Derek Pattinson, then secretary-general of the Church of England. He was a key influence on Johnson, acting as establishment father figure manqué, but also something of a lord of misrule. They shared a love of gossip and alcohol.

The Church had perhaps been a route for Johnson to plough his own furrow and make his way in life within a comparatively loose, not overly competitive, structure. It soon became clear that this would never work, in part because the ground had already shifted under him. Inside and outside Church House, the modernising church of the early 1980s was vastly different from that of 1960, or even 1970.

Johnson's church was the church of the Book of Common Prayer, not Common Worship; of livings and squires, and thus of a sense of place; but preferably all with smells and bells and proper Latin cassocks. His politics were almost wholly reactionary, including an array of Monday Club views, though he also had a curious ability to be colour-blind if he thought people interesting and worthwhile. His social or intellectual snobbery could then overcome any tendencies to casual racism.

After Church House, he was given his first parish in 1987, as rector of Gilmorton with Peatling Parva in the Leicester diocese. This was not a success, but took a while to unwind, in slow motion. He later became rector of Cogenhoe, Northamptonshire, in 1991, which was worse. ("Pronounced Cook-no," he would say, "spelt F-u-c-k!")

His parishioners were treated to some extraordinary visitors who were invited to preach, such as Enoch Powell. Typically, his style was to adapt his parish to his conception of how to order things, rather than adopt a more traditional pastoral manner.

He was fortunate in that wherever he was sent he managed to fall under the care of some of the more ostensibly sympathetic bishops. Yet he still alienated them in time, partly due to his inability to see that they were endeavouring to be on his side, but also because he could not help but mock those in authority. He would cross the street to bite the hand that fed, but he never seemed to repent.

In 1994 Johnson's highly amusing ecclesiastical riff on the Henry Root letters to famous men and women was published, co-authored with the Rev Toby Forward, a North Country cleric. This kind of thing did not help his cause, but it gave pleasure and mirth to many clergy and laity up and down the land.

In several memorable conceits, Francis (affecting to be the leader of an Anglican offshoot church) writes to princes of the church asking them to intervene to send him tickets for the royal enclosure at Ascot and royal garden parties, as well as to provide advice to "my nephew, Colin" about sexual matters. In one case, Johnson wrote to the canon of Coventry Cathedral, and adviser on evangelism to the archbishops of Canterbury and York, to ask if it was true that he really had a sofa "with a dip in the middle" due to his sexual exertions before seeing the light.

Another conceit was to try to get the support of the Bishop of Norwich for a new television programme based on *Baywatch*, only to be called *Beach Mission*. "I was a Group Scout Leader for several years … Scouting is not what it was, I regret to say, and there are many petty jealousies which can lead to unpleasant rumours!" The idea, which was not taken up by the bishop, though over several letters Francis insisted that it had been, was that "Young evangelists could patrol the beach in their skimpy costumes, attracting young viewers, then when they had got their interest, they could slam home the gospel message."

Johnson was in unlikely demand during this period as an after-dinner speaker at rugby club events, appearing in full clerical evening dress to unleash a slightly risqué routine laced with the odd, surprising common touch, which was then greeted with delighted, shocked surprise by those present. They were even more shocked when they realised that he was, indeed, not a vaudeville act but a serving priest.

By 1995 Johnson had used up his nine lives for a succession of derelictions and the church authorities decided to retire him with "a house for life" and a pension. He remained "licensed" but his permission to officiate at services was revoked.

In later life he moved to Oxford, seeking perhaps to recreate past glories in a new yet familiar setting, and he became in his fifties dean of the University Conservative Association. To this role he then added that of chaplain at Stringfellows, London.

Johnson was unmarried but not, despite the rumours, ever unfrocked.

The Rev David Johnson was born on December 5, 1953. He died of undisclosed causes on April 22, 2020, aged 66

MARGARITA PRACATAN

Colourful musical entertainer whose regular slot on The Clive James Show *brought new meaning to the word 'extrovert'*

Clive James was flicking through American television channels in New York, only pausing at Channel 69 when he caught sight, and sound, of Margarita Pracatan, a Cuban-exile chanteuse with a middle-of-the-road repertoire who could empty the M25 simply by opening her mouth. "The act was so unintentionally funny," James recalled. "She was more than just a singer. Everything she said and did was original."

Enthralled, James invited Pracatan on to his popular British television show from where in 1994 she burst into the homes of some 7.5 million unsuspecting viewers with an act that was so bad it was good. "He ask me to London. I sink he is crazy," trilled Pracatan in her treacle-thick Cuban accent.

In the studio she was let loose on unsuspecting guests, performing with Boy George, serenading Liza Minnelli or rounding off the programme with a mauling of Lionel Richie's *Hello* ("Ees it me ya looking fer?"). On one occasion she launched a vocal assault on *New York, New York* that would make Frank Sinatra fans weep, while on another she delivered a caterwauling *You Were Always on My Mind* accompanied by James and a bemused Freddie Starr. Gloria Gaynor's *I Will Survive* and Abba's *Mamma Mia* received the Pracatan treatment as the credits rolled.

From the outset Pracatan was a sensation. "Twirling her boas, shaking her spangles, hammering away at the helpless Yamaha, filling the screen to the very edge with her hair extensions, in every sense she was bigger than I was, and by the end of the first season I was a guest on my own show," wrote James in *The Complete Unreliable Memoirs*, describing her as "a yodelling bonanza".

If the voice was loud, so too were the glamorous outfits, a riot of primary colours resembling a tube of Smarties that had been left near an open fire. A matching feather boa was wrapped around her neck and she would be decorated with sequins and a towering wig. Depending on her mood, her false eyelashes might be a vivid green. Feathers were an integral part of her ensemble, with some of them being used to tickle James's balding pate as she admired his "bedroom eyes".

Extrovert was too dull a word for this exuberant songstress, who acquired a cult following among British television audiences. Once on a live discussion show with Ned Sherrin she told her host "I am into you already" before interrupting his reference to her talent with the disarmingly honest: "I don't have talent at all, honey."

Be that as it may, Cillian de Buitléar, James's producer, insisted that she took the business of being an entertainer seriously. "She wasn't messing around, despite her unorthodox time signatures," he said. "There was a certain amount of guessing you had to do when she started doing a cover version of a well-known song in rehearsal, but I suppose you could say she was reinterpreting it."

Off screen Pracatan was just as exuberant, with James recalling her squawking "Darling, I love you" to a passing police officer. Like many Cubans she sat down to dinner at midnight and would still be dancing on the table at dawn. "We had to provide one of our young men to look after her and she was using them up at the rate of one a week," James wrote. "The connection was purely platonic, but the guys had to eat amphetamines to stay with her."

Part of the joy of Pracatan was the way her syntax bore a close resemblance to random words plucked from a dictionary before being mangled through her thick accent. She spoke as she sang, with words tumbling out in such a way that they could be heard, if not always understood. When neither singing nor speaking she was howling with laughter.

The notes may have been flat and the phrasing incomprehensible, but Pracatan was a star. She received a rousing welcome at the Queen Elizabeth Hall and in 1995 sold out her televised show at the Edinburgh Fringe Festival, where she was billed as "Bob Downes meets Jackie Stallone" and her mere presence led to a near riot. Although she needed some hand-holding backstage, she insisted that nerves were never a problem: "The audience, they get nervy ... because they say, 'And what the heck she gonna be doing now?'" As James observed, "She never lets the words or melody get in her way," adding philosophically, "She is us, without the fear of failure."

Juana Margarita Figueroa was born in Santiago de Cuba in 1931, one of eight children of Buenaventura, a union leader in the sugar industry and Juana, his schoolteacher wife, who played the piano. As a child she adored Shirley Temple films and dreamt of living in New York, keeping scrapbooks bulging with pictures of the city cut out from magazines.

At the start of the Cuban revolution in 1953 her father fell foul of the communists and the family fled to Venezuela, though not before Pracatan had been briefly jailed. "They took all my *rrrings*," she said, her pain still evident. Turning up in the US, she made her way to Manhattan in search of fame and fortune. For the rest of her life she lived on the Upper West Side, a couple of blocks from John Lennon's old place, in a rent-controlled one-bedroom apartment that was a riotous celebration of reds, golds and mirrored tiles.

Depending on which version of her story she was telling, Pracatan might once have been a police officer. "I only have to take a knife from someone once and he didn't mind," she declared with pride. Her next career move was selling men's underwear at Saks Fifth Avenue, the department store. "I have to ask, 'What size are you? Is it small, medium or large?'" she would demand of her embarrassed customers.

One was Robert Brading, a second-generation German-American businessman who returned regularly to have his crotch assessed. They married in the early 1970s, but it was quickly dissolved. "He did not speak Spanish and my English was not good," she recalled with a shrug. "Sometimes he'd talk and I didn't understand him, but I say 'Yeah' anyway." She is survived by their daughter, Maria, a teacher.

Pracatan then had a seven-year relationship with a married man, later recalling how she also had emotional tête-à-têtes with his wife. "I said, 'Listen, don't worry, I love him too, but I don't want to get married, you can keep him. I can see him sometimes.'"

She was soon able to afford a Yamaha electric piano but never had a lesson in her life, not on the piano nor on singing. Her stage career began as Miss de Cuba in New York's small and steamy clubs, sometimes only in exchange for a meal, before she rented a video camera and started creating her own public-access cable shows, a form of make-your-own content in the days before YouTube.

It was on one of these that she was spotted by James and his team. At first they played clips of her performances on his show; later they flew her to London to appear in person. She was forever grateful, declaring: "He takes me seriously, and I am so happy that I want to do my 100 per cent."

The stage name Pracatan was, she explained, Cuban-Spanish for "wow". Pressed on the subject by James, she added: "When you do something and it comes out beautiful, you say, 'Prrracataaaan!' Or, when you have sex and it's fantastic, 'Prrracataaaan!'"

She went on to have a self-titled hit CD and was photographed perched on top of the new Daewoo Mya at the 1996 Birmingham Motor Show. There was even a Margarita Pracatan impersonator based in Brighton.

By then, Pracatan had become a gay icon, leading pride parades, headlining at gay nightclubs around the world and achieving success at the Mardi Gras festival in Sydney. On one occasion she was midway through her own inimitable rendition of Stevie Wonder's *I Just Called to Say I Love You* at the Pink Coconut club in Derby when an excited fan threw a gold G-string in her direction. A hail of men's underwear followed. "It was wonderful," she declared.

Her stage persona remained as wild and vivacious as ever: colourful, flamboyant and camp. However, she was indignant to be thought of as anything other than a fully-fledged woman. "These people think I ham transvessie," she told one interviewer. "I ask you, honey!"

Margarita Pracatan, entertainer, was born on June 11, 1931. She died of heart failure on June 23, 2020, aged 89

NAIM ATTALLAH

—————•—————

*Flamboyant publisher and parfumier who gave Nigella Lawson her
first job*

Naim Attallah never seemed to worry about the Fleet Street gossip
that wondered where he had made his millions. He would also meet
with an amused shrug the concerns of analysts who wanted to know
what he was going to do about the plummeting share price of his
jewellery company, Asprey. And he was quite delighted to be called
Naim Utterly-Disgusting by *Private Eye*.

What the enigmatic publisher and parfumier did care about was
loyalty. He demanded it, spoke often of society's need for it and seemed
at times paranoid that he was about to lose it. The demon of betrayal,
the ungrateful kind exacted by friends and beneficiaries, seemed to
him to skulk around every corner of his Soho fiefdom.

He had, it must be said, an individual sense of style, wearing two,
sometimes three watches at once and favouring mismatched socks and
dandyish ties, suits and even kaftans. The peculiarity that drew the
most suspicion, however, was his desire to be in the heart of the
Establishment, particularly the literary establishment.He acquired

Quartet Books in the 1980s and adorned the office with society's daughters: Lulu and Sabrina Guinness, Emma Soames, Georgia de Chamberet, Lady Cressida Ward, Anna Pasternak and Cosima Fry, all of whom he addressed as "beloved". He gave Nigella Lawson her first job.

He swore that they were all just friends of friends, their numbers were necessary and their uniform beauty mere coincidence. As Sophia Waugh, who described herself as one of "Naim's Girls", wrote: "We were young, pretty, had 'names' and we loved parties."

As he had a mild phobia about bodily functions, coughing or sneezing in his offices was said to be forbidden. It was also claimed that he found the thought that any of his "girls" might need to visit the lavatory truly upsetting.

His publishing list was equally picked for image rather than returns. *Conversations with Kafka* by Gustav Janouch was unlikely to become a bestseller, yet he did hit upon some nuggets too, such as Dennis Potter's *Pennies from Heaven*, Julian Barnes's first novel *Metroland* and Elizabeth Wurtzel's *Prozac Nation*. He had also acquired the Women's Press and had supported it through the zenith, and slow death, of feminist fiction, taking credit along the way for Alice Walker's *The Color Purple*.

Film production was another field in which he dabbled, most notably putting up the money to make a full-length film out of Potter's banned play *Brimstone and Treacle* starring Denholm Elliott and Sting. He also branched out into making the fragrances Avant l'Amour and Après l'Amour.

Attallah allowed his ventures, including *The Oldie*, *Literary Review* and its offshoot The Academy Club, to flourish creatively, even if they never did so financially. He no doubt enjoyed the way that Auberon Waugh, the editor of *Literary Review*, never passed up an opportunity to shower him with flowery, if slightly ironic, praise – "the sainted parfumier" and so on. He even let the magazine nominate him, or rather one of the 16 books for which he claimed authorship, for its "bad sex prize".

Born in Haifa, then part of Mandatory Palestine, in 1931, Naim Ibrahim Attallah had developed from childhood a willing dependence on women. His father Ibrahim was domineering, his mother Genevieve was doting and protective, and he was often too sick to avoid being either bullied or coddled. He was educated with his sisters at a convent school but, with partition, Haifa became a violent city and he was relieved to be sent to live with his grandmother in Nazareth.

He would later recall the abuses of British soldiers: being made to stand in a sports ground all day, without water, under the sun as part of a mass punishment for a sniper attack. "I was much relieved when I came here and found that the English were such cultured people," he said. "And that they don't represent the riffraff they send abroad."

He reached these shores in 1949, living with an uncle and studying engineering at Battersea College before taking a series of low-paid jobs, one of which was to slap luminescent paint on the electrical transformers along Battersea Bridge. He spent some time as a bouncer and as a steeplejack, repairing electrical switches. After three years of this he began work in a bank and moved from there to a business in foreign currency exchange.

The details of this phase remain cloudy, giving rise to such investigative works as *The Man from Nowhere: The Mysterious Life of Naim Atallah* (1996) by Frank Dobson and Ken Parrish. For his part the insouciant Attallah was more aggrieved by the refusal of writers and journalists to let him have two Ts as well as two Ls in his name.

In 1957 he married Maria Nykolyn, an interior decorator, after a proposal in a Wandsworth cinema. His eventual acquisition of Asprey – the company that owns Garrard, the crown jeweller – was, he said, partly fired by a walk home in straitened times, during which the young couple saw a bejewelled watch in Asprey's window. He promised her he would one day own it. He did, along with the company.

Although Attallah was an incorrigible flirt, there was never any suggestion that he was unfaithful to Maria. The couple lived in a house with brothel-red walls adorned with photographs of naked Edwardian women. Their son Ramsay is a director at the Namara Group, the umbrella company for Attallah's various business interests.

Precious, overbearing, vain and generous with both his money and his affections, Attallah had, somehow, both an enormous capacity for feeling slighted and an imperviousness to shame. He was willing to ask almost anything in his celebrity interviews, collated into a series of books. Thus he asked Harold Acton if he had ever held a naked woman in his arms; inquired of Enoch Powell "May I call you Eunuch?", and he was the first to accuse Laurens van der Post of making up his desert adventures. His strong accent, guileless demeanour and genuine interest were disarming, and few felt trespassed on by his questions.

In 2004, however, his editor and researcher Jennie Erdal, whose modest, Scottish Presbyterian background contrasted starkly with that of the exotic Attallah, revealed in her book *Ghosting: A Double Life* that she had written just about everything he had put his name to.

Ghosting spoke of the difficulty in writing around his eccentric ideas, such as the two cousins who share each other's orgasms in his novel *Tara and Claire*. When he had ideas for steamy scenes involving what he called "the jig-jig" she was expected to answer his calls at any time of day or night.

Attallah saw Erdal's autobiography as betrayal of the worst kind, compounded by that of journalists willing to believe her. "Et tu, Brute," he wrote to *The Times*'s Valerie Grove. "Betrayal is obviously the norm in the literary world, and I am beginning to question whether my contribution to that sector of the arts over the years has been worth the sacrifice."

After retiring from Asprey in 1996, Attallah struggled to repay a £4 million debt, and he lost interest in *Literary Review* after the death of his friend Auberon Waugh in 2001. He dropped *The Oldie*, too, while the book publishing went into stasis.

To rebut Erdal's claims that he could not write by himself, in 2007 he produced a new volume of memoirs, *Fulfilment and Betrayal 1975–1995*. It related his heyday in full, some might say tortuous, detail.

Erdal's exposé, though acclaimed, did perverse credit to Attallah too. Some critics said that Erdal was only entertaining when discussing him – showing his childish joy, his hilarious vanity, florid hand gestures, thigh-slapping and exuberant enthusiasm for everything he dabbled in. Perhaps, they suggested, the ghostwriter had lost sight of herself by living through someone more interesting.

Naim Attallah CBE, businessman, was born on May 1, 1931. He died in his sleep on February 2, 2021, aged 89

ROD TEMPERTON

———————•———————

Former fish filleter from Cleethorpes who made millions after writing the hit Thriller *for Michael Jackson, but refused to become a celebrity*

Rod Temperton defied every brash tenet of modern celebrity culture by writing some of the biggest-selling songs of all time, including Michael Jackson's "Thriller", while remaining almost totally anonymous.

Although his songwriting made him one of the richest men in the music business, he instructed his publishers not to release any information about him and never gave interviews. Few photographs of him exist in the public domain; he lived reclusively and shunned the limelight – popular music's answer to Howard Hughes or JD Salinger.

Dubbed "The Invisible Man", he remained virtually unknown outside those who read the small print on record labels, where they found "R Temperton" credited as the writer of Jackson's hits *Thriller*, *Off the Wall* and *Rock With You*, as well as a swathe of other funk and R&B classics, including *Boogie Nights*, *Always and Forever* and *Give Me the Night*.

The royalties from such hit songs ensured a luxurious lifestyle. His net worth was estimated at $125 million (£99 million) and he lived on Mulholland Drive in Los Angeles, where neighbours included George Clooney, Jack Nicholson and Bruce Willis. He also had homes in Britain, the south of France and Switzerland and owned an island in Fiji.

Yet he remained stubbornly beneath the radar, a man of strong principles, breaking cover only once – in 2006 – when he agreed to be interviewed for a documentary for BBC Radio 2 about his music. It took the programme-makers four years to persuade him to take part. Inevitably, it was entitled *The Invisible Man*. Many of popular music's greatest names, including Quincy Jones and George Benson, queued up to pay on-air tributes.

Asked about his personal life, he gave little away. "When I've finished a record," he replied, "I sit at home, watch telly, catch up on the news and maybe somebody will phone."

Modest and self-effacing to a fanatical degree, he "disappeared" after the programme was broadcast to sit undisturbed with his wife, Kathy Bucknall, a former record company assistant, in one of their many homes, safe in the knowledge that there were still very few people who really knew the enigmatic Rod Temperton – even though the whole world knew his songs.

Equally surprising was that this titan of Black American soul music, who worked not only with Michael Jackson but also with Aretha Franklin, Donna Summer, George Benson, Chaka Khan and Herbie Hancock, was a former fish factory worker from Cleethorpes with a north of England accent that made him sound uncannily like the politician William Hague. When Jackson toured Britain in 1988, a tabloid newspaper sent reporters to Cleethorpes and what little they were able to glean appeared under the headline "Grimsby fish filleter reels in fortune with Wacko Jacko". Temperton had the cutting framed and hung it on his wall.

Even in his home town it seemed that few knew of the existence of the famous son who refused to be famous. When a producer working on the BBC documentary approached the local council to ask if Cleethorpes had honoured Temperton, the official answer came back, "We think we have heard of the man but there's certainly no kind of civic acknowledgement of him."

His carefully preserved anonymity proved useful when Jackson died in 2009 and a Post-it Note was reportedly found on his mirror on which the singer had scribbled, "Call Temperton". A hue and cry followed as the world's press attempted to track him down. Nobody knew where to find him.

Rodney Lynn Temperton was born in the Lincolnshire town of Cleethorpes in 1949, the son of Les and Ida Temperton, who ran a garage. "My father wasn't the kind of person who'd read you a story before you went to sleep," Temperton said. He used to put a transistor radio on the pillow, and "I'd go to sleep listening to Radio Luxembourg. I think that had an influence." He attended De Aston Grammar School in Market Rasen where his music teacher, Ted Gledhill, encouraged him to form a pop group to enter the school's music competition. In later years he kept in touch with Gledhill, who described his former pupil as "very unassuming", and invited him to spend holidays at his Swiss home.

Temperton played truant from school and set up a snare drum and cymbal in the family's front room while his parents were at work. There he played along to the TV test card, which provided a surprisingly solid grounding, for the continuous background music was varied and eclectic. By the time he left school he was confident that he could play in almost any style.

While filleting fish at the Ross Frozen Foods factory in nearby Grimsby he taught himself to play keyboards and then moved to Germany where he formed a band, playing soul covers on a second-hand Hammond organ in the clubs and bars of Manheim and Frankfurt. After answering a small ad in *Melody Maker* in 1974 he joined the funk/disco group Heatwave, which was led by the Black American singer Johnnie Wilder. "He was the first British guy that I ever met and he spoke funny," Wilder recalled. "He had a good sense of humour and I knew he would fit."

Temperton swiftly became the group's main writer, starting with the disco-flavoured *Boogie Nights*, a top five hit in Britain and America. He followed with the swooning soul ballad *Always and Forever*, later covered by Luther Vandross. "We'd lock him up in a room at the end of a gig and leave him there all night to write," Wilder said.

"I'd sit there until the cleaner let me out at 7am," Temperton said. "Then I'd go back to the hotel and sleep for a few hours before a rehearsal at 2pm and then the gig."

When this punishing routine became too much for him in 1978, he stopped playing live with the group to concentrate on writing. He immediately came up with *The Groove Line*, another top ten hit for Heatwave in America, where the group had caught the ear of the producer Quincy Jones. He had just finished working on the film *The Wiz* with Michael Jackson and was preparing to make the singer's first adult album.

He rang Temperton and asked him if he would consider writing some songs for the record. "I was shocked and flattered," he recalled. "I wrote three songs for Michael and Quincy took them all." The three were *Rock With You*, *Burn This Disco Out* and *Off The Wall*, which became the album's title track. The two men immediately became friends.

"He's from Seattle, I'm from Cleethorpes – where's the meeting of minds?" Temperton asked. "But working in the studio, within an hour it was like we'd known each other since we were kids. We've got the same junkie work ethic. We'd smoke 160 cigarettes a night. People ran from us like we were vampires."

The album went on to sell 20 million copies around the world and established Jackson as "the King of Pop", the biggest-selling solo artist of his generation. The follow-up album was even more successful. "I wrote 35–40 ideas for songs," Temperton said. "From that we picked three to record."

One of them was called "Starlight". Jones liked the tune but was not taken by the title. "You managed to come up with the title of the last album," Jones told the writer. "Do it again."

When Temperton suggested "Midnight Man", the producer told him it was better but still not there. "The next morning I woke up and something in my head said, 'This is the title'. You could visualise it at the top of the Billboard charts. You could see the merchandising for this one word, how it jumped off the page – *Thriller*."

With the recording session imminent, Temperton had little time to come up with the lyrics and was still writing the spoken section for the actor Vincent Price in the back of a cab on the way to the studio. When he arrived, he saw Price getting out of a limousine and instructed his driver to drop him at the back entrance. He thrust his hastily written words into the hands of a secretary and asked her to photocopy them. "I put it on the music stand just as Vincent walked in. He sat down and hit it in two takes."

Thriller went on to become the biggest-selling album ever made. Temperton never needed to work again.

Rod Temperton, songwriter, was born on October 9, 1949. His death from cancer was announced on October 5, 2016. He was 66

MARQUESS OF BATH

Colourful aristocrat known as 'the loins of Longleat'

In June 2011 police were called to Longleat House, the Marquess of Bath's country pile near Warminster, in Wiltshire, to break up a fight: two of the polygamous peer's "wifelets" were arguing over whose turn it was to sleep with him. The eccentric aristocrat boasted of having slept with hundreds of women, known as the "wifelets of Bath", and he immortalised dozens of them in garish papier-mâché portraits that hung, in order of conquest, on the spiral staircase leading to his apartment in his 16th-century ancestral pile.

Alexander Thynn, as the marquess preferred to be known, was a writer, artist, founder of the Wessex Regionalist Party and entrepreneur, who transformed Longleat into one of the most visited stately homes in the country, complete with a safari park whose resident lions gave rise to his nickname, "the loins of Longleat". In his inimitable way, he did much to bolster the arguments of socialists who disapproved of inherited wealth and privilege: eating squirrels from his estate, believing in pantheism and rarely forgoing his turn when a cannabis joint or a line of cocaine was being passed around. There were, indeed, those who resented the licence that his fortune and class allowed him and viewed his way of life as offensively self-indulgent and egotistical.

The harder he fought to avoid conforming to the expectations of his family, the more he conformed to another stereotype – that of the eccentric peer. To meet him was to encounter a man who looked like an off-duty wizard or colourful hippy, with his snow-white beard, crimson crushed-velvet trousers and mauve hooded sweater. Yet behind all this lay a complex and deeply serious man, with an almost obsessive need to explain himself to the world.

He was born Alexander George Thynne in 1932, the third of five children of the sixth marquess and his first wife, Daphne, who was the daughter of Lord Vivian. In 1976 he had the "e" legally removed from the end of his surname so that it would rhyme with "pin" not "pine". His eldest sister, Lady Caroline, married the 11th Duke of Beaufort and died in 1995; an older brother, Thomas, died in infancy; a younger, Christopher, died in 2017; and his youngest brother, Valentine, was found hanged in the Bath Arms, a pub on the estate, in 1979 after a gala evening at Longleat attended by Princess Margaret.

Alexander's relationship with his father was problematic and a large proportion of the Longleat murals, which Bath described as "therapies", are concerned with exorcising the ghosts of his upbringing. He never forgave his father for beating him with a riding crop after he washed his dog in the bathroom at Longleat, which was built by their ancestor Sir John Thynne and set in 9,000 acres on the Wiltshire–Somerset borders, with grounds landscaped by Capability Brown. It has 128 rooms, 365 windows and 99 chimneys.

At Ludgrove preparatory school in Berkshire he distinguished himself by locking the headmaster in his study and forming a fascist society in a vain attempt to please his father, who was a collector of Hitler's paintings. Moving on to Eton he became a member of Pop and keeper of boxing, though contemporaries remembered him as being "straight up-and-down".

Viscount Weymouth, as he then was, read philosophy, politics and economics at Christ Church, Oxford, where his beliefs began to form, though his social life remained that of the typical young aristocrat and he was president of the Bullingdon Club, a boisterous dining club whose members wear tailored tailcoats with velvet collars. There was also National Service in the Life Guards, a period he recalled as his least successful although he became the army officers' welterweight boxing champion. From there he trained as an artist, rapidly metamorphosing into his ponytailed form, a process that was aided by long periods of withdrawal from the world, including a spell in an Amazon cave.

Despite the deteriorating relationship with his father, in due course the sixth marquess handed over Longleat to his eldest son to pre-empt death duties. The younger man set about transforming the walls of his wing of Longleat, dividing his murals into three categories: cocoons, therapies and fantasies. In 1973 they were put on show to the public and guests gradually became accustomed to guided tours appearing while they were having lunch in the dining room. While critical reaction to the murals was largely negative – his brother Christopher described them as "pornographic pizza" – viewers could only be impressed by the sheer scale of the project, while the tabloid press had a field day with the explicit Kama Sutra room.

Meanwhile, the estate had to pay its way. In 1966 his father, who had once been described by the headmaster of Harrow as "moronic beyond reach", had welcomed to Longleat the lions that today draw hundreds of thousands of visitors a year. Local people were opposed, fearing that the big cats would escape, while the idea of a safari park was scoffed at by *The Times*, which said that the "unbounded fecklessness" of the public was such that the enterprise was bound to end in tragedy. So far no one has been eaten. Instead, the safari park, said to have been the first outside Africa, has been a success and the lions have been joined by tigers, giraffes, gorillas, zebras and wolves.

LB, as he was known by some of his staff, was tall, broad and bearded with a look of the Viking about him, but with a gentle voice. He favoured ethnic quilted jackets, slippers and whimsical headgear. It was easy to be misled by his convivial manner and boyish exuberance. He had a hard edge, as was demonstrated by the removal of his brother Christopher from Longleat within a week of his father's death in 1992, and he was a shrewd and careful businessman.

In 1966 he contracted an "anti-marriage" with Tania Duckworth, a 17-year-old model from Sri Lanka. However, if he were to be able to pass Longleat on to any children he might have needed to be legitimately married, and in 1969 tied the knot with Anna Gyarmathy, a Hungarian soft-porn actress who later became a journalist. The couple reached an agreement whereby she would spend most of her time in Paris, leaving him free to be with his wifelets.

They had a daughter, Lady Lenka Thynn, who became a television researcher, and a son, Ceawlin, who succeeds in the title. In 2010 Bath, then 77, handed over Longleat Enterprises to Ceawlin, at the same time giving some two dozen longstanding retainers their marching orders. This father–son relationship was also fraught, with the pair falling out two years later when Ceawlin removed some of the erotic murals painted by his father. Three years later, when Ceawlin married Emma McQuiston, who is half-Nigerian, his mother suggested that the union would ruin "400 years of bloodline".

Lord Bath, who also had another daughter born in about 2000, divided his time between the house at weekends, a flat in London during the week and a sybaritic villa in the south of France, though he did not care for dining out because the cuisine was "too French". With advancing years, he wore a hearing aid. When asked in his seventies what he would have done had he not been born an aristocrat, he replied unhesitatingly that he would have been a lorry driver. He lamented not seeing enough of his children and in the evenings he would generally "consult with my doggy". A compulsive chronicler of his life he leaves an autobiography of some many million words in several volumes, as well as a complete photographic record of every guest to stay at Longleat.

After the fracas between his wifelets in 2011, one of them, aged 45, was arrested on suspicion of actual bodily harm but later released without charge; the second, aged 62, was treated in hospital for cuts and a suspected broken nose. As for Lord Bath, he had retired to his billet – a circular contraption on a podium in the middle of the room – telling the pair: "You sort it out, I'm going to bed."

The 7th Marquess of Bath, aristocrat, artist and writer, was born on May 6, 1932. He died on April 4, 2020, after contracting Covid-19, aged 87

CHRISTINA SMITH

———•———

*Idiosyncratic and colourful landlord, entrepreneur, property developer
and philanthropist known as 'the queen of Covent Garden'*

Christina Smith was walking through Covent Garden in the early 1960s when she spotted a "to let" sign on a former potato warehouse. Excited by its potential and enthralled by the "seedy atmosphere and the seedy people" of the bustling fruit and vegetable market, she borrowed £1,500 from her father and opened Goods and Chattels, importing and wholesaling colourful trinkets from South America.

It was the start of a multimillion-pound property and retail empire, with the former propping up the latter to create the quirky, colourful shops for which Covent Garden became famous. Although her attention could wander when not actively excited by a venture, she was by no means a dilettante and her philosophy was an eclectic combination of business and philanthropy. "I have always had a faintly maternal feeling towards my tenants, even when they're not paying their rent," she said. In the property sector, however, she had a reputation as a tough negotiator.

Known as the "queen of Covent Garden", Smith was also a restaurateur, philanthropist, conservationist, mentor, art collector and theatre angel. As Luke Johnson, the Pizza Express entrepreneur, wrote in *The Sunday Times*, she was "a renaissance woman … a woman who made things happen – always with style". She also marched to the beat of her own drum, once dragging a friend to an exhibition of works by the surrealist artist René Magritte with papier-mâché bananas round their necks.

She owned both freeholds and leaseholds, often acquiring tail-end leases and negotiating an extension. This made her the area's largest private landlord, with dozens of tenants including The Creative Business, Neal Street Restaurant and Lynne Franks PR. Sometimes she was simply the right person in the right place at the right time.

"I don't think I ever thought ahead very much," she said. "If I had, I would have expanded faster and probably made a financial mess of things."

Before long she was also importing goods from Asia. "China had an amazing impact on me," she said. "I found the people, the business methods and the commodities fascinating." These discoveries found an outlet in Neal Street East, her vast emporium of colourful textiles, fragrant incenses and tinkling wind chimes that became part of the Covent Garden experience. Many of Smith's businesses used her name, such as the Cas-bah, based on her initials. Smith's Galleries had an impressive roster of shows, including David Hockney's first public exhibition, while at Smith's Restaurant she employed Graham Norton as a waiter before he found television fame.

She was a tall woman with scraped-back hair, loud clothing and huge tinted glasses that matched her ego. She was, however, a terrible delegator, leaving many of her managers feeling underemployed and undermined. There was always a sense of drama. On one occasion she met a friend at the Tea House, another of her enterprises, entertaining him and the customers by chastising the manager because the mugs and teapot were cracked. Some days later the manager revealed to her friend his increasingly plaintive memos requesting new crockery, all of which had gone unanswered.

She was never short of things to do, berating people who approached her with their own ideas. "I say, 'Do them yourself. I've got plenty of ideas, I don't need yours.'" Yet cashflow was invariably a problem, especially in the early days, when banks were reluctant to lend to women, least of all an unmarried one. As she told *The Times*, "The bailiffs loomed on several occasions."

For more than 50 years Smith lived "above the shop" on Neal Street, with large bowls of dried flowers, old Chesterfield sofas, thousands of oriental artefacts and a red Aga. There was no bath or shower for the first dozen years. The wheels and pulleys that in the market's heyday hauled up boxes of potatoes were all but hidden by copious amounts of art and books.

She was an incorrigible hoarder, with old leather-bound volumes, enormous piles of newspapers and yellowing clippings all waiting to be read. Although irritated by the racket from the buskers below, she had her own ways of dealing with them, including on one occasion emptying her watering can over them. They turned out to be a gang of punks who cheerfully sat down and asked for more. At times she despaired of the crowds and the tat, fearing that she had been part of creating some sort of tourist hell.

Yet she insisted that the area had a special quality. "Covent Garden gathers momentum during the day," she said. "Suddenly, especially down James Street and in the piazza, and down Neal Street too, it's as if the Red Army is walking through the Forbidden City, great streams of people."

Christina Anne Smith was born in London in 1934, the second of three children of Ronald Smith, who was the doctor for Rugby School, and his Finnish wife, Maud (née Campbell), who was of Scottish descent and had come to England as a domestic worker.

Her love of art emerged at an early age and at 16 she bought her first piece, a Picasso print of a dancing girl. A year later she left St Mary's School, Calne. "I had got as far as taking my university entrance but didn't do it, which was a bit naughty," she said. She fainted during an audition for the Royal Academy of Dramatic Art, instead taking on several jobs "of the type well-brought-up girls do", including cooking on a Mediterranean yacht and working on a City switchboard. "It did teach me not to be afraid of banks," she said. On another occasion, she added: "I always thought that by the age of 30 I'd be married with two children, so I never sat down and mapped out a career plan."

In 1958 a friend helped her to find work in Fulham as a personal assistant to Terence Conran, the designer who in 1964 opened his first Habitat store. It was, she said, "a role that taught me a lot about running a small business". Conran's first marriage, to Shirley, was in its final stages and friends assumed that Smith would be her successor, as did the outgoing Mrs Conran, who accused them of having an affair. With feelings running high, Smith slipped away, "going to as many places as I could, Mexico, Seattle, San Francisco, Japan, Nepal, Hong Kong, Bombay and Greece".

During those travels she resolved to move into retail. "I'd been sending samples back to myself in England," she said. By the time she returned, Conran had a new partner, though 20 years later Smith was his landlord. She once claimed to have introduced him, and thus the rest of Britain, to the duvet.

After the fruit and veg market moved from Covent Garden to Nine Elms, in Vauxhall, in 1974, she was involved in saving the area from developers' proposals for a conference centre, a large hotel, offices and a new road layout. The market hall survived, as did another 250 buildings that were declared to be of historic and architectural interest. As a member of the Covent Garden Community Association, the Seven Dials Trust and the Covent Garden Forum, her beady eye scrutinised every planning application.

Much of her excess energy went into the Christina Smith Foundation, which supports theatre, architecture, and the advancement of gender balance. She went on to invest in Squire's Ambassador Theatre Group, an investment that was repaid tenfold when the business was sold in 2013.

She wanted to be a member of the Garrick Club, but, she growled, "they are still not letting women in".

Smith's one golden rule was never to answer the phone before 10am; other than that, she seldom rested. A couple of years ago she downsized, which meant parting with an art collection that included works by Hockney, Maggi Hambling and Henri Matisse. She never married. "I did actually say I'd get married to somebody once, but I changed my mind," she said. "After that I thought I ought to be extremely sure. And I never asked anybody to marry me. Perhaps I should have done."

Christina Smith OBE, entrepreneur, was born on March 27, 1934. She died from complications of Alzheimer's disease on March 11, 2022, aged 87

ZSA ZSA GÁBOR

———————•———————

Hungarian socialite and actress who made a success out of celebrity and
was best known for the regularity with which she got married

Provided that you were not married to Zsa Zsa Gábor – and many people were – she could be a lot of fun. Long before reality television she was proof that you could become famous for being famous. She may not have had much talent as an actress, but she did for being a celebrity. One wanted Zsa Zsa Gábor to play Zsa Zsa Gábor, right down to the pink mink and the diamonds and the Hungarian inflections. That, "dahlink", was the role of a lifetime.

It was the husbands, all nine of them, for which Gábor was best known. For each she had a pithy quip that disabused anyone who might have thought her motives were not purely mercenary. "I'm a marvellous housekeeper," she loved to say. "Every time I leave a man, I keep his house."

"I never hated a man enough to give him back his diamonds" was another gem. At her Los Angeles home, 1001 Bel Air Road, built by Howard Hughes and once owned by Elvis Presley, she kept a cushion embroidered with her favourite epigram "Never complain, never explain." Presumably somewhere else there was one with the line about the fool and his money.

Of course, Gábor did only what most women had had to do down the ages, obtaining security by trading what it was that men liked about her. She grasped what that was from an early age. "Daddy used to hold poker games with his friends," she told Wendy Leigh, who ghosted her memoir *One Lifetime is Not Enough*. "He would make me parade around the table and let each of them pat my ass."

Her father, Vilmos, was a diamond dealer in Budapest, then in the Austro-Hungarian Empire, where she was born in 1917. The chief influence on her, however, was her ferociously ambitious mother, Jolie, who lived to be 100. She was determined that her three glamorous daughters, Magda, Sári – as Zsa Zsa was christened – and Eva would make their fortunes. The sisters would rack up 17 divorces between them.

Zsa Zsa was sent to a Swiss boarding school and made her stage debut in Vienna at 16, supposedly having been discovered by the singer Richard Tauber. She and Eva claimed to have been crowned Miss Hungary, but as Cindy Adams, who wrote Jolie Gábor's autobiography, cautioned, "There was never any truth to anything." For example, Jolie and her daughters were Jewish, but ostentatiously wore diamond crosses.

In about 1937, when she was 20, Zsa Zsa met a 50-year-old Turkish diplomat and intellectual, Burhan Belge. She said that he had joked that he would make her part of his harem if she were a little older. Accordingly, when a few months had passed she turned up on his doorstep in Ankara with her terrier Mishka, which her father wanted out of the house. The marriage, such as it was, foundered within six months. Gábor claimed that this was because she had had an affair with Kemal Atatürk, the founder of modern Turkey. More plausibly, by then she had a diplomatic passport that, with war looming and the Nazis threatening Jews, allowed her to enter the US. There her sisters and mother soon joined her.

By now she had swelled into a chic if bosomy blonde, a Dresden shepherdess with an iron will. When she arrived in Hollywood in 1941, she had only an introduction to Basil Rathbone, the screen's Sherlock Holmes. Within a few months she was engaged to Conrad Hilton, the multimillionaire founder of the hotel chain. They had a daughter, Francesca, her only child, but the marriage was rocky for the five years that it lasted. "It was a little like holding a Roman candle," Hilton recalled. "Beautiful, exciting, but you were never sure when it would go out."

Gábor described their relationship as a fiasco. "He thought that I was after his money," she protested. She did admit to a fling with her stepson Nicky, who would marry Elizabeth Taylor.

Next up, in 1949, was George Sanders, suave star of *The Saint* films and *Rebecca*. ("I'm madly in love with you," she said when they first met. "How well I understand you, my dear," he replied.) In his *Memoirs of a Professional Cad*, Sanders made light of his five-year marriage to Gábor, but in fact it was disfigured by his violent jealousy.

This was demonstrated by her flagrant affair with the splendidly endowed playboy Porfirio Rubirosa, who may have been Gábor's only real love. She said Sanders was once so aggrieved that he dangled her out of a window by her dress; fortunately it was made by Balenciaga so did not fray. The evidence that Sanders did love her was perhaps his later, very brief marriage to her sister Magda, shortly before he committed suicide.

Zsa Zsa claimed that he was also jealous of her success as an actress, although in truth there was little of that. Her sister Eva did make a career on the screen, for instance as the voice of the Duchess in Disney's *The Aristocats*. Aside from starring roles in the Toulouse-Lautrec biopic *Moulin Rouge* (1952) and *Queen of Outer Space* (1958), Zsa Zsa was confined to small parts in films including *Touch of Evil* with Orson Welles. Later there were cameos on television in shows such as *Batman*, and in the sequel to the film spoof *The Naked Gun*.

Her fourth husband was Herbert Hutner, an investment banker. They were engaged in 1962 on their third date, her decision to accept perhaps influenced by the $3 million ring he had sent her after the second ("Daddy told me never to settle for less than ten carats"). Hutner lasted four years, for much of which Gábor was still dallying with Rubirosa, who was killed in 1965 speeding through Paris in his Ferrari. Husband No 5, in 1966, was Joshua Cosden, an oil heir. "I had gone into the marriage not really knowing him," said Gábor, when she came out the other side, after a year. "I left none the wiser."

"I know nothing about sex," she also said, "because I was always married." Neither of those claims was true, and she spent the decade until her next wedding entertaining Frank Sinatra, Richard Burton and Sean Connery, among others. These apparently included Richard Nixon. "A great mind. A big brain," she recalled, hinting that that was not the biggest thing about "Tricky Dicky".

In 1975, ensconced in Bel Air with her nine shih-tzus – Pasha Effendi, Genghis Khan and Macho Man among them – she married her neighbour, Jack Ryan. The designer of the Ken and Barbie dolls had a penchant for swingers' parties and was followed in matrimony after a year by the lawyer who handled their divorce, Michael O'Hara. Gábor's eighth husband, Felipe de Alba, a property developer, lasted only a day after their wedding in international waters in 1983. There was some doubt whether she was still married to O'Hara and, in any event, "he wouldn't have made a nice pet".

Presumably on occasion she was upset by some of these failures. Yet unlike, say, Pamela Harriman, Winston Churchill's daughter-in-law, who also made a career of snaring rich men, she was not a thwarted romantic. Nor was self-pity her style, any more than it was Scarlett O'Hara's. "A girl must marry for love – and keep on marrying until she finds it," Gábor held. She found her match in 1986 in Frédéric Prinz von Anhalt. Not the name he was born with, Prinz von Anhalt changed his surname after being adopted as an adult by Kaiser Wilhelm's daughter-in-law. Previously he had run a sauna.

Perhaps Gábor fell for the bogus title, or just for someone with as much chutzpah as her. Having hired a Rolls-Royce to convince her he was rich, and then showed his class by giving her champagne to drink, he soon moved into her $10 million mansion.

His new bride was rising 70 and, as her behaviour became more erratic, she began to need someone to see to her care. In 1989 she was jailed for three days after slapping a policeman who had stopped her for driving with an expired licence. Four years later a jury ordered her to pay Elke Sommer $2 million in libel damages after a long feud in which Gábor alleged that the German star was bankrupt.

In 2002 Gábor was left partially paralysed when a car driven by her hairdresser crashed. Having to use a wheelchair was said to have depressed her, as did the discovery that her daughter had fraudulently obtained a $2 million loan secured against her house. A lawsuit was dropped at the last moment. Francesca Hilton died in 2015.

"The secret to a long marriage is infidelity," Prinz von Anhalt said in 2008, gallantly confiding that he had enjoyed a ten-year affair with Anna Nicole Smith, the former *Playboy* centrefold. Whatever the spark was – he and Gábor liked to watch the film *Babe*, about a talking pig – they remained married for three decades until her death.

Her old age was marred by ill health, which stripped from her the last vestiges of glamour. She had several strokes, broke a hip and had to have a leg amputated – because she was paralysed she only discovered this a year later. She was also rumoured to have lost millions in Bernie Madoff's Ponzi scheme.

By the end, perhaps Zsa Zsa Gábor had accepted that one lifetime was enough for anyone, at least to learn the important things. "The only place a man wants depth in a woman," she concluded, "is in her décolletage."

Zsa Zsa Gábor, celebrity, was born on February 6, 1917. She died of a heart attack on December 18, 2016, aged 99

SIMON NORTON

———————•———————

*Maths genius with a passion for bus timetables who was worth a
fortune, got a first-class degree at 17 but turned his back on academia*

If, by the end, Simon Norton was concerned that his life had not
been what you would expect of one of the cleverest men in the world,
he did not show it.

This was the man who as a child was fêted as a prodigy in the *Daily
Mail* and *The Sunday Times*. Yet as he sat amid the accumulated detritus
of his basement – a tidy mind in an untidy world – he displayed little
worry that his was not the position of eminence most readers would
have predicted years ago.

He was the mathematician who gained his first first-class degree
aged 17, who began his second hailed as among the most promising
prospects of his generation – and who, indeed, had some notable
success in his twenties. In the dim half-light of his Cambridge flat,
however, he did not appear to be bothered whether after that he had
really fulfilled his potential – whatever that means.

Instead, if Norton's thoughts were occupied by anything as he ate
yet another meal of tinned mackerel and rice, it was probably the

subtleties of a mathematical problem known as the "Monster". Or maybe – a conundrum he considered just as important – the intricacies of improving one of Britain's many poorly designed bus routes.

If the word "genius" has any meaning at all, it must apply to Norton – mathematician, prodigy, group theorist, bus timetable enthusiast. After a childhood test gave him an IQ of 178, essentially off the scale, his mother was advised not to reveal the results to him, lest they prove an "unbearable mental strain". He cannot have been in any doubt about his skills though. The report from his Eton entrance exam read "Latin grammar: good. Greek grammar: very good. Latin verses: very good," and then, for mathematics, simply "!!".

"!!" is probably as reasonable an assessment as any of Norton's mathematical skills. Mathematics was how he saw the world; before starting school he began calling himself "5" and his mother "45". "45," he wrote in one letter to her, "I cried when you went out."

Three times as a schoolboy, he represented Britain at the International Mathematical Olympiad, the premier annual gathering of the world's teenage maths enthusiasts. Each time he gained the top grade – once with a mark of 100 per cent. While still at Eton he completed a mathematics degree at the University of London. Afterwards, at Cambridge, naturally, Norton collaborated on what would be his greatest work, the *Atlas of Finite Groups*, which for the mathematicians who followed became the bible of the discipline known as group theory. Then, at the age of 32, he largely parted ways with professional maths.

Eventually, maths, the obsession of his youth, was replaced by another: improving Britain's public transport.

Simon Norton was born in 1952, the youngest of three children. His parents owned an upmarket jewellery business, SJ Phillips, considered sufficiently part of the British establishment that, during the Second World War, it was enlisted for a top secret mission: Operation Mincemeat. When a supposed British agent washed up dead on a Spanish beach, with plans intended to disguise Allied attentions in the Mediterranean, an engagement ring receipt from SJ Phillips gave a touch of verisimilitude to the ruse.

The proceeds from the business sent Norton to Ashdown, then Eton, where he was so excited to finally encounter (relatively) testing mathematical problems that during his entrance exam he could be heard singing. Elsewhere, his performance was less impressive. A school report said: "During a game of cricket he spends his time counting blades of grass or calculating angles. He takes about as much interest in the proceedings as Archimedes did during the Siege of Syracuse."

The Cambridge mathematical sciences department, not a faculty renowned for the sporting and social prowess of its members, should have been a natural home for Norton. For a while, it was. After his PhD, Norton worked with the mathematician John Conway and others on their shared magnum opus, the *Atlas of Finite Groups*.

Group theory is the study of numbers or objects that share certain properties. If, for instance, you rotate one section of a Rubik's cube by 90 degrees, you still have a cube. The same goes if you do the same with another side, or if you rotate it by 180 or 270 degrees. If you rotate a section 45 degrees, however, the whole object ceases to be a cube. In group theory those actions that preserve "symmetry" in this way are "operations". For example, the Rubik's cube group becomes the set of "legal" configurations that retain its cube shape – all 43,252,003,274,489,856,000 of them. Group theory involves understanding groups such as this and the operations that can be performed within them.

The *Atlas* was Norton's attempt to bring further order to group theory, itself a study of order. On each of its pages, however, there was also a whole mathematical universe to get lost in. One of those pages, about which Norton would become a world expert, concerned the Monster group, also known as the Friendly Giant.

Rotating the same side of a Rubik's cube four times gets you back to where you started, to the "identity". This is a way of describing the size of the group. In the Monster group, the analogous operation would have to be repeated more times to achieve the same result. 808,017,424,794,512,875,886,459,904,961,710,757,005,754,368,000,000,000 times, to be exact.

In 1985, however, the symmetries and order in Norton's life collapsed. Among his fellow mathematicians, there were rumours of a full mental breakdown. Perhaps trying to understand the Monster would drive anyone to madness. More likely it was that his mentor,

John Conway, left to take up a position in the US. Alone, Norton floundered. When students stopped coming to his lectures, the maths faculty decided not to renew his contract. He kept his membership of the department, but afterwards never received a salary from it, nor did he produce any more work of note.

Depressed, Norton fell back on the family firm, his share of which would ultimately provide his main income until death. Not that he needed much. He loathed cars, subsisted on tinned fish, Bombay mix and rice, and he rented out most of his house to tenants. One tenant, Alexander Masters, would write a successful and affectionate biography of Norton in his later years, subtitled *The Genius in my Basement*.

By that time, however, in the 2000s, the depression had lifted and the transport obsession had begun. Masters said he considered a different subtitle, *The Biography of a Happy Man*.

He describes following Norton on long bus journeys around such exotic locales as Woking or Kingston upon Thames. This was not a pointless compulsion; Norton's goal was not to collect bus journeys, but to improve them.

For Norton, 1985 was a cataclysmic year. It was not just the year that he left top-level mathematics, but it was also the year that bus services were deregulated and, as a consequence of this, often disappeared.

Norton took it upon himself to fight back. For a mind that once considered the higher-order symmetries of N-dimensional space, calculating ways to optimise public transport was trivial. He fought to save bus and train routes, but also to integrate them.

With the excess income from the jewellery business, he endowed a charity: the Foundation for Integrated Transport. It receives £6 million from his will. Separately he also funded a £10,000 award for transport campaigner of the year. One alumnus, he was proud to tell people, was arrested for superglueing himself to Gordon Brown.

Simon Norton, mathematician, was born on February 25, 1952. He died of a heart condition on February 12, 2019, aged 66

'MAGIC ALEX' MARDAS

———————●———————

Inventor who was the Beatles' 'scientific guru'

If you watch the documentary series *The Beatles Anthology* you will see some grainy footage of a long-haired young man in a white lab coat in front of a screen showing pulsating psychedelic patterns. "Hello, I'm Alexis, from Apple Electronics. I would like to say hello to all my brothers around the world, and to all the girls around the world, and to all the electronic people around the world."

It was the late 1960s and a time when every self-respecting rock star had a guru. John Lennon had two, hedging his bets between the Maharishi Mahesh Yogi, who offered spiritual guidance, and "Magic Alex" Mardas, whom he lauded as his scientific guru.

To Lennon, Mardas was an electronic genius to rival Marconi and Edison. To others, he was a sham. At the very least he was a visionary. The truth is that he was probably a bit of both.

As the head of the electronics division of the Beatles' Apple empire, Mardas promised to deliver paint that would change colour at the flick of a switch; an invisible force field that would shield the Beatles' homes from fans; wallpaper loudspeakers; and a telephone that responded to its owner's voice and could identify callers. There was also a vague plan to build a flying saucer.

Little was delivered, including Mardas's pledge to create a futuristic studio far superior to EMI's Abbey Road. The equipment he built was scrapped as a disaster after a single session.

The group's producer, George Martin, complained that Mardas was an unwelcome presence at Abbey Road recording sessions: "I found it very difficult to chuck him out, because the boys liked him so much. Since it was very obvious that I didn't, a schism developed."

When Allen Klein took over as the Beatles manager in 1969 and was tasked with sorting out the chaos of Apple, he closed its electronics division and Mardas's involvement ended. His projects had cost the Beatles an estimated £4 million in today's money.

"Because John had introduced him as a guru, there was perhaps a little pressure on him to try and behave as a guru," Paul McCartney recalled. His words were perhaps carefully chosen because in later years Mardas won several libel actions against those who accused him of conning the Beatles. "I invented a large number of electronic devices, none of which had anything to do with music or the business of the Beatles," Mardas said in 2010. "Most of them are now in |common use."

Mardas often travelled with the Beatles and was part of the entourage when Lennon and George Harrison stayed at the Maharishi's meditation centre in India in 1968. Mardas told the two Beatles that their spiritual guru was a sexual predator and urged them to leave before the Maharishi invoked a "black magic" spell. Cynthia Lennon later suggested that in a fit of jealousy Mardas had invented the story to undermine the Maharishi's influence. Lennon believed Mardas and alluded to the Maharishi's supposed transgressions in the song *Sexy Sadie*. Lennon was the best man when Mardas married Euphrosyne Doxiadis, the daughter of the celebrated architect Constantinos Apostolou Doxiadis.

At Lennon's suggestion Mardas took Cynthia Lennon on holiday to Greece. When they returned, Cynthia found Yoko Ono ensconced in the marital home and asked Mardas if she could spend the night at his apartment, where he got her drunk, joined her in the spare bedroom and, according to Cynthia, attempted to kiss her until she "pushed him away". She later suspected that Mardas had been set up by Lennon so that the Beatle could accuse her of adultery in divorce proceedings.

For all his intriguing and failed experiments, Mardas did mastermind one of the rare non-musical ventures from which the Beatles made any money after Lennon persuaded his colleagues to buy a Greek island where all four of them could have homes connected by tunnels. Mardas used connections with the Greek government to broker the deal.

The Beatles had been keen on the project to begin with, their enthusiasm perhaps not unrelated to their consumption of LSD while visiting the island by yacht. But back in England they swiftly lost interest in owning an island retreat and a year later sold their purchase at an estimated profit of £11,000. "It was about the only time the Beatles ever made any money on a business venture," Harrison noted.

Born Yanni Alexis Mardas in 1942 in Athens, the son of a major in the Greek secret police, he arrived in London on a student visa in 1965. He found work as a TV repairman and became flatmates with John Dunbar, the founder of the Indica Gallery and Marianne Faithfull's first husband.

Through Dunbar and Faithfull he got to know the Rolling Stones, for whom he built a "psychedelic light box". After Brian Jones had introduced him to Lennon, Mardas then built a similar machine dubbed "the nothing box", which he filled with Christmas tree lights and which emitted random flashes that the Beatle spent endless hours staring at while tripping.

After the dissolution of Apple, Mardas went into partnership with ex-King Constantine II of Greece, selling bulletproof cars to clients who included the Shah of Iran, King Hussein of Jordan, Prince Juan Carlos of Spain and the Sultan of Oman.

"Magic Alex" Mardas, inventor, was born on May 2, 1942. He died of pneumonia on January 13, 2017, aged 74

EDDA TASIEMKA

●

Archivist whose cuttings were invaluable to generations of journalists

"The dead are in the loft," Edda Tasiemka would tell visitors to her home. Luckily, her suburban house in Golders Green in northwest London had a spacious attic. All downstairs rooms, even the kitchen and bathrooms, were filled with the living: the famous, the infamous, the mad, the sad, the bad. Sporting heroes were in the loo, except for David Beckham, who was in her bedroom. Tony Blair was beside the fridge-freezer.

In the lost era when newspapers prided themselves on their cuttings libraries, writers depended on them to appear omniscient. But when those libraries got dismantled in the Fleet Street diaspora, or went over to impenetrable microfiche and digital systems, despairing hacks turned to their favourite resource: the Hans Tasiemka Archive and its 6 million magazine and newspaper cuttings dating from the 19th century. Graphic contemporary accounts of the American Civil War, the death of Queen Victoria, the Russian Revolution, all squirrelled away at 80 Temple Fortune Lane.

Hans Tasiemka died in 1979, but his devoted widow, Edda,

immortalised him by carrying on the library in his name and running it with the utmost charm.

She was born Edda Hoppe in Hamburg in 1922 to Luise Hoppe and her married lover, Paul Frölich, from Berlin. Edda adored Frölich, a communist leader, but after holidays in Berlin with him and an interlude in Moscow she hardly saw him. She returned with her mother to Hamburg. Frölich – having been released from a concentration camp in 1933 – found a new wife and spent the war years in New York. After the war he returned to Germany.

In the 1930s, many of her mother's friends disappeared too. Edda refused to join the Hitler Youth, so she was excluded from her local school. She was interrogated by the Gestapo at 12 and had to travel to school in Hamburg. Her mother was arrested on New Year's Eve in 1938. Edda's plans to be a civil engineer foundered, but she trained as a draughtswoman and worked, after the war, as a secretary to the British Army of occupation in Hamburg, under Major Holt of the Royal Engineers. She claimed that this accounted for her command of English.

In 1949 she met Hans Tasiemka, a left-wing Jewish journalist 17 years her senior who had fled to Paris and joined the French Foreign Legion when war broke out. He was now an interpreter at the War Crimes Trials Centre, and Edda noticed that his pockets were always stuffed with newspaper cuttings, which he needed for his articles.

They moved to London and were married at Hampstead Register Office, with the film star Peter Lorre as best man. Storing their clippings in boxes under the bed in ever larger flats, and trawling antiques shops for vintage magazines, by 1962 they needed a large, three-storey family house to accommodate not a family, for they were childless, but the archive. And there they stayed, lending cuttings to friends, or letting them do research. Photocopiers and fax machines were added and they became a commercial enterprise. The Tasiemkas never advertised their services, but relied on word of mouth as hacks confided to one another about the increasingly essential archive.

Devotees valued the clippings collection's arcane reach. Any obscure story, tucked away in a long-ago feature page – Valerie Grove mentions her search to find the first newsprint mention of Caitlin Moran (in *The Sunday Times*), who had won a children's writing competition aged 12 – could be recovered. "The more difficult the task, the more she relished it," said Robert Lacey, the royal historian. Lacey had first met Hans, known as "Tasi". "You should see Tazzy's files," he was told. When Lacey started work on his first bestseller, *Majesty*, in 1974, he realised how deficient was the *Sunday Times* library.

It ignored magazines, whereas Tazzy's archive included cuttings from *Paris Match* and, most importantly, from *Stern*, which "had a forensic interest in our royal family, regarding them as German". Plus old *Picture Post* magazines, with photographs of the 1953 coronation, including Princess Margaret and Peter Townsend from every intimate angle. Tasiemka's name is gratefully acknowledged in most of Lacey's books.

"Calling [Edda] the human Google is a bit of a cliché, but she did have the international coverage nobody else had," Lacey said. "And you could ring beforehand, and park outside the house, and all your material would be waiting for you, with a smile."

When Lynn Barber took Alan Yentob to the Tasiemka library with TV cameras in 2014, *Culture Show* viewers saw the bulging manilla packets piled on open shelves and in every cupboard – never in filing cabinets – in a seemingly haphazard, random display. But Edda's index code was as rigid, in its way, as the librarians' classic Dewey system: Bigamy, Fraud, Incest, Honour Killings; Colds, Sneezing, Contraception. (Espionage occupied its own cabinet, as did Charles de Gaulle.) "So you're the human Google," Yentob said. "Never heard of them," Tasiemka replied.

Her slender elegance, her manicured fingernails, the clear delight she took in her library, differentiated her even further from dusty newspaper libraries as portrayed in Michael Frayn's play *Alphabetical Order*.

Her companion after the death in 1979 of Hans was Peter Knight, whom she met when he was in charge of syndication at Beaverbrook Newspapers and she was buying pieces for German magazines. Tasiemka referred to Knight, four years her junior, as her toyboy, although they never set up home together.

Edda Tasiemka, archivist, was born on August 5, 1922. She died on March 30, 2019, aged 96

WILFRED DE'ATH

---•---

Vagrant, scrounger, recidivist and ex-BBC producer turned
Oldie *columnist*

Wilfred De'Ath first became a guest of Her Majesty in 1993 and enjoyed it so much that he returned to jail on several occasions. The cause of his incarceration was usually his habit of waltzing off from hotels without paying the bill. It was, he said, preferable to sleeping on the streets of London or in the foyers of French shops, and his record was three months at the Queens Hotel in Leeds.

He found court appearances to be strangely enjoyable experiences. "I love being the centre of attention," he told *The Times* in 2003. "It's like being on stage. It's a battle of wits between you and the chairman of the magistrates, everyone is looking at you, and even though I'm in terrible trouble I feel very, very alive."

For much of the 1980s and 1990s De'Ath was homeless, drifting between Britain and France. He spent the whole of one Christmas in Limoges railway station, sleeping on the floor. He fleeced religious groups, raided church collection boxes and sold salacious stories about the clergy to *Private Eye*.

"A lot of my crime was economic; I just didn't have any money," he explained. "I didn't want to commit suicide, I was a Catholic in those days and suicide isn't allowed. So you have to find a way of surviving, and stealing things, not paying hotel bills, was a way of not being totally on the street. I feel no remorse about the shareholders of a large hotel group losing a few hundred pounds, no. I'd probably do it again."

Salvation came in the form of Richard Ingrams, a contemporary from Oxford and editor of *The Oldie*, who in 1997 spotted a rich vein of material in this devout recidivist. Thus was born the magazine's Down & Out column, in which De'Ath regaled readers with his shameless tales of life on the streets and behind bars, while never once making excuses for his behaviour.

Indeed, De'Ath's life was one largely devoid of contrition. What he regretted more than unpaid hotel bills were unconsummated passions. "You don't think about the women you've had," he said. "You think about the women you could have had but you blew it, or you chickened out."

Wilfred De'Ath was born in Elstree, Hertfordshire, in 1937, the son of a British travel broker of Huguenot descent also called Wilfred, who had met his German bride while on a business trip to Bremen and brought her back to Britain. She had once taken dictation from Hitler and during the war the family would listen to Lord Haw-Haw's *Germany Calling* rather than Winston Churchill on the BBC. "My father was an English gentleman – a really nice man, but rather reticent," De'Ath told *The Oldie*. "My mother was a very strong character – rather neurotic, and never assimilated into British life." He told of coming from "an intensely Protestant background", adding, "My mother wouldn't allow me to read to her from a novel if the characters were in bed together and not married."

From primary school, where he was known as the "little hun", he won a scholarship to Queen Elizabeth's School, Barnet, but was convinced that he had failed and had a "kind of nervous breakdown". His parents took him to a Harley Street psychiatrist who diagnosed that there was nothing wrong.

He "had a vague idea of being an Anglican priest" and won a place to read theology at Oriel College, Oxford, but first there was National Service, which came as a rude shock. "I'd never heard the word 'fuck' until my first night in the army," he said. "I didn't know what the word meant." Refusing to bear arms, he served as a medical orderly and was posted to Germany, where his fluency in the language came in handy: "Translator would be a polite way of putting it – pimp would be more down to earth."

At Oxford, where he switched to English, he was the only boy in his year to have been to a grammar school. "Everybody else was public school and nearly everyone was homosexual," he recalled. His revenge on the class system came by bedding lots of girls and imagining "that the whole of the British Empire was writhing beneath me". He became a theatre critic for *Cherwell*, the student newspaper, produced plays and emerged with an "actor's third". Yet the contrarian was already evident and in May 1959 *The Times* carried a report of him and Ken Loach resigning as producer and lead actor respectively from the Oxford Stage Group's *Othello* claiming a lack of cooperation from others in the group.

Joining the BBC he produced the *Today* programme, then in a lightweight magazine format, and shared an office with Melvyn Bragg. Determined to attract a younger audience he worked on *New Names Making News*, which became *The Teen Scene* and included appearances by John Lennon, Kenny Everett, Mick Jagger and Jimmy Savile.

In 1963 De'Ath married Erica Louis, his secretary and a former fashion model. They had two children: Emma, who is a commissioning editor at BBC World News, and Charles, an actor. He later took up with a schoolteacher called Sarah Hopkins and they had a daughter, Katie, who was taken off to Switzerland to be raised by her grandparents.

De'Ath quickly tired of the BBC's culture of meetings and bureaucracy. After a spell as press officer to Michael Ramsey, the Archbishop of Canterbury, he turned freelance, reporting on counterculture for his former employer, and writing book reviews and profiles for *The Times*. His 1971 BBC interview with Daphne du Maurier, her first for television, was a fine piece of work. He also shared a literary agent with Barbara Castle, which led to an invitation to write the Labour minister's biography. "I've never been terribly impressed by her soapbox manner, but she comes alive when you meet her," he insisted.

Towards the end of the 1970s everything fell apart for De'Ath, who converted to Catholicism around that time. He lost £4,500, all the money he had, in a libel action brought by former BBC colleagues whom he had described in a newspaper article as "intellectual pygmies" and in 1977 his marriage disintegrated. "I was literally on the streets and, unlike most people, who get their act together, I didn't, I remained dispossessed, bereft for many years," he said.

On one occasion he was placed in the stocks at Corby Glen in Lincolnshire, penance for making rude remarks about the village on local radio.

With gainful employment at *The Oldie* De'Ath was able to afford a room in Cambridge, but complained that it was "a mean little provincial town, with no bourgeoisie to speak of, with a snobbish university tacked on to it".

The places he was subsequently banned from in the town included the local WH Smith for stealing a copy of *The Oldie*; the University Centre for making homophobic remarks; a hotel for complaining about slow restaurant service; the Old Spring pub for flirting with a barmaid called Rose; M&S for shoplifting underpants; and a guest house for smearing excrement on a doorknob.

Wilfred De'Ath, producer and writer, was born on July 28, 1937. He died from complications following a heart attack on February 19, 2020, aged 82

RICHARD LUCKETT

———————●———————

*Unworldly and whimsical Cambridge don, polymath and
Pepys Librarian*

One of the fabled dons of his time, Richard Luckett came to embody Magdalene College, Cambridge. His fund of recondite knowledge was a continual source of comedy and delight to all who knew him, but it also enabled him to enhance the fabric and collections of the college, its music, its reputation, and the scholarly endeavours of others in many disciplines.

Always keeping an eye on catalogues and salerooms, and an ear to the ground, he made exceptional purchases and deals for the college – including the acquisition at a bargain price of an unknown oil painting of Pepys – as well as for his own valuable collection of books, musical manuscripts and keyboard instruments.

His unworldly charm made the college many friends, who were scarcely aware that their arms had been twisted when they contributed funds to buy this or that essential part of the Magdalene jigsaw.

Luckett's erudition seemed to promise a flow of remarkable books, but the promise was never fulfilled because his researches never ended. The one art with which he had no acquaintance was that of getting things finished. Yet he contributed richly, if always tardily, to the publications of others, not least the definitive, 12-volume edition of *Pepys's Diary*.

Though his excessively long legs were only perilously articulated to his body, and subject to regular breakages because he didn't look where they were going, Luckett was an elegant figure on a punt, and knowledgeable about sailing and naval history from Drake's time through Pepys's to our own. He claimed that he had once found plans for a kind of skiff that he had never seen and so constructed one to sail on the Cam. This may, however, have been one of his Walter Mitty interludes, for he was known for suiting the tale to the occasion. Yet that is not to say that he wasn't sincere in telling, for instance, of his part in disarming an aeroplane hijacker in South America.

His word was honoured sometimes more in the breach than in the observance. This was because he hated to say no to a challenge and was therefore always horribly overcommitted. And he would go through labyrinths to exculpate himself, without really expecting to be believed. It was a game. Not having had time to read something that had been faxed to him, for instance, he would claim that the machine had broken down but that the repairman had been called, and ask earnestly for another copy the next day. Twenty-four hours later, though no further fax had been sent, he would comment helpfully on the piece.

Friends for whom he promised to write had to endure serial frustrations. Reminders would bring apologies and new assurances. There was just one more book to consult, one more supervision to get through. Exasperation would grow as deadlines passed. Hopes died, and so, sometimes, did collaborators. Alternative writers would be canvassed. And then a meticulous piece would arrive, making remarkable connections between different realms of life or pointing out quite unexpected influences.

His absent-mindedness was so remarkable as to be a source of confusion, temporary embarrassment and later hilarity to everyone who knew him. He once gave a lecture on Tennyson in which he referred throughout to the poet as Dryden. He liked to pretend that no one in the audience noticed.

Richard Luckett was born in 1945, the son of Margaret (née Chittenden), a writer and PA to a local newspaper proprietor, and Rev Canon Gerald Archer Luckett, who himself had wide-ranging interests, from sundials to private printing. For reasons that remained obscure, Luckett attended what was essentially a private prep school for Rothschilds and the sons of a few tycoons, giving him useful early connections.

He was at home among the aristocracy and liked to boast of once entertaining the Roxburghe Club at Magdalene: "The only time I've sat down to dinner with five dukes." Yet he was rather self-effacing, and thought it only chance that others didn't share this or that piece of recherché knowledge. He would assume that undergraduates were following him through bibliographical thickets unless they had the good sense to confess their ignorance, when he would immediately apologise.

After St John's School, Leatherhead, which he loathed, he read English at St Catharine's College, Cambridge, where he also gained his doctorate. For two years he lectured at Sandhurst before returning to St Catharine's as a fellow for eight. In 1982 he was summoned by Magdalene, at 37 already obviously the antiquary it needed to be Pepys Librarian. He was also put in charge of the college library and the Old Library. Magdalene was to be his home for the rest of his life, more or less.

During the 1980s, he gave radio talks, mostly about music. On one occasion he was tickled to be telephoned by the BBC pronunciation unit, asking whether he could advise on the proper sound of a Norwegian word, wanted by someone preparing a talk. The someone was himself.

During the 1990s, Luckett's propensity to damage himself became life-threatening. He had many ailments, but specialised in breaking limbs. He had a poor sense of balance and was once seriously injured when a rollerblader whisked past and lightly touched his jacket. He said that he teetered for half a minute before toppling. His sister Helen, who survives him, claimed to keep track of what he had broken on a medical student's miniature skeleton. His mind was simply, sometimes disastrously, on other things.

He was, sadly, too busy ever to marry.

Richard Luckett was perhaps ironically aware of his own theatre. As he liked to point out, he never owned a house, car or mobile phone and his skills included the ability to tickle trout, but not how to use a computer – he preferred to write everything in an erratic longhand.

Yet he claimed to be hurt by the way he was once portrayed in a Cambridge novel. His own mix of fact and fiction was a finer thing. In an age of specialists, he advised experts in many fields about books and articles they had missed. His name in the acknowledgements of a book indicates that there was a good conversation in its making.

Richard Luckett, former Pepys Librarian at Magdalene College, Cambridge, was born on July 1, 1945. He died of cancer on November 19, 2020, aged 75

TED KNIGHT

Unreconstructed 'loony left' leader of Lambeth Council who wanted to overthrow first Mrs Thatcher then western capitalism

Ted Knight (right) with Ken Livingstone in 1981.

It was fitting that the death of "Red" Ted Knight in old age produced wildly opposed reactions. Jeremy Corbyn and John McDonnell saluted his life, with the latter claiming that Knight was "one of the finest and most courageous socialists I have known". They had been allies in London politics for more than 40 years. Other Labour figures complained that his activities as leader of Lambeth Council in the 1980s had divided the Labour Party, made it unelectable and paved the way for Conservative dominance.

Knight's political career began and ended in Lambeth, his efforts to become an MP or be elected to the Greater London Council having failed. Faced with tight Conservative government funding, Lambeth under his leadership steadily increased local rates to finance higher spending on services, to the anger of Margaret Thatcher.

The clash that was to end Knight's political career came in 1984 with the government's introduction of the Rates Act; this capped the rates or taxes that local authorities could levy on businesses and homeowners. Within local government a new generation of radical Labour leaders had emerged and were determined to take the fight to the Thatcher government. More than a score, including David Blunkett at Sheffield, Margaret Hodge at Islington, Ken Livingstone at the GLC and Derek Hatton at Liverpool, as well as Knight at Lambeth, vowed to defy the government.

Knight hoped the rebel authorities would combine to force a change of policy or of government. In his own words they would mobilise "a section of the state – local government – against the state itself". Eventually all backed down except Lambeth and Liverpool, both of which refused to set a rate. When the GLC caved in, Knight and Livingstone fell out.

His defiance led to Knight and 30 of his fellow councillors paying substantial fines and costs and being disqualified from office for five years. They sang *The Red Flag* and council workers walked out in support. But the protest had failed. Neil Kinnock and many Labour MPs blamed him and other hard-left figures for bringing the party into disrepute and damaging it electorally.

Edward Robert Knight was born in Brixton, south London, in 1933. His schooling began at Rosedale School in West Norwood but during the war he was evacuated to the northeast and then to Scotland. He returned home and attended Strand Grammar School.

His first job was as an insurance clerk but from an early age he lived for politics, encouraged in part by his Labour-supporting father. He joined the Labour League of Youth in 1949, aged 15, but seven years later was expelled for associating with a Trotskyist group, the Socialist Labour League; it was the forerunner of the Workers Revolutionary Party of which friends assumed Knight was a clandestine member. Not one to dwell on both sides of an argument, he saw capitalism as an evil to be overthrown rather than reformed.

He was readmitted to Labour in 1970, became chair of the Norwood branch and was elected as a Lambeth councillor in 1974. Knight formed an effective partnership with Livingstone, who had been elected a councillor three years earlier, and they worked to take over the leadership and move it leftwards. It was a heterogeneous party and Knight was only narrowly elected leader of the council in 1978.

Short, stocky and well-dressed, he had organisational skills, was single-minded and, despite internal divisions in the local party, retained substantial support in the community even after his disqualification.

A fellow Labour councillor colleague was the young Peter Mandelson. Mandelson acknowledged Knight's charm and skills but deplored his hard-left political gestures that gave ammunition to Labour's opponents. When the police intervened during the riots in Brixton, Knight complained that "Lambeth is now under an army of occupation". Asked for a comment, Mandelson replied: "Given the choice between having the Labour Party and Ted Knight in the borough or the police 99 per cent would vote for the police."

The activities of some left-wing Labour figures in London councils fed the image of the "loony left", in Knight's case, the Socialist Republic of Lambeth. Declarations of nuclear-free zones, expressions of support for the IRA and other minority groups and the setting-up of lesbian and gay committees were eagerly seized on by the tabloids.

Removed from frontline politics after 1986, Knight's influence waned. For a few years he ran a restaurant in Clapham, continued to support Labour locally and was active in the Unite trade union. New Labour under Tony Blair and Gordon Brown was unwelcoming but he was enthused by the election of Corbyn as Labour leader in 2015 and the prominent role of McDonnell, his friend. He joined Momentum. The tabloid press revived its "loony left" headlines in 2016, when it was reported that Knight had been elected as chair of his local ward party, which contained Momentum members.

He never married and lived alone. A journalist of his acquaintance recalled answering the phone one Christmas morning in the 1980s expecting to hear seasonal greetings. It was Knight asking him to write an article for *Labour Herald*. "I said to him, 'You do know it's Christmas Day, Ted?'" "Doesn't mean anything to me," Knight countered. "Christmas is a bourgeois deviation."

Ted Knight, council leader, was born on June 13, 1933. He died of unknown causes on March 30, 2020, aged 86

BERYL VERTUE

●

*Tough-negotiating, giant of British showbusiness who started out
making tea for Spike Milligan and ended up producing*
Men Behaving Badly

Cowed by the prospect of persuading Ike Turner to agree to his wife Tina appearing in the 1975 film *Tommy*, the impresario Robert Stigwood sent Beryl Vertue in his stead. Short, unassuming and rather, in her own words, "mumsie" looking, Vertue did not come across as the tough negotiator she most definitely was, still less as the most powerful woman in British showbusiness at the time. Even the abusive, paranoid, cocaine-addicted Ike Turner soon learnt not to underestimate her.

"I was driven to a hut outside LA by a girl who I later discovered was Ike's girlfriend. She had a gun in her handbag," the British comedy script agent turned film producer nonchalantly recalled. "When we arrived, Tina Turner appeared and dragged me to the ground – because there were surveillance cameras everywhere – and begged me not to make him cross.

"His office was like a bordello, maroon everywhere, and there he was, in a white suit, looking immaculate. He got out a cigarette and she [Tina] shot from one side of the room to the other to light it for him. I decided to be very British; I was wearing white gloves that day, and I told him not to worry, that we were going to take such good care of Tina. Well, he didn't quite know how to react."

The woman who had regularly calmed Spike Milligan during manic episodes, mollified Tony Hancock in foul, drunken moods, and persuaded the head of the Mafia-linked Teamsters union in Boston to let her make a film in the US city, got the deal done, as she always did. Tina Turner went on to give a pulsating performance in Ken Russell's *Tommy* as the Acid Queen. "I never did ask Ike's permission to hire her," she recalled, "but nevertheless thanked him when he hadn't quite given it."

Having started her career making tea for Milligan, Vertue told Kirsty Young on *Desert Island Discs* in 2013 that naivety had been her secret. "It's important not to know too many rules. If you don't know there's a rule against something you just do it."

Beryl Frances Johnson was born in Croydon in 1931 to Elsie (née Francis), and Frank Johnson, an engineer who worked in a munitions factory during the Second World War and later ran a garage where Beryl had her first job, manning the pumps.

She attended Mitcham County Grammar School with no great distinction and left at 15 to take a typing course. After this she spent six years in a shipping office before she was diagnosed with TB and sent to a sanatorium on the Isle of Wight. Not long after her recovery the *Hancock's Half Hour* writing team of Ray Galton and Alan Simpson, whom she had known at school, tried to recruit her as a secretary for Associated London Scripts (ALS), a writers' co-operative founded by Eric Sykes and Milligan.

Not fancying the one-hour trolley bus journey to their dingy office above a fruit and veg shop in Shepherd's Bush, Vertue refused. Simpson persisted and she was duly interviewed by Milligan, who was more interested in her tea-making ability than her typing or shorthand speeds. She was offered the job but asked for what, in the mid-1950s, she thought was the prohibitive sum of ten pounds a week. "To my horror they accepted."

In addition to her secretarial duties, which included typing Milligan's scripts for *The Goon Show* and dealing with the Goons' huge fan mail, she would fix the ever-faulty plumbing in the office and field calls from Milligan in the middle of the night asking her to type up his latest comic brainwave. Then one day Simpson and Galton asked her to call the BBC about their contracts, and she somehow succeeded in doubling their income for *Hancock's Half Hour*.

No martyr to shyness, comfortable with confrontation and rarely inhibited by sensitivity when it came to enforcing her will, Vertue went on to negotiate equally gilt-edged contracts for all the writers on ALS's roster, including an insurance salesman called Johnny Speight for whom she sold *Till Death Us Do Part* and a furniture salesman called Terry Nation who created the Daleks for *Doctor Who*. Showing an early aptitude for "exterminating" complacent male BBC bureaucrats, Vertue shrewdly altered Nation's contract to include merchandising rights, a first in British television. The popularity of

Dalek-related toys, comics and games made Nation rich.

She now turned her polite but steely attention to the flagging career of Frankie Howerd, who was considering giving up showbusiness and running a pub. Vertue was determined to dissuade him and suggested he try cabaret. She got him a booking at the Blue Angel, a London nightclub. Howerd was reluctant but gave in. "She was a dreadful bully. Thank goodness," he recalled. Entirely by default she had evolved into a highly effective agent for the cream of British comedy writers and actors in what was becoming known as the "fun factory".

In 1966, she formed an offshoot to ALS called Associated London Films, in partnership with Stigwood, an entrepreneur wanting to diversify from pop music into theatre, television and films. The two of them made big money. She wore fur coats, commuted to America on Concorde and had her own chauffeur-driven, powder-blue Rolls-Royce, though her embarrassed children begged her not to take them to school in it.

Much of the success was down to a lucrative and much-copied moneymaking idea she had that became known as "Vertuosity", a play on her name – selling successful British sitcoms such as *Steptoe and Son* and *Till Death Us Do Part* to US television networks to develop their own vernacular versions (*Sanford and Son* on NBC and *All in the Family* on CBS).

Along the way, she scored a coup by hiring Jack Lemmon to star in a 1975 American TV adaptation of John Osborne's *The Entertainer*, and earned notoriety by persuading US television networks to sanction the first use of the word "bastard" on terrestrial TV there.

American producers were so disarmed by her straightforward approach and, on first impressions at least, mild manner that they were unprepared for her idiosyncratic negotiating technique. In her matter-of-fact way, she told one that a script she was trying to sell "doesn't work in the middle, but we'll fix it". Used to dealing with Hollywood hustlers, he was stunned and perhaps even a little confused by her honesty.

It all made Vertue a wealthy woman. But the spiralling success of Associated London Films and her jet-set life style also put a strain on her marriage.

In 1951, Vertue had married her childhood sweetheart, Clem Vertue, who ran a travel agency. Keen gardeners, they had for years lived quietly away from the spotlight near Reigate, Surrey, with Vertue doing all the housework at weekends and raising their two daughters as a working mother. They remained friends but their divorce in 1984 destroyed her confidence for a while and, in her own words, she "spent five years not succeeding".

Having parted company with Stigwood as well, she set up a small independent production company at Shepperton Studios. Though Hartswood Films was not a success at first, her avidity was not easily dampened by failure and in 1989, Vertue, now in her late sixties, read an unknown comic novel called *Men Behaving Badly* by Simon Nye, a translator for Credit Suisse. After chuckling through the misadventures of two politically incorrect flat-sharers, she realised that it would make a great sitcom.

After selling it to ITV, the show was dropped in 1992, but undeterred, Vertue sold it to the BBC, where it ran for five series and became the highest-rated sitcom of the nineties, riding on the zeitgeist of the "laddish humour" then in vogue. It also appealed to women because of the underlying vulnerability of the men played by Neil Morrissey and Martin Clunes, and female viewers' empathy for the long-suffering girlfriends played by Caroline Quentin and Leslie Ash. *Men Behaving Badly* proved to be Vertue's redemption; forging a well-trodden path, she sold the format to the US.

She enjoyed more success with *Sherlock*, a quirky take on the Arthur Conan Doyle adventures that made a star of Benedict Cumberbatch.

Reflecting on her decades as one of the toughest and most enigmatic dealmakers in the business, Vertue described herself as "the world's worst feminist" – "I was just never aware of sexism in the office," she said. "I was having too much fun."

Beryl Vertue CBE, television and film producer, was born on April 8, 1931. She died on February 12, 2022, aged 90

JOHN LUCAS

———————•———————

Influential philosopher who argued against determinism and had a
reputation for being the most eccentric don in Oxford

In the paper for which he was perhaps best known, the philosopher John Lucas argued for the existence of free will and against determinism. Whether or not he himself possessed free will, he was certainly wilful.

Uncompromising in his eccentricity, he was both a man of settled habits and an enthusiast for new gizmos. The only car he ever owned was his father's 1929 open-topped Humber, the bashed bodywork of which provoked howls from passing car enthusiasts.

He rarely threw anything away, wrote with his father's fountain pen until its nib was too broad to write legibly, and had a collection of five raincoats, the age of each befitting a different task. The fifth-best raincoat was kept in the garage, for when he needed to do work on the bashed Humber. Another inheritance from his father was the tattered gown he wore for hall and chapel, which he held together by cloth tape. Together with his 6ft 6in stature, it made for a lasting impression.

Despite his conservative attitude to worldly goods, which was a mixture of wartime frugality and postlapsarian nostalgia for old England, he was quick to embrace technology. To save time in the morning, he would use his battery-powered razor to shave while walking the 50 yards from his house in Oxford to his college, Merton. An early adopter of computers, he always took a dim view of television, although this did not stop him becoming a member of the BBC commission on violent programmes. His fellow members, however, discovered that he had not watched television since the moon landings, and before that since the coronation, and had to give him a set.

For all his tendency to see the world in different colours, he was a leader in his field, especially on the subject of determinism, the idea that if you knew everything about a person you could create an algorithm to predict what they would do next, and hence that their free will is an illusion. Lucas noticed that determinism is undermined by Gödel's first incompleteness theorem, which proves that no algorithm can generate all the true sentences of arithmetic and no false ones. He pointed out that the corollary of Gödel's theorem is that it is possible for a person to have thoughts that no algorithm could predict, and hence possess free will.

He was also influential beyond his own area of expertise, notably with his argument that no single academic discipline could describe reality fully. Quantum mechanics might elucidate the building blocks of the universe, but he did not believe that meant it could explain all the ways of arranging those blocks. Only chemistry could explain their arrangement into molecules, while only biology could explain their arrangement into life forms. The pursuit of a theory of everything was, he thought, a hopeless quest, because reality is multifaceted and can only be comprehended from many angles.

Lucas was well placed to understand the incommensurability of different disciplines, because he understood so many. In a time when academia was growing ever more specialised, he was a true polymath. While a fellow at Merton College he wrote about epistemology, the study of how we know what we know, as well as about theology, quantum physics, the philosophy of time and of free will, about economics, and about the relative merits of Plato and Aristotle.

John Lucas was born in Lavender Hill, London, in 1929, the son of Joan (née Randolph) and Egbert, an Anglican clergyman who soon took a parish in Guildford. The family then moved to Durham, where his father was appointed archdeacon, and where John grew up in the shadow of the cathedral.

Educated first at the Dragon School in Oxford, where he was unhappy, he found the rigorous intellectual culture of Winchester College more congenial, and went from there to Balliol College, Oxford, to study chemistry on a scholarship. In an early display of his polymathy, he soon switched to maths, and then to Greats, to study the Greek philosophers. At Balliol he became friends with Peter Tapsell and Dick Taverne, future Conservative and Labour MPs. Having taken his MA in 1954, he spent a year at Princeton studying maths and logic, then in 1960 became a fellow of philosophy at Merton.

His tutelary style was sphinxlike. Instead of telling his students what he thought of their essays, he would question them in the Socratic manner, teasing out their assumptions and showing them the importance of arguing from first principles. It was in this way that they began to see that Lucas, despite his rather fusty appearance, had an anarchic cast of mind. He was frustrated by blithe belief in received wisdom and took impish delight in pretending to hold controversial opinions. Though he intended merely to make mischief by arguing that women should be denied the vote, not everybody was amused.

Yet he was no mere gadfly. His independence of mind led him to campaign ardently for several causes. Perhaps his most impressive sally forth from the quadrangle was his involvement in the work of the "Velvet philosophers", giving covert lectures in communist Czechoslovakia in the early 1980s. Along with Lucas, philosophers such as Roger Scruton (obituary, page 265), Kathy Wilkes and Jürgen Habermas responded to a plea from the Czech and Slovak intelligentsia to do so. He gave his lecture in a packed boiler room, handing out rapturously received copies of the Greek New Testament and Plato's *Republic*, both banned.

An implacable foe of communism, in response to any reference to "Eastern Europe" he would darkly intone, "Prague is west of Vienna." Lucas had married Morar Portal in 1961, having met her at a friend's wedding and they had four children, one of whom, Edward, became the first British journalist to base himself, at considerable risk, in Czechoslovakia.

As a tutor Lucas could be severe. When students asked him if they could rearrange their tutorials, he would innocently suggest meeting at seven the next morning.

John Lucas, philosopher, was born on June 18, 1929. He died on April 5, 2020, aged 90

BARONESS HOWE OF IDLICOTE

———————•———————

*Formidable chairwoman of the Broadcasting Standards Commission,
widow of a foreign secretary and nemesis of a prime minister*

Elspeth Howe could have fitted convincingly into a Trollope novel as one of those great "Whig ladies" who influenced the tone of Victorian public life simply by being there to stiffen the backbone of her man, whenever his posture needed correcting.

Her man was Geoffrey Howe, whom she married in 1953 and helped to develop from a shy young lawyer with a passion for Conservative politics into a powerful, if not always dynamic, cabinet minister. Elspeth had dynamism enough for both and in due course her forceful personality earned her important roles in public life on her own account, not least as chairwoman of the Broadcasting Standards Commission (BSC), where she had to take a view on topics such as explicit sex, crude language and violence. That role made her popular as a dinner guest, she said, when people found out that she spent hours every week in the course of duty watching recordings of "adult" scenes in TV programmes.

One BSC panel member, the *Times* columnist Matthew Parris, said that she was "wilful, but a terrifically good sport and not easily bruised". He described how on one occasion they watched a drama that had a scene featuring a naked woman astride a naked cabinet minister, bouncing up and down, as he moaned, "I only ever wanted to be foreign secretary." Aware that the chairwoman's husband had been foreign secretary, Parris recalled, "none of us dared catch another's eye."

That same strong personality also earned Elspeth a place in Tory mythology as the woman who helped to bring about the downfall of Margaret Thatcher in November 1990.

The scene for that rather more Shakespearean drama had been set a year or two earlier when she was one of many Conservatives who felt the time was approaching to find a new leader – and was convinced her husband was the obvious choice. She was angered when the prime minister deliberately demoted him by moving him from the Foreign Office to the grand-sounding but meaningless post of deputy prime minister.

The final straw came one day when Thatcher was thoughtlessly rude to him in Cabinet. He resigned and exercised his right to make a full statement explaining the seriousness of his differences with Thatcher over Europe. The speech was devastating, especially when, in reference to his negotiations on the Economic and Monetary Union, he compared himself to an opening batsman sent to the crease, only to find, as the first balls were being bowled, that his bat had been broken before the game by the team captain.

Thatcher's account of the episode in her memoirs is an example of a pen picture that reveals more about the author than about the man portrayed: "This quiet, gentle, but deeply ambitious man – with whom my relations had become progressively worse as my exasperation at his insatiable appetite for compromise led me sometimes to lash out at him in front of others."

Seemingly unaware of the irony, the Thatcher memoirs added: "I suspect he thought that he had become indispensable." It was only days after the Howe speech that the prime minister's colleagues made it clear to her it was she who was dispensable. Unsurprisingly, however, it was not to Howe that they turned to fill the gap – as both Geoffrey and Elspeth must have known.

Howe, a ponderous, monotonal speaker who had been compared

by Denis Healey to a dead sheep, would never have acted as he did without consulting his wife. Yet the comments in the corridors of Westminster went further than that. It was Elspeth, the wags said, who had written the speech: "It took her ten minutes to write it; it took ten years for Geoffrey to deliver it."

The Thatcher–Howe conflict was no more than one feature of the rift between the traditional and the radical, the "wet" and the "dry", wings of the party that was the story of Thatcherism. It was symbolic that, a few months before the 1990 resignation speech, Elspeth had embellished her reputation, in Thatcherite eyes, as a hopeless liberal by joining in a street protest against homelessness that involved sleeping rough in a cardboard box with bin liners. Thatcher was probably quite right in suspecting Sir Geoffrey of sharing many of his wife's liberal Conservative instincts.

On the night the IRA bombed the Grand Hotel in Brighton in 1984, the Howes were in the suite next to the Thatchers. Their door was jammed and they could not get out until they and their dog, famously named Budget, were rescued by the police.

Elspeth Howe was a formidable exponent of a kind of Toryism that contrasted sharply with that of the Thatcherites, who thought her political ideas downright old-fashioned. Some of them might have added that they thought the same of her sense of fashion, firmly based on sensible clothes, sensible shoes and sensible hairstyles.

She was in many ways, then, a traditional Tory, but she was also a Tory feminist who considered that Thatcher was "not interested in women's issues". When she became deputy chairwoman of the Equal Opportunities Commission she could strike alarm among head teachers with her powerful views on the importance of teaching boys to cook and girls to do metalwork. Her zeal for women's liberation dated from childhood, when she realised the need for women to be free to earn a fair income.

Elspeth Rosamund Morton Shand was born in 1932, the daughter of Philip Morton Shand by his fourth wife, Sybil (née Sissons, previously Mrs Slee). As such, she was a half-aunt to Camilla, Duchess of Cornwall (née Shand, formerly Parker Bowles), whose father, Bruce Shand, was Philip's son by a previous marriage.

Her mother, despite belonging to a social class who tended to be free of financial worries, had been obliged to become the family breadwinner. Her father – "I suppose he was a bit of a genius," Elspeth would say – wrote clever books on architectural history, which were highly regarded by the right people (Shand was, after all, a friend of Evelyn Waugh and John Betjeman) but they never made money. Father–daughter relations were often strained. He was "a powerful personality, quite prickly, with a sarcastic tongue", who did not approve of her engagement to Howe after they had met at a party. She recalled, "His view was that you should never marry a Welshman, a lawyer or a politician, and Geoffrey was all three." He reluctantly attended the wedding, but there was a greater frustration for Elspeth: she did not want to vow to "obey" her husband, but the clergyman refused to change the traditional wording for the service.

Elspeth was educated at Wycombe Abbey, where she captained the school cricket team and was head girl, but did not go to university until later in life. It was typical of her that she felt she could improve her already extensive conversational powers by deciding, at the age of 50, to become a mature student in social science at the LSE. She delighted in mixing with students half her age and when a reporter tried to gatecrash a class to watch how she was coping, she was impressed at the way her young classmates rallied round to protect her.

The Equal Opportunities Commission had been a creation of Harold Wilson's Labour government in 1975 and when the Tories won power four years later Lady Howe was not pleased to be told it would be inappropriate for her to continue in the job now that her husband had entered Thatcher's Cabinet as Chancellor of the Exchequer. "I wasn't all that amused at that moment," was how she put it. Thereafter, throughout the Thatcher years, the prime minister and her chancellor's wife did not take to each other. A former whip recalled how, when it was suggested to Thatcher that Elspeth Howe should become a church commissioner instead, the temperature in the room dropped and "she was unbearable for the rest of the day". Elspeth told Thatcher's biographer Lord (Charles) Moore of Etchingham: "We were like two wasps in a jam jar." Denis Thatcher referred to her as "that bitch of a wife" while other ardent Thatcherites dubbed her "Lady Macbeth".

In fact, her solid common sense probably discouraged the Equal Opportunities Commission from diverting energy into doctrinal flourishes, but it is easy to see why the founder of Thatcherism was suspicious. Granting rights to women by imposing new obligations on employers was out of tune with the laissez-faire instincts in the ascendant.

Lady Howe found her role as a statesman's consort congenial. She loved travelling the world and gained a reputation for kindness in finding ways to ease the lot of diplomatic families. She relished being hostess at Chevening, the foreign secretary's country residence, as she had enjoyed her social life in 11 Downing Street. The Howes were keen bridge players.

Her public life expanded after Geoffrey's career in government ended in 1992, when he stood down as an MP and was made a life peer. She had long since built up a portfolio of offices common to many Tory wives including party committees, work as a magistrate and school governor and, later, membership of the Parole Board. She became a governor of the LSE shortly after completing her degree course there and joined several company boards – Kingfisher, United Biscuits and Legal and General Group. She combined all this, moreover, with being the attentive mother of three children.

In 2001, she was made a life peer, as Baroness Howe of Idlicote, becoming one of the first "people's peers". She sat as a crossbencher and had a reputation for espousing unpopular, left-of-centre causes that, in the process, seemed to enrich public life. She and her husband were one of the few couples who both held a peerage in their own right. Having already been styled Lady Howe by dint of her husband's knighthood and then his peerage, it was quipped when she received her own peerage that she was, in the words of the Lionel Richie song, "once, twice, three times a Lady".

Baroness Howe of Idlicote CBE was born on February 8, 1932. She died of cancer on March 22, 2022, aged 90

BRIGADIER JACK THOMAS

———————————•———————————

Military police commander who survived a landmine, bullet, rhino and
faulty parachute and liked to watch TV with an owl on his head

Jack Thomas used up the first of his many lives by abseiling down a rockface to rescue a Canadian commando during a training exercise in Scotland. The Canadian jumped for Thomas's rope, sending his rescuer falling 30m down the mountain. Astonishingly, Thomas emerged with only bruises.

His next brush with death came during parachute training when his equipment failed to open and he plummeted to the ground in what is known as a "Roman candle". This time he suffered two broken ankles.

While in British-Mandate Palestine in 1947 he was the sole survivor from a Jeep carrying three people that drove over a landmine on the Ein Shemer airfield. "All I saw was a red flash and all I felt was a nasty taste in my mouth," he recalled. "I woke up in hospital."

The damage this time was more psychological than physical. He did not speak for a year and when he did his voice had changed so much that he became known as Squeaky Jack, a nickname that lasted for the rest of his military career.

Six years later he was shot in Korea and an X-ray revealed a 6mm gap between his collarbone and his shoulder. Subsequent surgery meant that he never again made it through airport security without setting off alarms.

Later, while serving with the Royal Military Police (RMP) in east Africa, his Jeep was charged by a rhinoceros. On another occasion he returned home to be greeted by a pride of lions on the doorstep, who hung around menacingly for an hour before moving on, and once a suspicious lioness kept him and his wife pinned against their Chevrolet as he struggled to get the children inside to "unlock the bloody doors" without antagonising the predator.

A tall man with a broken nose and a rugby player's cauliflower ears, Thomas went on to become the head of the RMP in Northern Ireland, with a title, provost marshal (Northern Ireland), that dates back to the 13th century; later he became provost marshal (army).

The one regret of his military career, he said, was helping to provide Idi Amin with a platform from which the "butcher of Uganda" terrorised his country in the 1970s. "I was a member of the commissioning board that decided that Amin, who was then a sergeant major, should be commissioned," he admitted gloomily.

John Francis Thomas was born in Margam, near Port Talbot, south Wales, in 1926, the son of John Henry Thomas, an Old Contemptible who had served with the Household Cavalry, and his wife Dorothy (née Gregory).

He was educated at Sandfields school, describing himself as "an ordinary Aberavon boy who went to school with patches on his trousers", before moving on to Port Talbot County School, where he was a contemporary of Clive Jenkins, the trade union leader, and Richard Burton, the actor. "I've not been as successful perhaps as Clive or gained as much recognition as Richard," he reflected. "And I've certainly not become as rich."

From there he was apprenticed to GH Page, a local joinery business, where he acquired the practical skills that would serve him well in later life. At 17 he followed his father into the Life Guards and learnt to drive a Humber Scout armoured car, recalling that he quickly mastered its tricky gearbox because whenever he crunched the gears he received a bang on the head from a coal shovel wielded by the Corporal of Horse.

He missed the Normandy landings because of a traffic accident but proved talented at rugby, playing at club, county and army level until the age of 38, including taking part in the army's first postwar tour to Japan in 1952.

He was also useful with a pair of boxing gloves, something that, according to family folklore, earned him his commission: having "boxed the ears" off the barrack room bully, he was marched in front of a far-sighted commander. Given the option of military jail or the officer cadet training unit he chose the latter and at 18½ was selected for an emergency commission. He joined the Commandos (badged to the Welch Regiment) and after basic training was assigned to No 6 Commando. On their disbandment in 1946 he was assigned to 1 Para and was sent to Palestine. Not long after recovering from the landmine blast he met Dorothea Williams, who was still a teenager. They were married in 1953, when she was 21. The car that was supposed to collect him on his wedding day failed to arrive and he made his way to the church perched on the handlebars of a bicycle, still wearing tails, with his best man pedalling furiously.

Unusually for a military wife of her generation, Dorothea worked throughout her husband's career, specialising in remedial and dyslexic education. They had three children.

After seeing action in the Korean War in the early 1950s, during which he frequently wrote home about his struggle to receive new army-issue underpants, Thomas remained in the Far East. He was promoted to major and in 1959 joined the RMP, serving with them in east Africa, West Germany and Wales. Wherever he was posted he endeavoured to learn the local language, acquiring a working knowledge of Cantonese, German, Russian and Spanish.

After retiring from the army he became director of security for the National Diamond Mining Company in Sierra Leone.

His first car, a grey Armstrong Siddeley Whitley, remained part of the family until recently, playing a significant role in their milestones, from births to weddings, and on one occasion was driven to Germany. He loved repairing it, especially when it meant visiting a scrapyard – he built his eldest daughter's first car, a Ford Anglia, entirely from salvaged parts.

His eccentricities did not weary with age and his family grew accustomed to welcoming unexpected guests, including a group of Austrians who Thomas found looking lost on the Aldershot ranges. As a grandfather he had an alarming line in bedtime stories for his eight grandchildren, invariably involving gunfire, explosions and plenty of blood and guts.

His other great passion was for Alsatians. In Hong Kong he kept 14 of them and as a subaltern he had one called Prince, who would ride pillion on Thomas's motorcycle with his paws on his master's shoulders. Prince "earned his wings" by once making an unaccompanied parachute drop.

One of his favourite animals was Hector, a rescued Alsatian/Great Dane cross who, according to Thomas, "weighed nearly 150lbs and stood 6ft 4in in his stockinged feet". Hector's party trick was "singing" along to his master's harmonica, an experience that was once heard on

BFBS Radio. One Christmas, Hector and Fred, a large beagle with a divergent squint, came home with two chickens they had stolen from the NAAFI. Thomas insisted that he had no option other than to dust them off and feed them to his family.

This peripatetic menagerie travelled the world with him, eventually settling at the family home in Aldershot, where they lived for nearly 40 years surrounded by Thomas's oil paintings. One later arrival was ET, an African wood owl he had rescued as a chick in Sierra Leone. He secured permission to fly ET home on British Airways, though objected to being charged for the bird's inflight meal. ET found a home in the family's inglenook fireplace, bathed in their bidet and watched television perched on Thomas's head. He had thought ET was a male and was taken by surprise when "he" laid an egg.

Brigadier Jack Thomas CBE, was born on June 25, 1926. He died of Covid-19 on January 29, 2021, aged 94

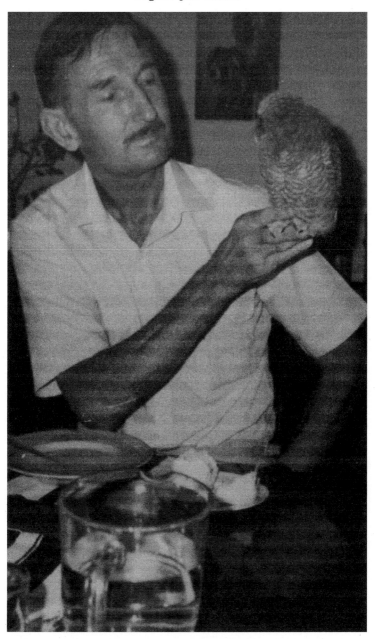

DIANA ATHILL

———————•———————

Grande dame of English letters who found literary fame in her eighties after writing about her sex life in unflinchingly frank memoirs

As she approached the grand age of 100, Diana Athill continued to speak as she had always done, with a booming voice that was all fruity vowels and tart consonants. She also remained a striking figure, with cheekbones like ledges and a high forehead that was still smooth. Such was her aura of immortality she would still be asked her beauty secrets at the readings she gave at literary festivals.

Although she did not find true literary fame until her eighties – as a bestselling and extremely candid memoirist – she was well known in publishing circles before that as an editor of a rare kind: formidable, closely engaged with her authors' writing and, above all, interested in literary quality rather than sheer volume of sales.

In 1952 she helped André Deutsch to found the independent publishing firm that bore his name, and one of her first successes was Norman Mailer's *The Naked and the Dead*, of which she later said: "No one else would touch it because of how rude it was."

She was also herself an elegant writer whose memoirs attracted the admiration of a younger generation of readers. Her *Somewhere Towards the End* won the 2008 Costa prize for biography and she published her ninth and final volume of her memoirs, *A Florence Diary*, at the age of 99.

Diana Athill was born in 1917, the eldest daughter of a family of Norfolk gentry. Her maternal grandfather had inherited an 18th-century house and 1,000 acres in East Anglia. Although the family fortunes had so declined that her father warned her that she would have to earn her living, she spent her childhood in surroundings of ease and privilege – to which she later attributed her "strong propensity for idleness" and a feeling that money ought to fall from the sky, like rain, rather than having to be tediously earned.

Until the age of 14, when she was sent to boarding school, she was educated by governesses, filling some of the gaps in their instruction by extensive reading in her grandfather's excellent library. In childhood the most important things in her life were, she later wrote, "falling in love, riding and reading".

At 15, she fell in love with an Oxford undergraduate employed by her parents to coach her younger brother for the Common Entrance examination. The affair continued when she went up to Oxford, where she read English at Lady Margaret Hall, and in 1938, at the end of her second year, she became engaged. Her fiancé, by then a pilot officer in the RAF, was posted abroad and, after a two-year silence, wrote formally asking to be released from the engagement because he was about to marry another woman. He was later killed in action.

The end of her engagement was to overshadow the next 20 years of Athill's life. "My soul shrank to the size of a pea," she wrote. Her long, flat unhappiness, she added, substituted her blood with "some thin, acid fluid with a disagreeable smell".

Leaving Oxford with a third, she took a wartime job in the BBC's information service, where she met, and later shared a flat with, George Weidenfeld. He in turn introduced her to Deutsch, a 26-year-old Hungarian with whom she embarked on a brief, tepid affair that rapidly turned into an enduring professional partnership.

Although she claimed always to value her private life more highly than her work, her role as an editor and director at Deutsch's newly established firm provided Athill with a modest but adequate income and a congenial occupation. While Deutsch kept the firm afloat financially with a mixture of flair and parsimony, Athill concentrated on the detailed editing of texts and the nurturing of authors, including VS Naipaul, Philip Roth, Margaret Atwood and John Updike. She also helped to retrieve the careers of Jean Rhys and Molly Keane from undeserved obscurity and neglect.

Publishing also brought Athill into contact with more raffish figures, such as Hakim Jamal, a Black American follower of Malcolm X who became convinced that he possessed Godlike powers, and Waguih Ghali, an Egyptian writer and exile. Both these men, younger than Athill and disastrously flawed, moved at different points in the 1960s into her life and her flat (where Ghali killed himself in 1969) and provided an outlet for a mixture of sexual and maternal feeling about which she later wrote, with characteristic candour: "I might have been quite a Jocasta, given the chance."

It was writing that eventually succeeded in dispelling the sense of failure that had permeated her life since her abandonment by her fiancé. In 1958, at the age of 41, she won first prize in a short story competition run by *The Observer*. The effect on her was transforming. Until then, she wrote, she "had never really wanted anything but the most commonplace satisfactions of a woman's life and these ... I had failed to achieve. The *Observer*'s prize woke me up to the fact that I had become happy."

Athill continued her work at Deutsch as a literary midwife to other writers until her retirement in 1993, eight years after the firm was sold by Deutsch to Tom Rosenthal, under whose ownership it was felt by its original partners to have suffered a painful decline.

However, between 1963 and 2000 she produced a series of books that established her as a distinguished author in her own right. Her first published work was a volume of short stories and she later wrote a competent novel. But her real gift was for memoir. She was a good, crisp writer so long as she stuck to the topic of herself. Once she strayed beyond that, she tended to become ineffable.

In 1963, several decades before self-revelation became a fashionable publishing formula, she wrote *Instead of a Letter*, an affectionate, ironic and ruthlessly self-revealing account of her childhood and adult life to the point at which it was transformed by the *Observer* prize and by a fond, enduring partnership with the Jamaican-born playwright, Barry Reckord. *After a Funeral*, about her entanglement with Ghali, followed in 1986, and *Make Believe*, about the sad and mad Jamal, in 1993.

Diana Athill never married or had children, although she did become pregnant when she was 43. As she wrote in her memoirs, she assumed she would arrange an abortion, as she had done twice before. But her body – that or the "pinheaded, pig-headed" tortoise of her subconscious – had other ideas. She would keep the baby. In the event she miscarried at four months. The father was Reckord, with whom she lived more or less happily for the best part of 40 years.

In 2000 Granta published her volume of memoirs, *Stet*, the subject of which was her working, rather than her emotional life. In this she gave a beady-eyed account of dealings with, among others, Moore and Naipaul, and Deutsch himself. In an interview with *The Times* pegged to its publication, she declared the sixties a media invention. "Most of the people I knew had been bedding each other for years without calling it a sexual revolution." The book was widely praised, although a rare dissenting critic described its brisk, Rousseau-esque revelations as being in bad taste, not least the book's standout chapter about the miscarriage she had in her forties. The book made her, at the age of 82, something of a literary celebrity.

Aged 98, she said: "As it turns out, I have never had one wistful thought about that child. I quite liked children, but I was never motherly. And nor, I realised, was I wifely. The role I was most comfortable with was that of the Other Woman, and I was good at it. I never wanted to wreck anyone's marriage."

That same year, in the pages of *The Guardian*, she talked about how she regretted her "nub of coldness at the centre". When asked to explain what she meant she said that she had always been "very interested rather than involved" in experiences. Having written about her lovers with unflinching scrutiny over several volumes of memoirs she then talked about faking pleasure during sex in her seventies. Why not run through men, she asked, even if "one no longer feels sexy about them"?

The consequences of having (and not having) sex remained the subject with which her writing was most associated. As *Growing Old Disgracefully*, a BBC documentary put it, "No one writes about sex as frankly as Diana Athill." For her own part she saw this reputation as having disadvantages as well as advantages. "It does get boring sometimes," she said. "But then I say to myself, well, I've asked for it, I suppose."

Her sometimes excruciating frankness even extended to her parents. In her fifth book of memoirs, *Yesterday Morning*, she described how they were sexually incompatible and how much angst this caused them: "To continue having sex, even if occasionally, with someone whose touch has become hateful, is nerve-racking; while on his side, poor man, to be unable to resist making love to someone you adore, even though you know she can hardly bear it, is misery."

She always characterised writing as a form of immortality, describing her memoirs as "the story of one old ex-editor who imagines she will feel a little less dead if a few people read it", but concluding more philosophically with the thought that intelligence, as represented by the good writing, is "evolution's peak", and mankind's only remedy against despair.

Athill opened the first volume of her memoirs – they weren't in chronological order – with a meditation on life and death. She concluded it with the thought that, in the absence of religious faith or surviving offspring, "to die decently and acceptingly would be to prove the value of life".

Diana Athill OBE, writer, was born on December 21, 1917. She died after a short illness on January 23, 2019, aged 101

STEPHEN JOYCE

———————•———————

Controversial keeper of the Joycean flame who brusquely rebuffed attempts to study his famous grandfather

No publisher, author, academic, producer, curator or politician who dared to invoke the name of James Joyce was safe from his grandson's strictures. None was ever sufficiently respectful. They were all, in their ineptitude and greed, seeking to reshape the Joyce inheritance to their advantage.

It didn't matter how sincere or serious applicants were. They were, without exception, seen as predators or as fools who had no idea what they were talking about. One hapless supplicant, a young Irish composer, was stunned by a vicious rebuke he received in response to his request to quote some words from *Finnegans Wake* in a choral piece on which he was working.

In his letter David Fennessy had foolishly assumed an apostrophe in the title of the novel in question, giving Joyce the younger the opening he needed to turn him down with extreme prejudice. "You cannot even spell the title of my grandfather's last work correctly: its [sic] Finnegans Wake," Stephen Joyce wrote, himself omitting an apostrophe. "To put it politely and mildly, my wife and I don't like your music."

In 2005 a Canadian professor, Michael Groden, hoping to make use of recently uncovered research material, was told by Joyce: "You should consider a new career as a garbage collector in New York City, because you'll never quote a Joyce text again."

More recently, in 2013, Joyce described an Irish commemorative coin minted in honour of his grandfather's contribution to world literature as "one of the greatest insults to the Joyce family that has ever been perpetrated in Ireland".

It cannot be easy being the son or daughter of someone who is routinely described as a genius. There is so much to live up to and it is almost always impossible. For succeeding generations, the burden is reduced. There is greater distance and less expectation. But for Joyce, grandson of the writer reckoned by many to have been the greatest and most innovative novelist of the 20th century, the responsibility of being heir to his literary estate weighed heavily upon him every day of his adult life.

If Joyce Jr, as the paranoid executor of the estate, was obsessed with preserving the centrality of his grandfather's published work, he was equally resolved to remove from its legacy all trace of scandal or insufficient piety. In particular he was bent on eradicating any reference to his grandparents' colourful private life as well as to the lifelong mental illness suffered by his aunt Lucia, the writer's daughter and sister to Stephen's father, Giorgio Joyce.

In 1988 he shocked a gathering of literary academics in Venice when he announced from the lectern that he had destroyed a horde of letters Lucia had sent to him, along with correspondence to her from Samuel Beckett while the author of *Waiting for Godot* was working as Joyce's secretary. "I didn't want to have greedy little eyes and greedy little fingers going over them," Joyce observed, referring to the letters. The work, he said, in the form of Joyce's established writings, was all that mattered. As time went on and his obsession deepened, he came more and more to resemble a puritanical Christian, the sort for whom only the Bible, pure and unsullied, can provide the necessary insight into God's creation.

While rejecting the charge that he was cashing in on the Joyce name, Stephen Joyce could not be said to have drawn upon the example of his grandfather's 1927 poetry collection, *Pomes Penyeach*. His own value judgments were markedly more mercenary. Not only was every attempt to quote from Joyce contested, but each hard-won approval came with a price tag attached. Like Father Coffey, the writer's take on Cerberus, the fearsome guardian of Hades, Joyce the younger was clear that there could be no entrance to the canon other than through his turnstile.

Over the years this uncompromising approach yielded him considerable dividends. But not always. Sometimes he came unstuck. On one occasion, a planned reading from the works of Joyce and Beckett to mark Bloomsday, the annual celebration of *Ulysses*, in 2000 was cancelled when the organisers were presented with a bill for £27,000. The Beckett estate, by contrast, had requested a mere £20.

It is no exaggeration to say that Joycean scholarship was placed in suspended animation by the machinations and avarice of Stephen Joyce, who will have known that the impediments he erected would not survive his death, but who appeared to believe that so long as he was alive he had no higher duty than to protect his grandfather's reputation.

The war, for that is what it was, between scholars and the object of their ire came briefly to an end in 1991 when the copyright on the Joycean corpus expired 50 years after the writer's death. Suddenly, academics and others were free to quote their hero's words as they chose and to speculate on their true meaning and origins. But four years later the European Union extended copyright from 50 to 70 years, allowing the grandson to resume hostilities.

From then on, he thundered, on pain of prosecution, no permission would be given, unless authorised by him, to quote from anything written by his grandfather. Dramatic adaptations were forbidden; universities and libraries that owned Joycean papers were prevented from displaying them without permission; new anthologies were rejected; the use of the internet to quote from the master was denied. Those who ignored the edicts soon found themselves facing costly litigation.

Nemesis was probably inevitable. In 2004, during events in Dublin to celebrate the centenary of Bloomsday, the Irish government decided that enough was enough and enacted legislation that allowed publishers, theatres and others the right, in Ireland, to mark the occasion as it deserved. Stephen Joyce was livid.

Then, a year later, Stanford Law School, one of the most richly endowed academic institutions in the United States, decided to lend its support to a suit brought by the scholar Carol Loeb Shloss against Joyce for opposing her use of certain Joycean quotations in her biography, *Lucia Joyce: To Dance in the Wake*. The result was a rare grandfilial defeat, made all the more painful by costs of $240,000.

It was not until January 1, 2012 that relief was rendered permanent when the extended copyright on Joyce's literary output finally lapsed. Since then there has been a free-for-all in Joycean scholarship, spearheaded in Britain by Gordon Bowker, whose biography of the writer, the first full-length study since that by Richard Ellmann in 1959, exposed publicly for the first time the full extent of the writer's intense and varied sex life.

Stephen James Joyce was born in Paris in 1932, the son of Giorgio, the Irish author's only son, who was a professional singer specialising in Handel, and his wife, Helen, an American heiress. He was nearly nine when James Joyce died, but he knew his grandmother, Nora Barnacle, and Lucia quite well until their deaths in 1951 and 1982. Young Stephen was schooled in France and later attended Harvard, where at different times he shared rooms with the Aga Khan and Paul Matisse, the son of the painter Henri Matisse.

It was in the middle of a successful career with the Paris-based Organisation for Economic Cooperation and Development (OECD) that he awoke, quite suddenly, to his heritage as keeper of the Joycean flame. Until then Lucia, who ended her days in an asylum in Northampton, had been executor of the Joyce estate, giving free rein to those, including Ellmann, interested in her uncle's work. Stephen's accession to the role changed that.

In his later years, having retired early from the OECD to concentrate on what had become the defining feature of his life, Stephen Joyce lived on the Île de Ré, near La Rochelle in France, with his wife, Solange, who predeceased him. They had no children and there are now no living descendants of Ireland's most acclaimed and controversial writer.

Stephen Joyce, guardian of James Joyce's literary estate, was born on February 15, 1932. He died on January 23, 2020, aged 87

CHRISTOPHER BOOKER

---•---

Quixotic, peppery and unfailingly bloody-minded right-wing journalist and co-founder of Private Eye *who delighted in teasing his enemies*

Christopher Booker (second from right) with colleagues from Private Eye *outside the High Court, London in 1963 where the magazine was being sued for libel.*

As a student at Cambridge, Christopher Booker announced that his ambitions were to edit a magazine, appear on television and marry the daughter of an aristocrat. By the age of 25 he had prematurely achieved all three.

On graduating he founded *Private Eye* with his old school chums Richard Ingrams and Willie Rushton and became the magazine's first editor. That led to employment as a scriptwriter and occasional performer on BBC television's pioneering satirical magazine show, *That Was the Week That Was.*

His aspirational hat-trick was completed in 1963 when he married Emma Tennant, the daughter of Lord and Lady Glenconner, and the half-sister of Colin Tennant, sometime suitor of Princess Margaret.

If it had all come too easily, it melted away just as quickly. While on honeymoon he was ousted as editor of *Private Eye* by Ingrams and within months had lost his TV income when *TW3* was cancelled at the end of 1963. With an election year looming, the BBC feared the risqué programme could compromise its impartiality.

Before long the aristocratic connection had gone too, and after their divorce, Tennant married the journalist Alexander Cockburn in 1968.

Such disruptions caused a rethink, during which Booker underwent a religious conversion and reinvented himself as an astringent critic of the permissive society. Yet he continued to write for the *Eye* for the rest of his life as part of the magazine's collaborative joke-writing team, "holding up a distorting mirror to all the political and social absurdities of our time".

One of his most famous *Private Eye* covers – which to his irritation was sometimes erroneously attributed to Peter Cook – depicted Enoch Powell at the height of the racism row that cost him his job in Ted Heath's shadow cabinet, holding his hands out wide and saying: "And some of them have got them this long."

Booker remained a prolific contributor under Ian Hislop, who took over from Ingrams in 1986, and co-authored such well-loved *Private Eye* institutions as the Secret Diary of John Major, the Rev ARP Blair's St Albion Parish News and Gordon Brown's Prime Ministerial Decree. Other columns to which Booker contributed regularly included the threnodies of EJ Thribb and the left-wing rants of Dave Spart.

Yet by the late 1960s he was also pursuing a parallel career as an intellectual contrarian and polemicist of the "young fogey" school. Falling under the influence of the conservative Christian commentator Malcolm Muggeridge, he stayed at the older man's home in Sussex for three months while he worked on a book in which he excoriated what he regarded as the decade's excesses of liberalism.

The Neophiliacs: A Study of the Revolution in English Life in the Fifties and Sixties (1969) bemoaned manifestations of modern life from rock'n'roll to supermarkets via the relaxation of the gambling laws, miniskirts and James Bond films. All, he claimed, were "fashionable absurdities".

The irony was not lost on Booker that his satirising in *Private Eye* of the old establishment personified by Harold Macmillan, Sir Alec Douglas-Home and their like had helped to fuel the social revolution of the 1960s that he was now attacking.

The Neophiliacs was serialised in the *Sunday Telegraph* and launched

Booker as a social commentator swimming against the tide of "modernism". Combining a sceptical populism with undoubted erudition, he attacked the "nanny state" and set himself against what he saw as a new and arrogant professional elite. His targets ranged from architects and town planners to scientists and doctors.

Although he had no scientific training, he wrote prolifically in denial of the consensus on issues including the link between passive smoking and cancer (Booker was a 30-a-day man) and the dangers posed by asbestos. We were being "scared to death" by the dire and unsubstantiated warnings of those who wanted to interfere with our life choices, he believed. Such ideas caused enough consternation for the Health and Safety Executive to issue refutations of several of his claims.

He was also a fervid denier of man-made climate change and included "teasing global warmists" among his recreations in *Who's Who*. In his book *The Real Global Warming Disaster* (2009) he suggested that the measures taken by the world's governments to reduce carbon emissions "will turn out to be one of the most expensive, destructive, and foolish mistakes the human race has ever made".

Needless to say, he was widely rebuked by the scientific community and he was sued by the United Nations' Inter-governmental Panel on Climate Change over accusations he made about its chairman. Booker was only encouraged by such skirmishes. If he was getting under their skin that much, he was convinced he must be doing something right. His campaigning was consistent and his message, unlike the climate, never changed.

Even when he entered into the more sedate waters of literary criticism, his ability to engender controversy did not desert him. In *The Seven Basic Plots: Why We Tell Stories* (2004) he managed to condemn Chekhov, Proust, Joyce, Kafka and DH Lawrence while praising *Crocodile Dundee*, *ET* and *Terminator 2*.

A fiery academic debate followed the book's publication, but even his sternest critics were forced to concede that the 700-page opus was as "stimulating" and "ambitious" as its conclusions were adversarial and perplexing.

Unsurprisingly, he was one of the first seriously to question Britain's membership of the European Union and in his way was one of the architects of the Brexit vote in 2016. Together with Richard

North he wrote *The Mad Officials: How the Bureaucrats Are Strangling Britain*, which was published in 1994 just as the Maastricht Treaty was ushering in a new era of expanded European integration.

His writings in *The Daily Telegraph* on the subject exasperated the paper's editor Max Hastings, who wrote in his memoir that "Booker's fanatical hostility to Europe increasingly distorted his journalism".

When he was removed from his column in the paper he became a resident Euro-scourge at *The Sunday Telegraph*, filling his weekly column with denunciations of European perfidy and meddling, although the veracity of some of his wilder assertions – which included a claim that the EU wanted to abolish double-decker buses from the streets of London – was frequently challenged.

Dubbed "the patron saint of Leave", he should have viewed the result of the EU referendum as one of the crowning moments of his career. Yet the conduct of the campaign dismayed him. "He could see that the politicians who proposed to take us out of the EU hadn't a clue how to go about it and he wasn't afraid to say that in his columns," one newspaper colleague noted.

Opinion was divided on whether his influence as a social and political commentator was harmless or pernicious. His fellow conservative commentator James Delingpole saw him as a heroic crusader who "speaks truth to power without fear or favour". The writer and critic Adam Mars-Jones regarded him as "near-barmy", yet it was said without malice.

Those who abhorred Booker's views tended to take a gentler view of the man and indulge him as an archetypal English eccentric, with his soft voice, unfashionably long hair and a face that crumpled into a winning smile at any excuse. The glasses he wore had lenses so thick they looked bulletproof and he had a disconcerting habit of tilting his head back in order to study people's faces through them. He was out of sorts with so much of the modern world, so it was perhaps fitting that he made his home in an old rectory in Somerset, where he lived with his third wife, Valerie (née Patrick). They married in 1979 after the annulment of his second marriage to Christine Verity, who was remarried to the historian Norman Stone. They had two sons.

Christopher John Penrice Booker was born in 1937 in Somerset. His parents, John and Margaret Booker, ran a private prep school in Ilminster that they subsequently moved to Knighton House, Dorset.

He was one of three children. His sisters Joanna and Serena predeceased him.

Booker attended the Dragon School, Oxford, but it was as a pupil at Shrewsbury School that he formed life-changing friendships with Ingrams and Rushton. All three had spells editing the school magazine, as did another friend and future fellow journalist, Paul Foot. The divergent political leanings that would shape their respective careers were already mapped out in a school debate in which the motion was proposed "that this House deplores the decline of the landed gentry", when Booker and Foot took opposing viewpoints.

Described by his headmaster as "an extraordinarily staid young man, reserved and studious, who used to spend his Sundays collecting fossils", Booker went up to Corpus Christi, Cambridge, where he read history and met Peter Cook, another future *Private Eye* collaborator, while Ingrams went up to Oxford.

Excused National Service owing to his poor eyesight, Booker worked briefly for the Liberal Party on its newspaper and in 1961 landed his first Fleet Street post as jazz critic for the newly launched *Sunday Telegraph*. Among the reviews he wrote during his three-year tenure was a fulsome account of a concert by the pianist Erroll Garner, which never took place after a last-minute cancellation.

Also that year, "between Supermac and the rise of the Beatles", Booker reunited with his fellow Old Salopians Ingrams and Rushton to found *Private Eye*. Early issues were assembled and pasted up in Rushton's flat, with the cartoonist's mother keeping them going with supplies of tomato soup and coffee.

As an editor, Booker was a perfectionist, highly strung and prone to temper tantrums. Pages were ripped up, telephones smashed, and on at least one occasion Ingrams felt compelled to lock him out of the office.

His ousting from the editor's chair by Ingrams was symptomatic of a feisty relationship. Booker once wrote dismissively in *The Spectator* that *Private Eye* was "on its day a strong candidate for the most unpleasant thing in British journalism". Yet a few days later he was happily back in the magazine's Soho office for a joke-writing session.

Christopher Booker, journalist, was born on October 7, 1937. He died of cancer on July 3, 2019, aged 81

PAUL CALLAN

— • —

Fleet Street all-rounder and model for Private Eye'*s* Lunchtime O'Booze *whose scoops included Kray confessions and two words from Garbo*

Paul Callan (second from right) with fellow columnists.

When Paul Callan met Greta Garbo at Hotel du Cap-Eden-Roc in Antibes he thought the scoop of a lifetime was about to land in his lap.

The reclusive actress had not granted an interview in decades and Callan, in town to cover the Cannes Film Festival for the *Daily Mail*, saw the headline "GARBO SPEAKS!" flashing before him on a world exclusive that was bound to be syndicated around the globe. His sense of elation lasted no more than a few seconds. "Miss Garbo, I wonder ..." he began as he framed his first question. "Why wonder?" she interrupted and walked out.

Resourceful as ever, Callan got a full-page feature out of his two-word interview and a fine anecdote with which to regale his fellow hacks over a glass or three in El Vino. His reputation as one of the last of the old-style Fleet Street "big beasts" parodied in *Private Eye* as "Lunchtime O'Booze" was hard earned.

Sent to Belgium by the *Daily Mirror* in 1987 to write a piece on the victims of the Zeebrugge ferry disaster, he freely admitted that he had arrived "too pissed to file", yet his byline was considered such an asset that back in London the news desk composed a piece in his colourful style and put his name on it.

He could survive such occasional mishaps thanks to a vast back catalogue of enviable front-page exclusives. Without bothering with the formality of seeking Home Office permission, he interviewed both the Kray twins for the *Mirror*. In Broadmoor he cajoled Ronnie Kray into recounting with an alarming relish how he had calmly murdered his fellow gangster, George Cornell, with a bullet to the forehead, adding: "I done the earth a favour."

In Parkhurst he persuaded Reggie Kray to confess for the first time to the murder of Jack "the Hat" McVitie. "I heard he was going to kill me, so I killed him," he told Callan. "He deserved it."

He also talked Bobby Kennedy's murderer, Sirhan Sirhan, into singing during a two-hour interview in a maximum-security cell in California's Soledad prison. In a front-page *Mirror* splash headlined "Kennedy Killer Speaks", Callan dramatically reported how Sirhan had coiled his fingers around an imaginary revolver and pointed it at his interviewer's head to show how he had assassinated the man who might have become president.

One of his crowning triumphs came in 1995 when the *Express* sent him to cover the 50th anniversary of the liberation of Auschwitz. Callan, who was Jewish, filed a moving piece which his executive editor said brought tears to his eyes, as did the expenses claim which followed a few days later.

By then Callan had adopted the airs of a patrician, which belied more humble origins, his frame well-upholstered after a lifetime of long and bibulous lunches. "He looked more like a judge having a quick snifter after a tricky fraud case, all pinstripes, bow tie and large vodka," Alan Frame, executive editor of the *Express* observed.

Gregarious, rarely less than ebullient and proudly politically incorrect, he was in his element holding court to his peers in El Vino, even after the ending of its males-only policy, a change of which he deeply disapproved. He had been to the fore in an infamous battle in 1970 when feminist journalists invaded the Fleet Street watering hole in protest at their exclusion.

As he shouted "repel boarders!" and aimed a soda siphon in the direction of the insurgents, one of them kneed him in the groin. Typically, he claimed £50 compensation for an industrial injury from his then employer, the *London Evening Standard*. Needless to say, it also provided him with a good story for the following day's paper.

For many years he posed as an alumnus of Eton and Cambridge, fictitious claims that he even propagated in the notices of his 1973 marriage. One of those who saw through him was the Prince of Wales. At a reception at the British embassy in Delhi while covering a royal tour of India, Callan fell into conversation with the heir to the throne, who noticed his striped Old Etonian tie.

"Surely a man from the *Mirror* did not go to Eton?" Prince Charles inquired. "Certainly not, sir," Callan admitted. "But it's a nice tie!"

His Fleet Street reputation was initially made as a gossip columnist. After editing the Londoner's Diary in the *Evening Standard* he arrived at the *Daily Mail* in 1971 to create a column intended to rival the pseudonymous William Hickey diary in the *Daily Express*. One of the contributors to the Hickey column was the 29-year-old Nigel Dempster, whom Callan promptly recruited as his deputy. It was an appointment he came to regret, for within two years Dempster had taken his job in a coup d'état, turning in humdrum stories when Callan was editing and keeping his best tales for when Callan took a day off.

He is survived by Steffi Fields, his American wife, who for many years was desk editor for NBC's London bureau. He is further survived by their two children.

Paul Stanley Lester Callan was born in Redbridge, Essex, in 1939. His mother was Jewish and his Irish father, James, was a musician whose academic achievements, according to his son's not always reliable testimony, included professorships at Harvard and Cambridge. Educated at Cranbrook School, Ilford, he studied cello at the Royal Academy of Music before joining the BBC Overseas Service.

By 1964 he had joined the *Yorkshire Evening Post*. One of his favourite stories involved being dispatched to London to cover Winston Churchill's funeral by a news editor who was convinced that the great man must have had Yorkshire blood. Callan was instructed to solicit tributes from only "salt of t'earth" mourners from God's Own

County. Shortly after, he moved permanently to London to join the *Evening Standard.*

After his ousting from the *Mail*, he returned briefly to radio, fronting a morning chat show on the newly launched LBC in an unlikely pairing with Janet Street-Porter.

Callan considered her common, and revelled in telling listeners that his co-host looked a complete fright, with a bad hangover and bags under her eyes. She considered him "a snooty slimeball" and moaned on air about his "suede shoes, the stench of his French cigarettes and his ceaseless harping about his houses in the country and in 'town'". Their contrasting accents earned the nicknames "cut-glass" and "cut-froat" among broadcasting colleagues. "Day in and day out the morning was spent settling scores and trashing each other's taste," Street-Porter wrote in her memoir, *Fall Out.*

It made for entertaining listening but was short-lived. In 1975 Callan joined the *Mirror* to write a gossipy column called "Inside the World of Paul Callan" and later "Close-Up". His flair for self-projection meant that, as his star rose, he was given free rein to write colour pieces about the biggest news stories of the day and to jet around the world conducting celebrity interviews, more often than not "around a sparkling swimming pool in Beverly Hills".

Away from the typewriter and the lunch table, his abiding passion was music. Few assignments in his long career gave him more professional pleasure than the weekly *Celebrity Choice* show he presented in the 1990s on Classic FM. His knowledge of the classics was extensive, if not quite flawless. While covering Cowes Week one year he got into an argument over dinner with a fellow journalist, Christopher Wilson, about whether the baroque music playing in the background was by Tartini or Scarlatti. The dispute became so heated that the proprietor threw them out, adding tartly that they had both been wrong.

Paul Callan, journalist, was born on March 13, 1939. He died of a heart attack on November 21, 2020, aged 81

ROD RICHARDS

Colourful Welsh Tory MP and minister known as 'Randy Rod' who did much to undermine John Major's 'back to basics' campaign

Many Conservative MPs seemed resolved to undermine Sir John Major's "back to basics" campaign in the 1990s. Rod Richards, who was burdened by occasional irregularities in his private life and apparently revelled in being known as "the most hated man in Wales", appeared determined to outclass them all in word and deed.

"Rottweiler Rod", as he was known, accused the Welsh of having an "inferiority complex", denounced New Labour as "nothing more than a wooden horse called Tony the phoney pony [Blair]", and during his first big speech in the Commons had to be restrained three times by the deputy Speaker because of his intemperate language. Even that could not prevent a walk-out by a dozen Labour and Liberal Democrat MPs as Richards ploughed on with claims of Labour "sleaze, corruption and gerrymandering".

At Westminster, Richards became something of a pioneer of new technology by holding surgeries via video call linked to a computer in his constituency office. He championed the concerns of his constituents, opposed further European integration and, as a Welsh-language speaker, was particularly proud of securing funding to support the language in the South American region of Patagonia, where it has been spoken for more than 150 years.

Even by Westminster standards, his was a rollercoaster of a career. After a couple of years in Parliament he was appointed minister in the Welsh Office, and presumably this had more to do with his political than diplomatic skills as he promptly marked his arrival by referring to Labour councillors in Wales as "short, fat, slimy and fundamentally corrupt". Such disdain lost him friends in local government at a time when John Redwood, the Welsh secretary, was trying to cosy up to them. Richards, the only member of the government to speak Welsh, was ordered to apologise.

Although Richards's frank style, described as being "as abrasive as sandpaper", endeared him to Tory activists, they took a less generous view when in 1996 the *News of the World* published details of his extramarital "bondage romp" with Julia Felthouse, a former public-relations executive for the National Canine Defence League, who was 20 years his junior.

"Randy Rod", as the tabloids called him, was considered fair game by the media because of the way he had used his family to promote his election prospects in 1992.

He was immediately sacked by a furious Major without the customary exchange of letters, instead just an announcement from No 10. There was little sympathy from MPs on any side of the Commons, where a distinct whiff of schadenfreude emerged at the departure from ministerial office of an MP described by one colleague as a "sanctimonious and arrogant" man. A year later Richards, who was no flincher from the glass, faced ruin after losing his seat in the Labour landslide.

"It was ghastly, absolutely ghastly," he told *The Times* when recalling that election night. "I was standing there doing the usual gracious stuff, but my guts were churning because I had two kids in private school, a home in north Wales and a home in Richmond, and you just do this mental arithmetic while you're trying to congratulate the chap who's won. It was one of the worst experiences I've ever had in terms of stress, and I've been an officer in the Royal Marines."

Returning to his former occupations of military intelligence and TV news reading were not options. "So I fished around for some work, and being an ex-Tory MP and an ex-Tory minister was about as popular as a rat on a Communion plate," he said. "There wasn't a door that I pushed that would open."

He wanted to get back into the Commons, but that would mean a wait of five years. The next best thing available was Blair's new Welsh Assembly, even though he had campaigned vigorously against it. After giving himself a makeover with a military-style regime of swimming and working out in the gym, he was chosen as leader by Welsh party members.

At the first elections to the assembly, in May 1999, he was defeated in his constituency, but gained a seat through the regional top-up list and became a footnote in history as the first member of the assembly to be sworn in. Yet, priapic fellow that he was, trouble still followed.

A couple of months later he met two sisters in a pub near his home in Richmond, southwest London. The three had dinner in a pizzeria before taking a cab back to the sisters' home in Kew where, one of them claimed, he smoked cannabis and made unwanted sexual advances and flung her against a parked car.

Although Richards was cleared of grievous bodily harm in a court of law, in the court of public opinion the jury was still out. He did himself few favours by using a long interview in the *Daily Mail* to claim that he "didn't fancy" either of the young women, but admitted that he had "moved in on them and chatted them up". He also said that he and his wife, who had stood by him after his previous indiscretion, were "in an open marriage".

During the court case Richards stepped aside as leader of the Welsh Conservatives, but the party refused to back his choice of acting leader, and instead picked Nick Bourne, with whom he had a fractious relationship. That descended into outright acrimony when Richards failed to vote with his party on the assembly's budget and had the whip withdrawn. The row reached the floor of the assembly, where Richards referred to Bourne as a "prat".

Meanwhile Richards's debts, estimated at more than £300,000, were becoming overwhelming. Knowing that he was about to be declared bankrupt, he resigned from the assembly in 2002 on the grounds of ill health, speaking openly about his drink problem. Eventually he found political solace in UKIP, claiming that many of the things the party stands for chimed with his own views, but he continued to feel nostalgia for Parliament. "I loved the House of Commons," he told *The Times*. "I had found my niche in life. I was going to stay there till I died."

Roderick Richards was born in Llanelli in 1947, the son of Ivor Richards, an engineer and fitter at Llanelli docks, and Lizzie (née Evans), a nurse. He was educated at Llandovery College, Carmarthenshire, and at Llanelli grammar school. He left Aberystwyth University after a year, having dedicated much of his time to sport rather than study, and in 1969 joined the Marines on a short service commission.

After a few odd jobs, including driving a taxi in east London, he returned to university in 1971, achieving a first in economics at the University of Wales in Swansea. There he met Elizabeth Knight, who became a clinical child psychologist, and they were married in 1975.

The marriage was dissolved in the early 2000s, and he is survived by their children, who knew him as "Spags" because of his love for spaghetti bolognese. They are Rhodri and Trystan, who served as officers in the Welsh Guards and are now management consultants, and Elen, who is an accountant. She recalled how while her father was an MP he would accompany her on her Sunday paper round on dark mornings, even when he was being tormented by the very newspapers that he was helping to deliver.

From university he worked as an economic forecaster for the BBC, before joining the security services in Northern Ireland. In 1983 he moved to S4C, the newly launched Welsh language TV channel, as a newsreader.

Richards, scarred by the way that the trade unions had failed to protect his father after an industrial accident, was a dedicated Conservative and keen to get into frontline politics. He stood in Carmarthen at the 1987 general election, and then the Vale of Glamorgan by-election in 1989 after the death of Sir Raymond Gower, the Conservative MP, but lost to Labour by more than 6,000 votes. David Hunt, the Welsh secretary, took him on as a special adviser, before parliamentary success finally came his way in 1992, when he held on to Sir Anthony Meyer's former seat of Clwyd North West by 6,050 votes – the biggest Tory majority in Wales.

After boundary changes he stood for the new seat of Clwyd West in 1997, losing to Labour by fewer than 2,000 votes. After leaving the Welsh Assembly he was essentially retired and living on what he described as a meagre pension, although there were occasional fees for radio and TV work around election time.

There was a brief flash of the old firebrand once more when in 2008 Richards was given a caution after "clipping" a Conservative canvasser who called at his home.

Rod Richards, Conservative politician, was born on March 12, 1947. He died from lymphoma on July 13, 2019, aged 72

FENELLA FIELDING

———————•———————

Velvet-voiced actress who ranged from Carry on … to Chekhov

As an actress, Fenella Fielding was more than the sum of her parts, but not much more. She nevertheless made the most of what she had – a doe-eyed gaze, a deep husk of a voice, a posturing manner – and, in the heyday of the intimate West End revue, she made her mark.

Since the writing was already on the wall for revue when she started in the mid-1950s, what would she do when it finally fell from favour? The ever-poised Fielding was untroubled, and continued as a straight actress for 30-odd years. Whether it was Wilde or Ibsen, Chekhov or Coward, the same bodily principles, often hilariously obvious, applied and she stretched her elegant gifts.

She reprised her vaudevillian talents most memorably in the 1966 comedy *Carry On Screaming*. As the vampiric, seductive, velvet-clad Valeria, she reclines and asks a visiting detective played by Harry H Corbett: "Do you mind if I smoke?" With permission granted, smoke begins to billow from the length of her lounging form.

She and her co-star Kenneth Williams had already sparked off each other to great effect on stage. In the 1959 revue *Pieces of Eight* at the Apollo Theatre, written by Peter Cook and Harold Pinter, they scored point after point off one another in various sketches. She remembered his eccentricities fondly, but his jealousy less so. If she had a good review, he would be enraged. "Kenneth came out of the wings and he had the paper in his hand and he had the most terrible temper about it. I thought, 'God! I can't help the fact they've said something nice about me.'"

Fielding had starred the previous year in Sandy Wilson's musical version of *Valmouth*, taken from Ronald Firbank's novel. Rich in knowing humour, gowned in Edwardian costume and with a characterisation as the mincing Lady Parvula de Panzoust to draw laughter first at the Lyric in Hammersmith, and then in the West End's Saville theatre, the assured insinuation of her humour was a constant joy. Her suggestive improprieties were so subtle in song that no one could seriously object to the fun. It was one of the performances that earned her the sobriquet, "England's first lady of the double entendre".

Valmouth proved to be the springboard for a distinguished career in theatre over the next two decades, which, much to her chagrin, was overshadowed by *Carry On Screaming*. "People still think of me in a certain way because of the Carry On films," she said, although she did not demur from pinching her "Do you mind if I smoke?" line as the title of her memoirs.

Fenella Marion Feldman was born in London in 1927, to a Romanian-Jewish mother, Tilly (née Katz), and a Lithuanian-Jewish father, Philip, who managed a cinema. She grew up in Lower Clapton and was educated at the North London Collegiate School in Edgware.

Her father was, in her words, "a respected member of the community" who hit his daughter while her mother egged him on. Despite Fenella's obvious intelligence, he forbade university, telling her "I'd rather see you dead at my feet". He also disapproved of her attending RADA.

"I had to wait until he had gone to work in the morning and then stay out late to try to avoid him in the evening. Because of these terrible rows, Mummy would come and try to get me to go back home in the middle of the day. After about a year the school said, 'Look, this cannot carry on.' I had to leave."

Aged 27, working as a typist and still living at home, she began to secure small acting roles. Hours spent hanging around Vidal Sassoon's hairdressing salon in London, which had opened in 1954, had begun to pay off. "You had to go," she explained, "otherwise it was social death. Everybody spent their entire time there, and anybody who was looking for an actress to cast in a play would come to Vidal Sassoon."

The sixties and early seventies were a characteristic mix of serious, silly, and seductive. Highlights included her haughty Madame Arkadina in Chekhov's *The Seagull* at the Nottingham Playhouse, and the title role in *Hedda Gabler* in Leicester's Phoenix Theatre in 1969, which was described by *The Times* as "among the theatrical experiences of a lifetime".

On the big screen, Fielding appeared in *Carry On Regardless* in 1961, alongside Tony Curtis and Zsa Zsa Gábor in the 1966 farce *Drop Dead Darling*, and in *Doctor in Clover* with Leslie Phillips.

Through it all she captivated figures such as Kenneth Tynan, Noël

Coward and Federico Fellini. The latter once offered her a part in a film playing the incarnation of six different men's desires. "Not a bad role," she reflected. Pre-booked by Chichester Theatre, she declined.

As she entered her fifties, her career began to suffer. After a dishonest agent embezzled some of her earnings, she was declared bankrupt and had to sell her house. "It's rather awful," she said, "sitting in a room waiting for benefits when everybody knows who you are."

As luck would have it, she was offered the chance to reprise her signature role as Lady Parvula de Panzoust at the Chichester Festival Theatre in 1982. The critics loved it. Fielding was "so far over the top as to be almost out of sight," wrote Sheridan Morley.

Fielding worked in a period when male co-stars had to be managed carefully. Male comedians "got very uncomfortable if they couldn't make you laugh," she recalled. "So I would fake being unable to stop myself laughing, and the relaxation in their eyes was absolutely amazing". Norman Wisdom was not so easily dealt with: "Hand up your skirt first thing in the morning, not a lovely way to start a day's filming."

Fielding never married but once revealed that she had two lovers concurrently for 20 years. "It was simply lovely to be loved by two very different but such lovely men." Asked how she kept them apart, she would giggle and say, "I think it's just an art". She did not divulge their names but one lover she did admit to was the journalist Jeffrey Bernard. "It wasn't a really serious fling – he was always so pissed."

She is survived by her older brother, Lord Feldman, the former Conservative peer.

In old age she was delighted to find herself much in demand and remained an engaging figure in bright red lipstick and a black wig. She had a daily routine of yoga and she kept her mind active, she said, by reading philosophy books every night before going to sleep.

Fenella Fielding OBE, actress, was born on November 17, 1927. She died on September 11, 2018, aged 90

FRED HAMBLIN

—————————•—————————

Wodehousian chemist who was a key figure in the development of plastics at ICI, once stole a steamroller and almost blew up his school

It was clear from his schooldays onwards what Fred Hamblin would end up doing for a living. In one chemistry lesson at Kingswood Grammar in Bristol he managed to create enough TNT to blow himself clean through an asbestos wall into the next classroom. He went on to run ICI Germany, where he was instrumental in the early development of the plastics industry.

A man of buoyant personality throughout his long life, he delighted in giving colourful accounts of his exploits. He never slowed down, having a second family in his fifties, and was a serial retiree who, unbowed by age, continued to work into his eighties. In his spare time he was chairman or president of a wide range of societies, among them the Brighton West Pier Trust, the Brighton Lifeboat Association, and, most significantly, the British German Association. For him, Anglo-German fellowship was a lifelong mission.

Frederick Thomas Hamblin was born in Warmley, near Bristol, in 1914 to John Hamblin, an engineer, and his wife, Ethel. At his small primary school run by elderly women, one of the last of the "dame" schools, he wrote on slates with slate pencils. At Kingswood Grammar, after making a strong impression on the explosives front, he was allowed to matriculate (the equivalent of O levels) at the age of 13. His continued fascination with chemistry led him to set up apparatus for experiments in the loft at home. "Looking back," he reflected in later life, "I'm amazed at the tolerance of my parents to the horrible smells and noises I often made."

Fearing that he was becoming too much of a swot, his father sent him to work on his uncle's farm in Dorset. There he collected fossils from around the local mines and became an accomplished mole catcher, selling the fur at Yeovil market. He also made it into the local paper by demonstrating a novel way of trapping rats using his boots.

Satisfied that he had become more "rounded", his father allowed him to return to his education and, after passing his higher school certificate, he went to the University of Bristol to read, inevitably, chemistry.

There he became addicted to mischief and on one occasion pulled off a prank that was to enter university folklore. He and his co-conspirators stole a steamroller one night and managed to drive it under its own steam, with clearance of only a few inches, into the auditorium of the Victoria Rooms, which, with its eight-columned portico, is considered the symbol of the university.

After an extensive search, the steamroller was eventually found the next morning by a surprised porter, who rushed outside and said to the police superintendent: "Did you say you were looking for a steamroller?" The superintendent's exact reply is not recorded. As the boiler had cooled down and it was too much of a fire risk to restoke it indoors, it had to be pushed out by a small army of the Somerset Constabulary. The operation was eventually accomplished, amid much cheering from the students who had gathered to watch, Hamblin among them.

He graduated with a first and went on to study for a doctorate in artificial radioactivity, which was such a new field that he got to know Ernest Rutherford, the father of nuclear physics, personally. He was also able to build the first neutron source outside Cambridge, Oxford and London. As was becoming a pattern of his life, however, this endeavour was not free of complications. It was housed in a lead apparatus located in the quadrangle of Bristol's chemistry department. The source was a glass tube containing beryllium powder and radium bromide. One day, when Hamblin lifted the tube out, it burst with a loud pop, dispersing radium bromide around him.

He took a shower immediately, but was not sure if he had inhaled (if he had he could expect a lingering death). The nearest working Geiger counter was in London, at Imperial College, but the last train that night had left. He spent what he later described as a "somewhat restless night", before taking the morning train. En route to the station he asked Audrey Lawrence, known as Derry, a fellow student and girlfriend, to marry him if all was well, and to forget all about him if not. The professor at Imperial gave him the all-clear and took him for a strong drink.

Insouciant of manner and untroubled by self-doubt, Hamblin seemed to adopt a Woosterish persona as he went from one scrape to the next, and he always seemed to emerge with his optimistic spirit undimmed, perhaps because there was often a fortunate outcome from his tribulations. During his university holidays, for example, he took his first trip abroad, getting a job on a coal ship as a deckhand to work his passage. A collision with a tug when leaving Bordeaux badly damaged the ship. The master managed to bring it to shore and they stepped on to dry land, resulting in him being "shipwrecked" without getting his feet wet, and, happily, stranded in a vineyard.

After completing his doctorate in 1937 Hamblin applied for a job with the plastics division of ICI. The interview small talk over, he was asked about his hobbies. When he said "keeping fish", the man interviewing him, a retired colonel called Sampson, beamed and said that he was constructing a pond in the garden. For the rest of the interview, all 45 minutes of it, they discussed how it should be stocked and what plants would be required. The door of the office then opened and the research director, a man who rejoiced in the name of Dr Caress, came in. When Dr Caress asked Sampson how the interview was going, he replied: "He's a splendid fellow, knows all the right things – we should take him on!"

And so they did, with Hamblin joining a small team at Billingham, Co Durham. His first task was to develop a commercial process for the production of Perspex for the windscreens of RAF aircraft, vital work that meant he was in a reserved occupation. He helped to put up barrage balloons over the Billingham chemicals site, only for them to come down in flames after a lightning storm. Hamblin described this as "somewhat disconcerting".

In 1941 he moved to Welwyn Garden City in Hertfordshire, where ICI put him in charge of a unit preparing plans for postwar developments. They tried to develop plastic bottles for whisky. It didn't work, but he had to taste a lot of whisky to find that out.

After the war, and by then a fellow of the Royal Institute of Chemistry, Hamblin became ICI's export sales manager for plastics, travelling extensively. On one trip he was driven from Entebbe to Nairobi by the ICI sales manager for Uganda and Kenya. At Jinja on Lake Victoria they stopped to camp. Hamblin wanted to take some pictures of the lake, so walked down to the edge, but no one had told him about the hippo traps placed to prevent the animals getting on to the golf course. As he was walking while looking through the camera viewfinder the ground gave way and he fell into a pit with stakes and barbed wire. He climbed out, lacerated and dirty, and hobbled back to camp. He washed his leg in gin and tore a shirt into strips to bandage it. As it was their only bottle of gin, this did not endear him to his colleague.

Hamblin had a singular dress sense, not only favouring bow ties and a military moustache, but also sometimes wearing his large spectacles upside down on his nose (he was always losing his reading glasses and remedied this by reversing his ordinary spectacles because his left eye was weak). He was not one for toying with his food.

With his first wife, Derry, he had three children. He later married Christa Schmidt and had two more.

Hamblin's mother used to say of him and his brothers that Robert got the brains, Cyril got the charm, but Fred had all the luck. During the war she used to worry about Cyril and Robert, but she told friends she never worried about Fred "because if he was in an aircraft and had to jump out he would land on a feather bed and find a beautiful blonde in it".

Fred Hamblin CBE, chemist, was born on October 14, 1914. He died on February 16, 2018, aged 103

CELIA HENSMAN

Eccentric social scientist who led research on links between poverty and addiction and once forgot to cook for a dinner party

The social scientist Celia Hensman was a foremost authority on the link between poverty and addiction. She was also delightfully scatty. At one of her supper parties in the 1980s, it was almost ten o'clock before her friends realised that no food had been prepared. Their hostess had forgotten. A raid on the fridge and kitchen cupboards ensued with the 20 guests, including West End actors, charity fundraisers and foreign diplomats, taking out whatever they could find and cooking an improvised meal of hummus, dates and buttered pasta with paprika.

Hensman's book-lined garden flat in South Kensington, west London, was usually shared with a lodger, godchild, waif, stray or refugee, who paid little or no rent but instead performed the role of general factotum. Tidying was, however, no mean feat, as Hensman had a tendency simply to throw decorative Indian fabrics over her many piles of clothes, books and paperwork and pretend they were not there. Once, after seeing that the front door had been left wide open, the police called round to announce that her home had been burgled. When Hensman told them that they were mistaken, an exasperated officer replied, "Can't you see that your flat has been ransacked?"

These eccentricities disguised a keen intelligence. Celia Caroline Stuart Hensman was born in 1936 to Catharine and Stuart Hensman. Stuart was a successful private London GP. Celia attended Benenden School in Kent, and then read history and economics at Newnham College, Cambridge, before starting her career as a social scientist.

She worked with Griffith Edwards, the noted psychiatrist and pioneering expert on addiction, at the Maudsley Hospital in southeast London after developing an international perspective by working in hospitals and prisons in Harlem, New York City.

She was quick to understand the links between poverty and addiction at a time when this was under-recognised, co-writing a book with Jim Zacune entitled *Drugs, Alcohol and Tobacco in Britain.* Their work used economic data and international comparison to encourage the World Health Organisation to develop improved preventative treatment and rehabilitation programmes in the field of alcohol and drug dependence.

A late service entrant to the DHSS, she became a senior principal in the Department of Trade and Industry before working on social and community projects with the Prince's Trust, the Charity Commission and the Port of London Authority.

A sociable woman with a quick wit, understated glamour and hair always styled in a sharp 1920s bob, Hensman never married. However, she was adored by many men, even those who, in her words, "must have a perfectly good wife somewhere".

One suitor sent her a specially composed sonnet every day for 15 years. But she could never quite decide with whom she might settle down. She embraced the idea of "missing the boat" with a wry amusement tinged by only a hint of melancholy.

Singledom gave her the freedom to cultivate an eclectic circle of friends; she often attended three separate social engagements on a single night: drinks, dinner and a nightcap. Friends, who included Yehudi Menuhin, tolerated her ability to fall asleep with her eyes open, even during the most compelling conversation, as "typical Celia".

Hensman was the role model for Amanda Kendall, the maddening and unrequited love interest in her godson James Runcie's *Grantchester Mysteries* book series, televised as *Grantchester*. This infuriated her: "Ruddy cheeky if you don't mind my saying so."

Celia Hensman MBE, social scientist, was born on January 29, 1936. She died of Covid-19 on January 3, 2021, aged 84

BETTY DODSON

Artist and sex therapist who was hailed as 'the guru of self-pleasure' and was so frank she even made Gwyneth Paltrow blush

Betty Dodson's mantra was "better orgasms, better world". The sexologist made her name as the woman who "brought masturbation to the masses" through her books, videos and sex workshops, which she started in the 1970s and continued to host until she was in her nineties.

As she argued in her enduring how-to guide *Sex for One* (1987), "The most consistent sex will be the love affair you have with yourself. Masturbation will get you through childhood, puberty, romance, marriage and divorce, and it will see you through old age."

Dodson's frankness about self-pleasure even made the actress Gwyneth Paltrow blush in an episode of *The Goop Lab*, a Netflix series about Paltrow's wellness and lifestyle brand, Goop, which has famously touted the benefits of vaginal "detoxes", from steaming to Jade eggs. In the episode featuring Dodson, Paltrow declares that "vaginas" are her favourite subject matter. "The vagina's the birth canal only," Dodson says, correcting her. "You wanna talk about the vulva."

In the aftermath of her divorce, against the backdrop of the 1960s sexual revolution, Dodson began experimenting with group sex, experiences that made her realise that even in such a liberal setting, women were "performing their orgasms" and had no idea how to climax on their own; invariably they ended up in Dodson's bedroom examining her collection of vibrators while the men talked, usually about sports and stocks, in the sitting room.

"We'd push the furniture against the wall. I had two double beds side by side and a little couch. The sex was taking place in the back room. I'd have coffee, cookies, cheese, crackers. They'd be socialising. And then somebody might be fucking over by the fireplace. It was just a natural way to socialise," she reflected with some understatement years later.

As her interest in erotic art and sexual activism developed, with the encouragement of her friend Gloria Steinem she set up a group to raise "physical and sexual consciousness", hosting masturbation workshops in which she taught women how to use vibrators. The genital show-and-tell part of the BodySex workshops, as they became known, involved all the women sitting naked on the floor examining one another's vulvas. She viewed the classes as a force for social good, a way of ending women's sexual dependence on men. Women were "so addicted to romantic love," she said. "It's the heaviest drug in the world and we make long-lasting bad decisions because of it."

Born in 1929, Betty Anne Dodson was one of four children to Bess (née Crow), who worked in a dress shop, and Frank Dodson, a painter. Growing up in Wichita, Kansas, she credited her three brothers with always treating her as an equal and imbuing her with a sense of entitlement as she got older. The family had little money but the house was a spirited and loving one, except for one episode that never left Dodson. During her teens one of her father's drinking companions put his hand into her underwear after she asked to drive his car; she told no one at the time out of a feeling of shame and complicity. Shortly afterwards she witnessed the same man trying to grope one of her friends. It fuelled her conviction that women must learn to love their bodies and understand that sex was not a transaction owed to a man.

In 1950, aged 20, she moved to train at the Art Students League of New York and supported herself by working as a freelance illustrator of lingerie adverts. In 1959 she married Frederick Stern, an advertising director, but it was not a happy union, emotionally or sexually. Frederick returned home one evening and told her he was in love with his secretary; she pretended to cry but in fact felt relief. They divorced after six years and she remained wary of marriage, once quipping, "You get married, you give up sex. Pretty much count on it."

Her unhappiness during that period brought her to drinking, until she met Grant Taylor, an English professor from New York University, through a support group for alcoholics. He helped her to build her website and promote her sex education business. Their relationship lasted until his death in 2008, though Dodson said she was agnostic about the gender of a partner and once described herself as a "heterosexual bisexual lesbian".

Her first book, *Liberating Masturbation: A Meditation on Self Love* (1974), which featured her own artwork and sketches of the vulva, became a feminist classic. Before the rights were bought by Random House she sold 125,000 copies herself. It was followed in the eighties by *Sex for One*, since translated into 25 languages. Her last book, *Sex By Design: The Betty Dodson Story* (2016), chronicled her experiences within America's sexual revolution and the women's movement. "Instinct told me that sexual mobility was the same as social mobility. Men had it and women didn't," she wrote.

The internet buoyed her fame as "the guru of self-pleasure", with her videos and "sex-positive" teachings being watched by millions. Women continued to flock to her workshops. As one Dodson acolyte, the 1970s porn star-turned-sex therapist Annie Sprinkle, told *The New York Times*: "To teach sex in such an explicit hands-on way requires enormous courage, experience and conviction. Betty had it all. She gave the clitoris celebrity status."

The apartment where Dodson started her sex teachings in earnest remained home for the rest of her life, its walls lined with her nude paintings including portraits of herself and Taylor. Her doorman knew the golden rule: if it's a woman always let her up, if it's a man then ring the buzzer.

A woman who, as one wag put it, both did and did not beat around the bush, when not giving talks in her direct style, or organising her next class with her business partner, Carlin Ross, Dodson sat in her robe drinking champagne, reading *The New Yorker* and chain-smoking, a habit from her youth which she took up again in her eighties. "I've lived a great life, there's nothing left for me to do," she told Ross. And the reason for her longevity, she had no doubt, was a life full of pleasure.

Betty Dodson, sex educator, was born on August 24, 1929. She died of cirrhosis of the liver on October 31, 2020, aged 91

KEITH MURDOCH

———•———

Mighty All Blacks prop who had a tempestuous relationship with the press and 'disappeared' after a post-match brawl in Wales

Keith Murdoch (front) training with the All Blacks at Porthcawl in 1972.

In December 1972 the All Blacks had beaten Wales 19–16 in Cardiff, thanks to a try from the mighty prop Keith Murdoch. Later that night, as Murdoch and his teammates celebrated at the Angel Hotel, he went to the kitchens in search of more food, or drink, depending on who is telling the story. A fight ensued and a baton-wielding security guard emerged with a black eye.

On the Sunday evening Murdoch, who was just over 6ft, weighed 17st and had an imposing walrus moustache, was named in the team for the subsequent game, but the next morning, after a meeting with the team manager, he told his teammates, "I'm off." He had won the last of his 27 caps. "Wild man sent home" was the headline in the *London Evening Standard*.

Yet Murdoch did not make it home. During a stopover in Singapore he took another flight to Darwin and disappeared into the Australian outback. A year later he rang his mother to tell her that he was alive and well; a year after that he paid her a fleeting visit. Otherwise, he spent his time apparently wandering from job to job, happy to live in obscurity.

Journalists who tracked him down were sent packing. One found him working at an oil well near Perth. Brandishing a monkey wrench, Murdoch growled: "Keep fucking moving."

However, Murdoch, being somewhat deficient in the appreciation of the humorous, had always had a troubled relationship with journalists. In 1971 after a club game, one breezily asked him for an interview. Murdoch pointed to the changing rooms. Once in there, he grabbed the journalist and held him under a shower.

In Peebles, Scotland, another journalist, the New Zealander Norman Harris, made the mistake of correcting him at a hotel desk when Murdoch had given a false name to avoid attention. "It's K Murdoch," the journalist told the receptionist. Recalling the incident, Harris said Murdoch "reached out a huge hand, grasped my scalp, and with a swift downward movement deposited me on the floor".

Yet there was another side to Murdoch. Lin Colling, his All Blacks teammate, said he was "a terribly considerate team man. Whenever there was a function Keith made sure everyone had a drink, and afterwards he was the one who tidied up." After training, another teammate said, Murdoch was always the one gathering up the flags and balls.

Little is known of Murdoch's private life. He was born in Dunedin in 1943 and attended the local King Edward Technical College. Teased about his size, he would snap and strike out, and was branded a bully.

He played for Otago, Hawke's Bay and Auckland, then made his international debut in 1970, playing in the final Test of the tour to South Africa in great pain because of a rumbling appendix. During the trials for that tour he had clashed with Colin Meads, urging the legendary hard man to "have a go". Meads lashed out, Murdoch did not flinch. Meads broke his knuckle.

With hindsight, there was always going to be trouble on the tour to Britain. The fires had been stoked when a *Daily Telegraph* journalist tried to interview him. As was his way he told the journalist to "fuck off". Murdoch's teammates believed that from then on he was a marked man. They regretted, they said, not standing up for him after his altercation in the kitchen. The New Zealand captain, Ian Kirkpatrick, said he should have stood his ground and said, "If Keith goes, we all go."

During his decades of self-imposed exile, Murdoch went home for a while in 1980 and worked on a farm in Otago. When journalists began to descend after he had saved the life of a young boy in a swimming pool, Murdoch took off again.

He came to public attention once more in 2001 in Tennant Creek, Northern Territory, during the inquest into the death of an Indigenous Australian named Kumanjai Limerick, whose body was found in an abandoned mine. Murdoch was called on because he had found Limerick breaking into his home a few weeks before, but no charges were laid against him for Limerick's death.

In 1990 a TV journalist, Margot McRae, managed to talk to Murdoch in a bar in Queensland. "I felt like I was stalking an endangered species," she recalled. Murdoch was, she said, "a deeply shy person, not very articulate. He felt it was better to be quiet than be embarrassed." He was happy, not bitter, he told her. He refused to let the interview be filmed, but the next day she and her film crew went to the banana plantation where he was working.

"He was out in the bush, slashing away with a machete," she recalled. "Then he heard me. The slashing stopped and there was this moment's silence. Then he just ran away."

In 2007 she turned the encounter into a well-received play, *Finding Murdoch*. Its hero did not attend.

As far as is known, Murdoch never married and had no children. At every All Blacks reunion a chair would be left empty in his honour, and whenever the team visited Wales a pilgrimage would be made to the Angel Hotel bar. There, recalled Tane Norton, a former All Blacks captain, "We'd go for a quiet beer and talk about Keith. We never leave Wales without doing that."

Keith Murdoch, rugby player, was born on September 9, 1943. He died of undisclosed causes on March 30, 2018, aged 74

VINCENT POKLEWSKI KOZIELL

*Much-married Polish aristocrat, vacuum cleaner salesman, advertising
executive, banker, tireless raconteur and committed bon viveur*

Although he gave his memoir the arresting title *The Ape Has Stabbed Me*, Vincent Poklewski Koziell was not the recipient of the stabbing in question. That was Taylor, the imperturbable butler. The chimpanzee belonged to the mother of a friend of his who lived in grand if lazy style, rarely rising before four in the afternoon. During one of her dinner parties, at which Koziell was a guest, Taylor approached her and muttered with as much dignity as he could muster: "Madam, the ape has stabbed me." He then passed out, revealing that there was indeed a butter knife lodged in his back. The butler recovered, but, as Koziell, a masterly and tireless raconteur, noted, his tailcoat was ruined.

Born in St John's Wood, London, in 1929, Koziell was the son of Alfons, a scion of "rundown Polish nobility" whose estate in what is now Belarus had "only 56 peasants". Much of the family's fortune was lost overnight during the Russian Revolution in 1917. The family relocated to London, where they moved into Claridge's as an "economy measure", together with their ladies' maids and valet.

It was at a party of Lady Cunard's that his father, Alfons, met Zoia de Stoeckl, a former maid of honour to the last empress of Russia. They wed in 1919 and returned to Poland, where he briefly became a diplomat before realising how little they were paid. As debts mounted he took a job running a smelting and zinc-mining business in Katowice, the capital of Polish Silesia. Vincent considered it a city of "remarkable ugliness".

Fortunately the family had friends nearby who still had their Polish estates intact, so they moved into Lancut Castle, which had a ballroom, library, billiard room, chapel, theatre and Turkish bath. It also had 11 dining rooms so that a house party never had to dine in the same one twice. In the church there was a family box enclosed in glass, which was opened so that communion could be received through it. Vincent was told the reason was to "avoid the smell of peasants, especially on a damp day".

When Hitler invaded Poland in 1939 this life of luxury came to a juddering halt and the family became refugees for the second time, returning to London, where Alfons became a commercial counsellor at the Polish embassy and the family were housed in a grace-and-favour chauffeur's cottage on the estate of their friends the Duke and Duchess of Kent. Here, on more than one occasion, Vincent's playmates included Princess Elizabeth and Princess Margaret.

A plump boy, Vincent was schooled at Downside where he quickly traded in his Polish accent for a plummy English one. When the social climbing headmaster's wife found out about the Duchess of Kent link, she pressured Vincent's mother into bringing her to the school's sports day. In return for this, Vincent was made head boy, a role for which he considered himself "totally unfit", not least because he had no leadership qualities. He was proved right, as he was unable to get any boy to obey him because he was "too wet" to have them beaten by the headmaster.

Well-connected they may have been, but the Koziell family had little money, so when he finished at Downside they were unable to buy him a place to study at Cambridge, as he wished. He also failed his army medical for National Service on the grounds of his eyesight being poor. Instead he got a job selling Electrolux vacuum cleaners for £2 15s (£69.27) a week in Wandsworth. After this he bought a motorbike and headed for Glasgow to sell washing machines. He was "a born salesman", he was told, and seemed to find the work fulfilling, until the day he was called in by the sales director and told that, if he continued to work hard, he could expect to take over from him in as little as 20 years. He resigned.

Always with a buoyant self-belief that came from knowing his family had once owned "half of Siberia", Koziell decided to tackle his impecunious circumstances head-on and arranged to meet his bank manager. A Midland Bank loan of £50 was duly refused and with the rebuff came a lecture on living within your means. Koziell thanked the manager for his advice and left resolving to try to live well beyond his means for the rest of his life. His next stop was Sutton & Co, pawnbroker to the gentry. There he handed over a pair of silver Georgian candlesticks given to him by the Duke of Kent. They made £50.

For his next attempt at gainful employment, he headed across the Atlantic on a liner, only to be put on a "purser's report" halfway across after his dancing proved to be a triumph of enthusiasm over co-ordination. While attempting a pirouette he had held above his head a woman he had smuggled up from steerage. He then tripped and hurled her across the dancefloor, an action that damaged not only the woman, but also the tables. In New York he slimmed down and found work as a butcher's assistant in the Bronx.

After a year he returned to England and used his family contacts to find work as an advertising executive at Colman, Prentis and Varley. His first job there was keeping the creative department sober enough for long enough to meet their deadlines and he proved so successful at this he was handed the Jaeger fashion account. He soon blotted his copybook, however, when he blew the department's budget on what he thought was an inspired wheeze: a trip to Kashmir to photograph models wearing cashmere. He left the company unlamented after getting the giggles during a catwalk featuring plus-size models.

His next job was running a nightclub in Mayfair, where the food was so bad the head waiter dimmed the lights so customers could not see it. This ended badly too, when he was raided by the police for serving drinks after hours.

At this stage in his so far unglittering career he finally fell on his feet when he landed a job with a private bank run by a Romanian friend. This led to him becoming a property developer in Sardinia, where he was known as "Il grande banquiere Inglese" and he found himself, he said gloomily, for the first time in his life in danger of having to do some hard work.

To avoid this he headed for Ireland, where he set up a mushroom nursery, which duly failed.

Although he described himself as a late starter with women, something he put down to once glimpsing a nanny naked, he did consider himself a late finisher. There was a brief, year-long marriage in 1958 to a Polish aristocrat called Natalie Potocka and a happier second one to Annabel de las Casas, whom he married in 1962. They had three children.

Annabel died of cancer in 1977 and Vincent married for a third time in 1982: Vicky, a daughter of the Raj who described herself as "an Anglo-Irish horse Protestant from Co Carlow". She recovered bravely, he said, at the change of name from Wimborne to Poklewski Koziell.

Life in Ireland suited Koziell, not least because there were so many grand and bohemian parties to attend, at some of which he got to know assorted members of the Rolling Stones. He also hosted a few memorable parties. On one occasion he lent Stacumny, his country house, to friends who wanted to hold a party for Brian Mulroney, the prime minister of Canada. Koziell couldn't resist visiting his dressing-up box and coming downstairs as a Mountie. The gesture did not go down well. He hadn't realised that the head of the Mounties had recently been forced to resign, after a scandal.

A man with an easy conscience, Koziell led a mostly directionless life that can only be described as picaresque. He was a dedicated hedonist given to colourful turns of phrase such as "I felt like a hooker in a Nevada brothel". Above all else he will be remembered for inventing a cocktail, the Knickerdropper Glory (a mix of Frangelico, a hazelnut liqueur, and lemon juice) and for accumulating a sizeable collection of hats and uniforms. In later years, after losing his licence for drink-driving, he became a keen cyclist. Often seen with a travelling cocktail shaker and a pug that he liked to dress up in hats, Koziell was a kindly sybarite who described himself as "dysfunctional" and "greedy by nature". He loved an audience, had a keen sense of the ridiculous and liked to wear a mask of ruthless frivolity and joie de vivre at all times.

"Vincent never does things the same way as others," Vicky once said, somewhat patiently. She was referring to one of his extravagant parties, held at the Duke of York's barracks in Chelsea. He had decorated the place with gilded pineapples and Indian silk, and populated it with actors dressed as Venetian birds who walked on stilts between guests while a reggae band played.

Vincent Poklewski Koziell, aristocrat and businessman, was born on June 30, 1929. He died after a fall while on holiday in France on September 1, 2017, aged 88

TONY NASH

●

Short-sighted and alcohol-fuelled British bobsledder who overcame problems with fogged-up glasses to win gold in the 1964 Olympics

In more ways than one it was hard to envision a path to bobsleigh glory when Tony Nash took up the sport. One problem was that Britain had no track, and scant funding. Another was that his eyesight was terrible.

Nash's glasses fogged over as he put on his goggles at the beginning of each run. Experiments with a visor failed to forestall the mist and trying to sleigh without his spectacles proved virtually suicidal. The solution was contact lenses but in the fifties and sixties they were hard and uncomfortable. Nash decided it was worth the hassle as he set his sights on becoming an Olympic champion driver.

"Tony was as blind as a bat," his brakeman, Robin Dixon, recalled, adding that Nash kept losing or dropping the contacts. "But I was never worried when we were on the bobsleigh. I had absolute confidence in him."

Sturdy of frame, the balding, 5ft 7in, 14-stone Nash had strength, sharp reflexes, a calm personality and an appetite for risk. Dixon, now

Lord Glentoran, his slender partner in the two-man sled, could sprint 100 yards in 10.3 seconds, helping them get off to a fast start.

Targeting gold in the 1964 Winter Olympics, Nash seized his chance to become the leading British driver when the first choice, Henry Taylor, was gravely injured while racing in the 1961 British Formula One Grand Prix at Aintree. He teamed up with Dixon and they became Britain's top pair, also competing in the four-man event.

The season was brief in the days before artificially refrigerated tracks but Nash kept in shape playing rugby, sailing, rowing and working long days on a farm. "You get really fit shovelling 50 tons of manure before breakfast or loading 28 trailers of hay," he remarked. Nash and Dixon would go shooting in the autumn and agree on tactics and schedules, then drive a Land Rover to the Alps in January for training.

Long before the phrase "marginal gains" entered the sporting lexicon, Nash paid close attention to details. He visited Innsbruck on a reconnaissance mission months before the Games, scouted opponents and fine-tuned his equipment using engineering know-how gleaned from working in his uncle's cigarette machine factory. Since warmer blades zip faster across ice, he wrapped sled runners with tea towels and warm blankets and heated them on radiators. But, convivial to a fault as he was, schnapps was as important as science.

Fraternising with rivals at courses and in bars aided the underdogs. Nash nurtured close relationships with other racers, especially the highly rated and well-funded Italians. They shared equipment and knowledge and invited the British pair to their training camp in 1963 even though it was clear they would be medal contenders.

The star Italian pair of Eugenio Monti and Sergio Siorpaes were favourites for gold in Austria. Nash and Dixon, their nerves calmed with a whisky or two before bedtime, posted the second-fastest run in the opening heat, much to their delight. "When the Brits' splendid time was announced [Nash] bounded out of the sled, rushed up to a pretty girl he didn't even know and kissed her," the author Brian Belton wrote in his 2010 account of the competition, *Olympic Gold Run*.

That heady optimism evaporated shortly before the second heat, when they discovered that a bolt had broken on the sled's rear axle and there was not enough time to source a replacement from the Olympic

Village. Monti found out and offered to let the British team use a bolt from his sled as soon as the Italians had finished their second run. Siorpaes quickly removed the bolt and handed it to a British team member who rushed back up to the start. With the sled duly repaired, Nash and Dixon made another quick run and moved into the lead.

Seeking to highlight the kindness of their friend, Nash told reporters about Monti's extraordinary act of sportsmanship and credited him with saving their medal hopes. The tale passed into Olympic folklore and the Italian was awarded the inaugural Pierre de Coubertin Fair Play Trophy the following year. Nash and Dixon did not publicly admit until they spoke to Belton more than four decades later that they had not used Monti's bolt because they had already sourced another. Monti, who died in 2003, was also unaware of the truth.

The next day the British pair slipped to second overall after a mediocre third heat. Their final run also underwhelmed, as they misjudged a bend known as the "witches' cauldron" and the sled lost time when it bumped off the side wall. Expecting only the bronze and feeling dejected, Nash and Dixon headed to a café at the bottom of the track.

The weather came to their rescue while they sipped coffee with schnapps. As they drank, they were interrupted by journalists who urged them to return and watch the closing stages. The rising temperature softened and slowed the track for the fourth runs of the two Italian teams. They posted sluggish times and Dixon and Nash took gold by 0.12 seconds.

Celebratory fizz flowed at the team hotel; Nash claimed that the British contingent drank 64 bottles of champagne. The driver, who took four baths over the course of the day in an attempt to sober up, was unsurprisingly effervescent when interviewed by the BBC presenter David Coleman that evening. The broadcast over, Coleman whipped out a bottle of whisky and a glass for Nash from under the studio's table.

The medal ceremony was unexpectedly stressful: the winners could not find the right way into the stadium. "The Austrians had policemen everywhere but they were very Germanic and uncooperative," Nash told the BBC. "We saw another chap we knew [the Marquess of Exeter] milling about and said to him, 'Excuse me, sir, where do we get in?' He said, 'Don't worry chaps, they can't start without us. You're getting the medals and I'm giving them to you'."

Back at home in Little Missenden, Buckinghamshire, Nash was honoured with a party in the village hall.

It was Britain's first medal at a Winter Olympics since 1952; the next did not arrive until 1976. Joy was not unconfined, however. Nash noted that after spending weeks overseas for training and competition he was "£500 out of pocket" (about £11,000 today) because of meagre financial support from the British Olympic Association.

Anthony James Dillon Nash was born in Amersham, Buckinghamshire, in 1936, to James and Gladys (née Dillon Bell). His father ran breweries; his grandfather, Francis Bell, was briefly prime minister of New Zealand in 1925.

Nash excelled in heavyweight boxing at Harrow then entered the army for his National Service. On his return he worked in the family brewery. After it was sold, he went to work for his uncle, who had a factory near High Wycombe that made light machinery. He was introduced to bobsleigh aged 19 when he visited St Moritz, Switzerland, on leave while stationed in West Germany. The teenager was hooked, seduced by the adrenalin rush and the alcohol-fuelled camaraderie of the cosmopolitan crowd. "If you needed someone for a four-man bob in those days you got him pretty drunk the night beforehand, then the next day you'd insist that he'd given his word to go on the sled – cannon fodder," Nash told Belton.

Noting Nash's history of speed-related car crashes, his father offered to bankroll his son's alpine pursuits on the condition that he abandon any motor-racing ambitions, though bobsleigh, its participants sliding down sinuous icy inclines at 80mph, was hardly any safer. Sergio Zardini, an Italian who won the silver medal in the two-man event in 1964, was killed at Lake Placid two years later when he lost control on a turn and his head was crushed by a retaining wall.

Dixon, an Old Etonian officer in the Grenadier Guards who was in St Moritz on a ski trip in 1957, had never even seen a bobsleigh before he was recruited to the British squad over breakfast in his hotel by a cousin, Richard John Bingham, better known as Lord Lucan.

In 1966 Nash married Sue, an international skier he met at a dance in Dorking, Surrey. The union ended in divorce. He remarried three years later, in 1992, to Pam, a dressage competitor and former British

Airways flight attendant. She survives him along with two children from his first marriage.

Strange but true, in 1965 Nash took the equally short-sighted John Lennon for a bobsleigh ride, the two having bumped into one another in St Moritz and fallen into conversation about their respective careers.

That year Dixon and Nash won gold in the World Championships in the Swiss resort, adding to their bronze at Innsbruck in the 1963 event. They also came third in Cortina in 1966. When they retired after the 1968 Olympics they were each appointed MBE.

Nash moved to Devon, where he owned a timber yard in the Tiverton area and became a stamp collector and dealer. The inability of subsequent generations of British bobsleighers to equal his success only burnished his legend.

"A few years ago I got a postcard from the organisers of a bobsleighing event in Canada," he told Belton. "It was addressed to 'Tony Nash, Olympic Gold Medallist, England', and it got to me!"

Tony Nash MBE, bobsleigh champion, was born on March 18, 1936. He died in his sleep on March 17, 2022, aged 85

BARON CLEMENT VON FRANCKENSTEIN

Colourful Eton-educated son of an Austrian ambassador who moved to Hollywood and became a bit-part actor, socialite and roué

It may be unkind, if not untrue, to say that Clement von Franckenstein's boisterous life would make more riveting viewing than most of the dozens of films and television shows in which he appeared during a 40-year career as a bit-part actor on Hollywood's fringes.

What, however, should the tone of the script be? How best to portray the picaresque, Rabelaisian journey of a nobly born but impoverished Anglo-Austrian Old Etonian orphan with a taste for the arts and a love of cricket, tireless in the pursuit of *jeunes filles sportives*?

Was all of this tragedy, or comedy, tipping frequently into bedroom farce? Yet, whatever the director's take on it, that would not have mattered to the born performer that was von Franckenstein. He was, after all, a pro.

In this, he was helped by a lifetime's experience of introducing himself by that name, in a voice that carried. Family legend, which he was happy to burnish, had it that Mary Shelley had borrowed it, with a slight amendment, for her book after meeting an ancestor of von Franckenstein's, who was consul in Geneva when she was there.

What was unambiguously true was that the Franckensteins could trace their roots to medieval Germany, even if there was debate about when their branch had gained their title. To his friends, he was always known as Clem.

Not of course that that proved a bar if protocol demanded otherwise, such as at dinner with his fellow Austrian Arnold Schwarzenegger, the former governor of California. "I rarely use my title in LA," von Franckenstein divulged, "but Arnold always calls me 'Baron'." In fact, when he arrived in the city in the early 1970s, he was so worried that casting directors would not take him seriously that he called himself Clement St George. Before turning to acting, he had spent several years training as an opera singer, eventually admitting his baritone was not up to Covent Garden's standard.

The lessons did not go to waste: the first job that he landed in America was as a singing Henry VIII in a Tudor theme restaurant in Anaheim, California. 1520AD had been opened by the ex-tycoon John Bloom after his business, Rolls Razor, went into liquidation.

Franckenstein's first role on camera, improbably, was as an extra in Mel Brooks's spoof *Young Frankenstein* (1974). He went on to appear in films such as *Death Becomes Her* (1992) and another Brooks parody, *Robin Hood: Men in Tights* (1993), as well as much fare destined for video only.

Perhaps his biggest part was as France's head of state in *The American President* (1995), with Michael Douglas and Annette Bening. The script allowed him to show off his French, although his Teutonic accent led to complaints from Gallic patriots.

While resting between parts, von Franckenstein became a notable figure in his community. He was an opening batsman for the Beverly Hills Cricket Club and often read the lesson at its Episcopalian church, All Saints – this doubled as an audition for any agents and directors in the congregation.

With his stentorian voice and garrulous tendencies von Franckenstein sometimes talked himself out of roles. Yet his remarkably wide range of friends could overlook the bombast, admiring his resilience, his commitment to his work, his kindness to animals and his willingness to put himself out for others. He was a rarity: a larger-than-life character who also liked other people.

In his quieter moments, he showed a touching vulnerability, the façade of human hurricane concealing a spirit compared by some to Peter Pan or the Little Prince. Undoubtedly, he had a need to be loved and it was his unceasing search for a physical manifestation of this that led to the escapades of a roué with which most associated him.

There was the time when he had to sit through dinner with friends having discovered that the young lady he was expecting to meet later had cancelled, though not before he had taken Viagra. Meanwhile, the tale of who unsuspectingly drank the contents of a bottle of Spanish brandy that von Franckenstein had been using to sterilize himself after dalliances with women in Tijuana is, perhaps, a story for which the world is not yet prepared.

Clement George von Franckenstein was born in 1944 at Sunninghill, near Ascot, Berkshire. His father, then 66 years old, was Georg Freiherr von und zu Franckenstein and, until 1938, had been Austria's ambassador for many years in London.

Appalled by the rise of the Nazis, however, he had refused to return home after the Anschluss and had taken British nationality. He was knighted by King George VI and, a year later, married the much younger Editha King, who had herself tried acting.

Clement, their only child, carried the name of his paternal uncle, a former director of the Munich Opera. When he was nine his parents were both killed in an air crash at Frankfurt. Much to his sorrow, Clement was not allowed by his prep school to attend their funeral.

Yet he never appeared to be sorry for himself, aided as he was by being fostered by friends of his mother's, the Taylors, a rumbustious Oxfordshire farming family. Like them, he rode and hunted, and at Eton particularly enjoyed athletics. There he also appeared in a noted production of *The Birds*, Aristophanes's comedy, staged by the actor John Wells, who was on the staff, and Brian Rees.

Franckenstein was commissioned into the Royal Scots Greys, with whom he served in Germany and Aden. A harbinger of things to come was when he was discovered in a Hamburg nightclub "in full mess kit – boots, spurs, the lot" with two ladies of the town.

"I was supposed to be guarding Kuwait from Nasser," he recalled. "I was very much a soldier's officer. I would have been fine in a war, but I was lousy in peacetime." A love of gambling meant that he quickly ran through his inheritance – he was short of money for years afterwards until his nanny left him a legacy. Before leaving for America, he worked for the nightclub owner Harry Meadows, who had London haunts such as Churchill's and 21.

While he enjoyed the limelight, he was happiest among his close-knit circle, with whom he could verbally spar; or when simply enjoying his love of painting and the company of his cats. He was a dandy dresser, who did not think twice about leaving his house in a designer suit and a pair of fancy slippers.

Sometimes he enjoyed social events too much, once telephoning a friend to confess that he had woken up in hospital after passing out from the effects of consuming 15 double vodkas in a bar in Santa Monica, California. In reply to the friend's query as to what was the noise in the background, von Franckenstein said that he was now at a party.

All this took its toll on his health, although after a heart attack some years ago he had curbed his irrepressibility. In 2016 he enjoyed appearing in the Coen brothers' comedy *Hail, Caesar!*, in which George Clooney got to share a scene with him.

The passing of time did, however, prompt him to seek a wife at the turn of the millennium – "one doesn't like to see an old title die out". *People* magazine nominated him one of America's top 50 bachelors and he told an interviewer that he would prefer a spouse who was "smart, independent and buxom".

He did not find one, but at the start of his funeral, a woman in her twenties matching von Franckenstein's requisites and known to his friends placed herself in the front pew. Then another arrived and announced it was she who was Clem's girlfriend. Something of a contretemps ensued.

Baron Clement von Franckenstein, actor, was born on May 28, 1944. He died from a hard-earned heart attack on May 9, 2019, aged 74

NICHOLAS MOSLEY

Masterly novelist who bore with grace and fortitude the burden of being the oldest son of the fascist leader Sir Oswald Mosley

When Nicholas Mosley joined the Rifle Brigade straight from Eton in 1941, he gave his name to an adjutant who, without looking up, asked: "Not any relation to that bastard, are you?" Mosley replied: "Yes, actually." "My dear fellow," the adjutant spluttered, "I'm so frightfully sorry!" The decency of the comment made the young man feel even more patriotic.

The bastard was of course Sir Oswald Mosley, the leader of the British Union of Fascists. By joining up to fight fascism the first chance he got, the young Nicholas was making a none-too-subtle point about where he stood politically. "I knew after that there would been no point people asking me if I was for or against Hitler."

If this seemed like an extravagantly symbolic gesture, it was as nothing compared with the Freudian psychodrama of his youth. Whereas his "ferociously fluent" father had been considered one of the most powerful orators of his generation, Nicholas suffered from a chronic stammer. It developed when he was seven and never left him.

He was a tall, bespectacled figure with an amiable manner and, when it worked for him, a cultivated voice. In later life he won acclaim within the literary world as the author of more than 25 books, mostly unashamedly highbrow works of fiction, and in 1990 he received wider recognition when his novel *Hopeful Monsters* was named Whitbread Book of the Year.

As a memoirist he was a master of self-mockery who recalled his time in the army with a mixture of affection and ennui, the latter to do with his stammer. When giving orders on the parade ground, "It seemed that I, standing with my mouth open silently like an Aunt Sally at a fairground, might unwittingly become like Emperor Christophe of Haiti, who used to march his crack troops over a cliff for his amusement."

He remembered his platoon trying not to laugh while he gagged and contorted his way through a lecture. His sergeant eventually banged on a table with his stick and shouted: "Don't laugh at the officer!"

Mosley nonetheless enjoyed the anarchy and poetry of war, recording in his diary how there was much affected homosexuality, with men, himself included, dancing with each other and wearing women's clothes. "There is a tradition in armies for this sort of thing on the fringes of war – presumably as a counterbalance to the brutal business of killing ... homosexuals were seen as paragons of wit and fantasy; such qualities were life-giving in wartime."

Mosley turned out to be not only a good and brave soldier, but also a fine and disturbingly vivid writer about war, describing, for example, "German bodies hanging like rag dolls from burning tank turrets". If Spike Milligan wrote the definitive account of what the Italian campaign was like from the squaddies' perspective, Mosley's engagingly matter-of-fact memoir *Time at War* gave a flavour of the officer's lot.

In 1944 he was ordered to undertake what amounted to a suicide mission, or "an MC job" in army jargon. He led a charge against a farmhouse occupied by Germans. Outnumbered and with bullets fizzing all around him, his biggest fear was not death, but that he would not be able to stand the fear. Afterwards, as he and his men were lying exhausted, an officer who had not been in the battle told him to get up and move on. Mosley told him to "fuck off". In war, men were judged only on their bravery. Nothing else mattered. He was, indeed, awarded the MC.

Nicholas Mosley was born in 1923, the eldest son of Sir Oswald and Lady Cynthia Mosley, the daughter of Lord Curzon of Kedleston, once Viceroy of India. "It was difficult to be a child of my father's," he reflected in later life. "People regarded me as a bit of a freak." There was some teasing at his prep school, where he was nicknamed Baby Blackshirt, "but people were fairly civilised really, in an English way."

Sir Oswald and Cimmie, as she was known, were both elected MPs on a left-wing socialist platform and, as Sir Oswald was incapable of marital fidelity, he used to joke: "Vote Labour; sleep Conservative." (Sir Oswald would even boast about having slept with his mother-in-law and sister-in-law before his wedding to Cimmie.) He formed the British Union of Fascists in 1932 and, a year later, Cimmie died of peritonitis, perhaps not uncoincidentally around the time Nicholas developed his stammer. For his part he always attributed the timing to growing up in a household where language and silence were used like bullets. "I had the feeling that all grown-ups were fairly mad," he reflected. Like the future George VI, he was for a time a patient of the Australian speech therapist Lionel Logue, whom he used to visit weekly in his Harley Street practice.

Years later, after watching the film *The King's Speech,* he said that Logue had not been a great help to him except that he gave him a certain confidence and hope. At one point the therapist had asked if it had ever occurred to him that he might not want to get rid of his stammer because it might be a form of self-protection.

After the death of his mother, his father married Diana Guinness, née Mitford, in 1936 in Berlin at a ceremony at Goebbels's home attended by Hitler. When in 1938 Nicholas learnt about the wedding from a newspaper, he put as brave a face on it as he could. "I was naturally very surprised," he wrote to his father, "as I had gone round telling everyone that it was not true."

When war was declared, the same newspapers ran headlines demanding: "Hang Mosley!" Sir Oswald was duly interned, along with his wife Diana, only 11 weeks after the birth of her son Max. When he was on leave from the army, Nicholas would go and visit them in prison.

Along with his speech impediment, Mosley had by then developed a distrust of spoken words that flowed too quickly. He realised that he preferred expressing himself through the written word, especially when he discovered that he was good at it. Writing also helped him overcome the strange sense of loss he felt when the war ended and he went to read philosophy at Balliol College, Oxford, only to drop out after a year. Although largely uninfluenced by his father's political views, he did admit as a matter of enormous shame that during his time at the university he wrote to his father complaining that Balliol was "stiff with Jews", simply to ingratiate himself.

In 1947 he married Rosemary Salmond, an artist, and with money he had inherited from his mother he bought a smallholding in Wales and tried his hand at a "spot of sheep farming". He also penned three novels, which he later dismissed as "rather romantic and overwritten". By his late twenties he considered himself a devout Christian, having come under the influence of a monk, Father Raymond Raynes, who became a sort of guru to him.

After this religious phase his writing became more assured. One of his novels, *Accident* (1965), set in the brittle and amoral world of academia, was made into a film starring Dirk Bogarde with a screenplay by Harold Pinter. After that, Hollywood tried to get him to write a screenplay about Trotsky, but they only gave him three weeks to finish it, with the producer turning up at his house "in a Cadillac" to take away pages as they were written. He was eventually dropped from the project.

His relationship with his father, meanwhile, had soured after Sir Oswald had returned to the fray as a far-right politician in the late 1950s. Nicholas found this harder to explain than his prewar fascism. "I faced him and said, 'You're not only being immoral, wicked and crazy, but self-destructive.'" Sir Oswald replied, "I will never speak to you again."

The impasse lasted for six years, and Sir Oswald eventually cut his eldest son out of his will because he was "not my sort of person". He did find it in his heart to leave to him his archive when he died in 1980, and from this Nicholas was able to write a seminal if highly critical two-volume biography in 1982–83 (later adapted into a four-part drama series on Channel 4).

The biography was unflinching in its portrayal of his father as a womaniser and an egotist. Before it was published, Diana Mosley denounced this "dastardly" book as "the degraded work of a very little man". She went on: "It's all very well having an Oedipal complex at 19, a second-rate son hating a brilliant father, but it's rather odd at 60. Nicholas wants to get his own back on his father for having had more fun than he's had." She never spoke to her stepson again.

Relations with his half-brother, Max Mosley, the former president of Formula One's governing body, were strained after the biography was published. As was his equitable way, Nicholas allowed the years to heal, and the two men had a reconciliation in 2015, in defiance of their respective emotional legacies.

Mosley's first marriage to Rosemary produced four children. One of them, Ivo, a potter turned novelist and composer of operas, said of his father that he could be very powerful verbally, even with his stutter. "When words do come out, they can be very creative and very cutting. He oozes emotion like some kind of sticky plant."

Rosemary died in 1991. By his second wife, Verity, a psychotherapist 20 years his junior, Nicholas had a son, Marius, a set builder at Pinewood Studios.

Nicholas Mosley's own political career was brief. When, in 1966, he inherited the title Lord Ravensdale, he thought he should begin to take politics seriously. "I went to the Lords under the Liberal whip and I got on to an arts committee," he recalled, before adding with typical self-deprecation, "I was frightfully bad at it."

Lord Ravensdale (Nicholas Mosley) MC, author, was born on June 25, 1923. He died on February 28, 2017, aged 93

HANNAH HAUXWELL

—— • ——

Dales farmer who found fame in the 1970s when a film was made about her hard and solitary life

For many years after her mother's death in the late 1950s, Hannah Hauxwell scratched a solitary and subsistence living from the rugged 78 acres of her farm, Low Birk Hatt, a thousand feet up in the remote upland fastnesses of the North Yorkshire Pennines.

She was the fourth generation of her family to live in Baldersdale, which had once been a thriving community. As its farmers died, however, or gave up the unequal struggle against a hard-favoured soil and a harsh climate, Baldersdale died, too.

After her mother's death Hauxwell, its sole inhabitant, carried on the dour struggle to sustain life on an agricultural property whose technology owed as much to the Middle Ages as to the 20th century. A handful of milk and beef cattle, and the income from "eatage", fees paid by local farmers for the right to graze on her land, were bringing in, by the early 1970s, an annual income of somewhere in the region of £200 (about £3,000 today). Her daily life was one of unrelieved, grinding labour. At that stage Low Birk Hatt had neither electricity nor running water. Hauxwell – who was a highly literate individual – read by gaslight, and in the winter months frequently had to break the ice over the neighbouring beck to obtain drinking water. It was not uncommon for her to go a fortnight without seeing another living soul.

This solitude and way of life ended abruptly in 1973 when a Yorkshire Television film-maker, Barry Cockcroft, was on the lookout for subjects for a new series about people working in the Dales, called *The Hard Life*. A researcher had come across an interview that Hauxwell had given to the *Yorkshire Post* three years earlier. The cutting had the headline: "How to be happy on £170." "Her life has been hard," it noted, "yet she has a smooth pink and white face and a curious out-of-this-century grace and courtesy in speech and manner."

Cockcroft set off from Leeds to seek her out. Leaving his car at the bottom of Baldersdale, he scrambled over a series of drystone walls until he came across what he at first took to be an abandoned farmhouse and, as he later recalled, "a woman with hair as white as a pensioner's wearing what appeared to be several layers of carefully laundered rags". It turned out this "old lady" was only 46.

It was the beginning of a professional relationship that was to transform Hauxwell's life, making her the heroine of a succession of television documentaries and transforming her economic situation out of all recognition. Books of the series, celebrity status and tea with the Queen at Buckingham Palace followed, as did a televised Grand Tour of European capitals and even a *Hannah in America* documentary for the woman who had previously never been as far as Leeds.

The last two programmes might look suspiciously like the exploitation of an innocent, but Hauxwell enjoyed her new-found fame and never felt herself merely used. When she felt that *The Commonsense Book of a Countrywoman* (1999) was taking things a bit too far, and ascribing to her a rural wisdom to which she had no pretensions, she did not hesitate to say so. As she admitted, she was not a particularly good farmer.

Hannah Bayles Tallentire Hauxwell was born in 1926 at Sleetburn and her father moved into Low Birk Hatt Farm when she was three. He died in 1933 when she was seven, but Low Birk Hatt was in the early days always alive with the presence of relations: her grandparents, great-uncles, mother and her father's brother who came to live with them after her father's death. When she was still a young child Baldersdale boasted more than 20 farms, a school and a pub, as well as a Methodist chapel. Over the next few decades she was to witness the slow death of the community and see its farms fall into disrepair and be pulled down as men died or lost heart. The young married and moved away.

When her uncle and then her mother died, she soldiered on single-handed, never marrying, hermetically sealed from the 20th century by the absence of its most basic amenities. Only her wireless and the rare visits to market to sell livestock kept her in touch with the outside world, and in fact she struck all who met her as a well-informed woman with articulately argued opinions.

The year 1973 changed her life beyond recognition. Cockroft's documentary, *Too Long a Winter*, projected her image into millions of sitting rooms. She was shown walking with a bale on her back, washing in a bucket, and repairing drystone walls. A natural in front of the cameras, she explained that her bread deliveries were left three fields away, that she liked to drink warm milk in the byre and that she sometimes snuggled up to a cow during freezing blizzards. She said she wasn't much good at cooking because "so much of my life has been spent outdoors".

Although she protested that she was "just a plain Daleswoman", viewers were charmed by her accent and strangely eloquent, almost Victorian, way with words. "I keep expenditure down to the bare essentials," she said. "I put a brake on and keep it on." Of her status as a spinster she mused that a good marriage was a privilege and that she could not imagine anything worse than a bad marriage that involved "living under the same roof as someone you are utterly at variance with".

After it was screened, Yorkshire TV's phones were jammed for three days with viewers wanting to find out more about her and to offer financial help. Her name become synonymous with a kind of dignified, Yorkshire stoicism and she made her first visit to Leeds, where she was taken by helicopter. Coach trips began to descend and the local branch of Woolworths started selling postcards featuring her picture. She found herself opening fêtes and appearing at steam rallies.

The immediate effect of her exposure to publicity was the electrification of Low Birk Hatt. Workmen at Eccles, Lancashire, who were moved by her plight, raised £600 towards the £800 cost of carrying electricity 600 yards to her farmhouse, YTV paying the rest. Hauxwell, who had endured her primitive arrangements from necessity not choice, was delighted with the improvement. A television eventually made its appearance, but she had no difficulty in rationing its use.

In 1976 she made her first visit to London to attend the Woman of the Year lunch and stay at the Savoy, an experience she did not particularly enjoy, although in general she was far from overawed by her contact with the second half of the 20th century. She took tea with the Queen in 1980 at a Palace garden party. "It was all very dainty," she said. "There were little pancakes and tiny cakes; which, for the occasion, I suppose was quite nice, but if you'd been doing half a hard day's work, it would have left quite a gap."

All this time she had continued to farm at Baldersdale, but in 1988 she finally gave up the struggle against the elements. Her hard life had prematurely aged her and she sold Low Birk Hatt and moved to a cottage in the village of Cotherstone (by this time through boundary changes in Co Durham) six miles down the Dale. There, she was able to lead a more comfortable life, although visitors noted that it always looked as if she were merely camping there, littered as the place always was with the heterogeneous possessions she had brought from Low Birk Hatt.

Her working relationship with Cockcroft continued to flourish. In 1992 they made a series in which Hauxwell travelled abroad for the first time and recorded her impressions. Although she was the subject of *This is Your Life* with Michael Aspel that year, she remained unspoilt. Those who met her found her level-headed and forthright, modest about the immense interest her life had created and retaining a sense of true proportion about her worth.

Hannah Hauxwell, farmer, was born on August 1, 1926. She died on January 31, 2018, aged 91

RAYMOND BUTT

Gleeful physics teacher who could recite pi to 3,500 places and memorised the entire timetable of British Rail

Raymond Butt was one of life's enthusiasts. He chased eclipses, sang with the Kent Police Male Voice Choir, was a steward at Henley for half a century and never missed a British Physics Olympiad or a meeting of the Transport Ticket Society, having been a member since 1958. His unexpected areas of expertise included theme park rollercoasters.

For 30 years his day job was teaching physics and astronomy at King's School, Canterbury. There he was known for his habit of drumming his thumbs excitably against his jacket or gown as he talked as well as the way he would make unexpected train horn noises as he passed pupils in a corridor or on a staircase. If he noticed eyes glazing over in his lessons, he would willingly perform one of his party pieces, such as inviting requests to work out any train journey in his head, because he had memorised the entire British Rail timetable. Another of his classroom turns was to recite the value of pi to 3,500 decimal places, all the while grinning broadly. The boys relished his grandiose turns of phrase: his laboratory was "the Emporium of Discovery", while pieces of work that disappointed him might "describe a parabolic trajectory" as they were thrown in the bin.

Raymond Venimore Jack Butt was born in Colchester, Essex, in 1941, the son of Herbert Butt and his wife, Kathleen (née Upchurch). The family circumstances were modest, but he was a bright pupil, blessed with a good singing voice, and he went as a chorister to the King's School in Peterborough, Cambridgeshire. Although not a natural sportsman, he discovered an enjoyment of teamwork, which drew him to the river where he was keen on rowing.

His lively temperament would express itself as gleefulness. One drowsy Sunday the Archdeacon of nearby Oakham preached in the cathedral. The choir did not divine the entire import of the sermon, but a passage in which mention was made of inviting young devils to tea struck home. Raymond afterwards presented himself at the vestry at the head of a large deputation and announced that they were accepting the invitation.

At Edinburgh University he read four subjects in his first year, among them natural philosophy (or physics). He was taught by a postdoctoral student named Peter Higgs, who was yet to predict the existence of the boson that would win him a Nobel Prize.

After teacher training at Cambridge, Butt joined Abingdon School in 1965. There he taught physics as well as coaching rowing crews. Having rowed at university, he competed in the Silver Goblets (for coxless pairs) at Henley in 1968 and was elected the next year to membership of the Stewards' Enclosure. He took part several times in the Boston rowing marathon, a 31-mile race for crews along the River Witham to Lincoln, and twice won.

In the same year he moved to the King's School, Canterbury, which dates its foundation from AD597 and is claimed to be the oldest school in the world. Butt's ultratraditional, no-nonsense style of teaching physics and astronomy was perhaps welcomed most by the ablest pupils. They in turn responded to his obvious erudition and ability to produce top grades, as well as entertaining diversions.

Butt established the observatory at King's and his students included Michael Foale, who in 1995 became the first Briton to walk in space. He also created a sculling school, but such was his commanding manner that when he told two novices to "jump in", the next thing he heard was a resounding splash.

His relationships with those closest to him were not always easy and he seemed to many to be one of life's bachelors. Yet he did marry, in 1980, when Jane Woods became his wife. When a colleague went round for supper, they found Butt knitting while his wife prepared the food. They had two children but in 1989 the marriage ended in divorce.

Butt's interests outside teaching were manifold. In 1972 he was awarded cum laude a master's degree in astrophysics, and five years later was elected a Fellow of the Royal Astronomical Society. In 1995 he published his *Directory of Railway Stations*, a monumental work listing every halt and stop built. He collected train tickets for many years, moving into a larger house on retirement to have more space for them, and latterly had specialised in computer-generated ones.

On retiring from teaching in 1998, Butt became usher for ten years at Ashford county court, where judges sometimes drew informally on his scientific knowledge.

Troubled by changes in the Church of England, he decided to convert to Orthodoxy.

"I don't know why my miserable little life should be of such interest," he wrote to a friend asking for details of it for any posthumous appreciation. He knew his number was up. "That's me. Over and out."

Raymond Butt, schoolmaster, was born on February 26, 1941. He died of pancreatic cancer on March 23, 2018, aged 77

PROFESSOR NORMAN STONE

—— • ——

Bacchanalian and waspish contrarian who wrote speeches for 'Mrs T'
and liked to drink and gamble with his adoring history students

No other leading British historian of the Cold War could draw, as Norman Stone did, on the experience of spending three months in a communist jail. As a research student in Vienna in the early 1960s, he was imprisoned in Bratislava after being caught trying to smuggle a Hungarian dissident across the Czech–Austrian border in his car boot. The man was in love with a girl Stone had met and he had tried to reunite them; the *Daily Express* dubbed Stone the "Tartan Pimpernel".

At his best, as in his first book *The Eastern Front 1914–17*, the multilinguist displayed a mastery of sources in several languages, a flair for technical and economic detail and a shrewd eye for the underlying reality of events, personalities and trends.

He was also fearlessly iconoclastic, whether in his attack on the professional and private reputation of the celebrated historian EH Carr or in insisting that the 1915–17 massacre of Armenians by Ottoman Turks was not genocide.

As a fellow at Gonville and Caius College, Jesus College and Trinity College at Cambridge in the 1960s and 1970s and then Worcester College, Oxford in the 1980s and 1990s, Stone made a point of creating a young school of right-wing historians in his own image, including Orlando Figes, Niall Ferguson and Andrew Roberts, who recalled: "I was told you have to wear a gown to supervision, but the first thing Norman said was, 'Take that bloody stupid gown off.'"

At the end of one academic year, Stone listed his students as "weedy", "quite weedy", "very weedy". They would timorously enter his office for supervision to be greeted with the fumes of several recently stubbed-out cigarettes mixed with the aroma of a double espresso that would help him through the day after heroic alcohol consumption the night before.

"I want a long, detailed analysis," he told one student, asked to assess why the First World War went on so long. "You can start with the 100-odd volumes of the official British war history."

Never a man from whom opinions had to be wrenched, he was, most unapologetically, of the right in an academic field that was populated with lefties. As such he was the favourite historian of Margaret Thatcher and especially useful to her as an adviser on foreign policy and a speechwriter during her premiership. In turn, he admired her because "Nobody is interested in John Major or David Cameron, or any of these transitional nobodies. Mrs T stood up and turned this country around."

He was among the coterie of historians that Thatcher invited to Chequers for a seminar on German reunification. With wartime memories still strong, she feared the enlarged Germany would become a "Fourth Reich". Stone sought to reassure her, arguing that in taking over East Germany, West Germany was only getting "six Liverpools".

Chequers was a relatively agreeable environment for Stone from what he viewed as the oppressive atmosphere of Oxford, where, according to his former student Petronella Wyatt, he "loathed the place as petty and provincial and for its adherence to the Marxist-determinist view of history". It did not help that he had a "horrible little office" and had to share a bathroom with a feminist philosopher.

Stone also celebrated Charles de Gaulle and General Pinochet and gave vent to pet hates such as the welfare state, men with beards and the smoking ban – he did once give up smoking but it turned him, he said in his gravelly Glaswegian brogue, into an "ugly drunk". Edward Heath was his bête noire. Stone dismissed him as a "flabby-faced coward" along with another former prime minister Sir Anthony Eden. Sir Anthony, he said, was like a former Guards officer who, "through force of circumstance, must earn a living selling vacuum cleaners. Heath was the same, although an NCO."

Stone's waspish views made him a lucrative second career in newspapers and television, which enabled him to supplement what he regarded as a paltry £27,000-a-year academic salary. He reckoned that in the decade after 1985 his media work brought in £500,000.

When working on one of his columns at *The Sunday Times*, his editor would place a bottle of whisky out of his reach with the promise that he could get his hands on it when he finished his column. Stone would finish his piece with alacrity.

His enemies deprecated his later academic output as thin and weakened by prejudice, particularly his Cold War history, *The Atlantic and its Enemies*. For his part, Stone grew disillusioned with British academia and – perhaps appropriately – at the dawning of the New Labour government in 1997, he began a self-imposed exile in Turkey. He held a chair in international relations at Bilkent University near Ankara, where he felt his talents were given appropriate financial reward.

A chain-smoker who once had to leave a party for a cigarette despite wearing five Nicorette patches, he knew he would fit in as soon as he touched down; as he walked through the airport he saw six policemen "grimly smoking away" beneath a sign saying "No Smoking". As a lifelong challenger of convention, he felt an instant bond.

He was born in Kelvinside, Glasgow, in 1941. The next year his father, a Spitfire pilot, was killed in a training accident and he was raised by his mother, a teacher, Presbyterian and Labour voter. She was tough and he was devoted to her. "Family closes round," he recalled years later, "so I wasn't conscious of anything. But the point came in my late thirties when I began to realise what damage it had done. Not having your daddy is a very bad thing. If I read about women bringing up children on their own, deliberately making babies, I get very angry indeed. I think, 'Why don't they just buy a dolly?'"

With financial support from the charity set up by his father's squadron, he attended Glasgow Academy. Brought to history by an appetite for the military side, he also developed an early interest in central Europe. Although he won a scholarship to Gonville and Caius College, Cambridge in modern languages, he switched to history after a few weeks.

His ability as a linguist started at school with French, German and Spanish. He learnt Hungarian while a research student in Vienna, taught himself Russian during a lectureship at Cambridge and later added Polish, Italian and Serbo-Croat.

Thanks to all-night poker games he gained only a 2:1 in part one, but compensated with a first in his finals. From 1962 he spent three years as a research student in Vienna and Budapest, examining archives on the Austro-Hungarian army in the run-up to 1914 for a PhD that was never completed. His adventure with the Czech border police won him brief stardom.

In 1965 he returned to Caius as a research fellow, soon marrying Nicole Aubry, whom he had met in Vienna. She was from Haiti and was the niece of Papa Doc's finance minister. interracial marriages were still frowned upon and it took him six months to tell his mother.

In 1967, having won a state grant to learn Russian, he became a university lecturer in Russian history. In 1971 he became a fellow of Jesus College and director of studies in history. He also made strong demands on himself, though his first book, *The Eastern Front 1914–1917*, did not emerge until 1975. It won the Wolfson prize for history and netted £4,000, establishing him at a stroke as one of the country's leading young historians. Meticulously researched, although Stone had no access to Russian archives, the book filled an important gap in the historiography of the First World War and remained the standard work for at least two decades.

In the mid-1970s his marriage began to break down. "It was a wonderful disaster," he later recalled. His wife did not easily adjust to a Cambridge academic ambience or share her husband's passions. They divorced, acrimoniously, in 1977 and he lost custody of the children. They had two sons, Sebastian and Nick; the latter is a bestselling thriller writer.

His alcohol consumption was legendary, especially red wine. His student Niall Ferguson recalled coming into a tutorial once to find him flat drunk on the floor and Stone once appeared on radio "having drink taken", but scorned the presenter for suggesting that it affected his expertise. On occasions it led to physical collapse and threatened to derail his career.

Stone also enjoyed an energetic private life. One female undergraduate recalled: "He has this belief that women will never understand eastern Europe. We ended up having an affair." He settled down in 1982 with his second wife, Christine Booker, former wife of the journalist Christopher Booker. Herself a journalist, she later became a barrister. They had a son, Rupert, who is also a journalist.

His long marriage with Christine, with whom he owned a house in Oxford until her death, was a notably open one with regular ménage à deux, trois, quatre "whatever", according to a friend.

Early in 1983 Stone launched a no-punches-pulled attack in the *London Review of Books* on a fellow historian, EH Carr, who died on the day of publication. Carr had won praise for a multi-volume history of the Soviet Union, but to Stone he had been an apologist for a brutal regime that had sent millions to their death in the name of modernisation. He also attacked Carr personally, labelling him a "dreadful monster" for ill-treating his wives.

His academic masters, meanwhile, argued that his media

involvements and his heavy drinking meant that he was neglecting his academic duties.

Certainly, outside interests took more of his time. He became a television personality, making documentaries including one on Russia and a look at the Nazi theft of art treasures. He interviewed Albert Speer on Hitler's cache of paintings, the day Speer died. He made videos on Russian history. He appeared in French and German TV programmes, talking freely in those languages, as few other British historians were able to do.

As a journalist he moved far and wide for copy. The communist collapse in eastern Europe was an obvious subject for his punditry. His predictions were often right. Months before the Berlin Wall came down, he saw East Germany as finished and he predicted that Mikhail Gorbachev would be back within days during the brief attempt at a neo-Stalinist coup in August 1991. He wrote and broadcast extensively on the collapse of Yugoslavia, offering a pro-Muslim line, like many others, but also a pro-Croatian one.

Meanwhile, his academic output all but dried up and for more than 20 years he published no original, book-length work. A study of the USSR's handling of reactions to Hitler's death was one of several aborted projects. For it, Stone burrowed in the newly opened KGB archives and satisfied himself that he had held Hitler's skull.

A few weeks after arriving in his adopted home of Turkey he was asked why he was the only foreigner who never complained about Ankara. In his answer he managed to insult Scotland and Turkey in the same breath: "You have to understand that, in the depth of my being, I'm a Scotsman, and I feel entirely at home in an enlightenment that has failed."

When in Turkey at the time of the anti-Erdogan coup, he posted on Twitter that he had been woken in bed by the noise of "the good guys" aircraft going overhead. When the coup failed he rapidly moved to Budapest, where he was writing a history of Hungary.

However, part of this reason for moving was that the university in Ankara tried to ban him from drinking. When he retreated to Budapest he took with him a younger male Turkish student, who became his partner, looking after him as his health declined.

He felt at home in Hungary despite being a longstanding

Eurosceptic who voted for Brexit and believed that the EU should never have allowed mass immigration.

When asked when he was happiest he answered: "When I'm smoking, reading and writing, and, er, with a glass of red wine – I'm careful these days."

But not that careful. On being told of his death, a former (married) mistress of his said she felt devastated, but was not totally surprised as of late he "was drinking three bottles a day".

Professor Norman Stone, historian, was born on March 8, 1941. He died in his sleep on June 18, 2019, aged 78

GEORGE PINTO

Merchant banker who was sometimes forbidding, often eccentric, rarely convivial but always droll

When George Pinto came upon a couple in flagrante in a bunker on the golf course of Royal St George's, Sandwich, he had only one question: "Are you members?"

A two-handicapper, he was good enough to get to the fourth round of the English Amateur championship. He preferred playing alone and, as an observant Jew, his favourite golf day was December 25, when he had the course to himself. If wet, he played in wellington boots. "Some like golf mostly for the companionship. I don't," Pinto said. As PG Wodehouse remarked, to find a man's true character, play golf with him.

Once, playing a round, he and his opponent came across two women making what in Pinto's view was a lot of noise. He asked them to be quiet, prompting one to reply: "I wouldn't want to be married to you." Pinto shot back: "I don't suppose they are queueing up to marry you."

He played backgammon and was also a terrifying bridge partner at the Portland Club, a high-stakes establishment in London where, under even the most charitable circumstances, missing a trick is not received sympathetically. In 1993 he won the club's Pro-Am tournament with British international Andrew Robson.

Although he never married and also belonged to Brooks and the Cavalry and Guards clubs, the words "clubbable" and "Pinto" rarely appeared in the same breath. Offered a drink at the bar, he was liable to request a pint of milk.

He could be an alarming travelling companion, as his obsession with not wasting time meant that he liked catching trains as the doors were closing to leave the station.

Amid these diversions, Pinto was a highly respected merchant banker who spent 42 years with Kleinwort Benson, now part of the French group Société Générale.

A former colleague, John Nelson, described him as "the heart and soul of the machine" behind Kleinwort's success in scooping much of the advisory work in Margaret Thatcher's wave of privatisations. Among its scalps were British Aerospace, Cable & Wireless, Associated British Ports and British Telecom, a company that soon became associated with "Beattie", a Jewish grandmother played by Maureen Lipman in a series of BT adverts.

Like all professional investors, Pinto made the occasional mistake. He once put money into a Chinese film finance scheme and went to Leicester Square to see the movie he had helped to produce. He was the only cinemagoer.

Tall and slim, Pinto always walked outside with a rolled-up umbrella, wearing a dark grey suit, double-breasted waistcoat, dark blue tie and blue shirt. Declining to remove his jacket in the office, he sat at a lectern on his desk illuminated by an Anglepoise lamp as he pored over the minutiae of lengthy legal documents for bond issues and stock-market flotations.

Many a budding Kleinwort executive would arrive for work in the morning to find their document crawling with Pinto-esque corrections, down to the last dot and comma.

Nelson, a devoted Pinto pupil, said, "He was fearsomely bright, eccentric in the most wonderful way. He had a pedantic mind. Split infinitives were one of his pet hates."

Pinto liked to work or play bridge late into the night, arriving in the office at midday. Sir Simon Robertson, one of the bank's star financiers, said, "I left a message for him once, asking him to call me. I heard nothing, and went out with my wife. At 1am the phone rang. 'This is George.' I said: 'Do you know what time it is?' He replied: 'Yes.'"

However, not everyone at Kleinwort bought into Pinto's demanding peculiarities. One said: "He was a bit forbidding, but I learnt to work around him."

George Richard Pinto was born in 1929 to Major Richard Pinto, who won the Military Cross in the First World War, and his wife, Gladys Hirsch. Richard left the army to go into business with his father Eugene, a London stockbroker and early cinema proprietor who owned one of Brighton's piers and the Academy cinema on Oxford Street.

George grew up in Queen's Gate, near the Natural History Museum, apparently sleeping undisturbed when the house was bombed in the Second World War. He had been evacuated to New York at the outbreak of hostilities, but returned in 1942.

He went to Eton, where he boxed for the school. After two years' National Service as a 2nd lieutenant with the Coldstream Guards, he went up to Trinity, where he read history and economics.

After Cambridge he took accountancy articles with Cooper Brothers, now PricewaterhouseCoopers. In 1957 his uncle Jimmy Rothschild got him into Model, Roland and Stone, a City stockbroker. The next year he joined the merchant bank Robert Benson, Lonsdale, which merged with Kleinwort in 1961. As a director of the bank from 1968 to 1985 he was not known for people skills.

Among Pinto's many charity interests, he was treasurer of the Anglo-Israel Association, chairman of the Central Council for Jewish Community Services, chairman of the finance committee of the Jewish Blind and Disabled Society, vice-president of Jewish Care and a governor of the Oxford Centre for Hebrew and Jewish Studies.

An art lover, Pinto displayed a select collection of paintings he had inherited at his homes in Kent and Knightsbridge. They were otherwise austere. He became a man of fixed and fastidious habits, always turning out the lights before leaving a room. While his dinner guests would savour his Château Lafite, they were unlikely to become inebriated.

He enjoyed female company, but he was not keen on marriage. A true loner, he liked his own company too much.

He would have been hard to live with. He always resisted the urge to self-deprecate and among his papers he left sheaves of complaints to plumbers, food and drink merchants, chocolatiers and other suppliers. Nevertheless, it is a measure of the regard in which Pinto was held that when he died Royal St George's golf club unusually flew its flag at half-mast in his honour.

George Pinto, merchant banker, was born on April 11, 1929. He died in a road accident on September 10, 2018, aged 89

LEE EVERETT

•

Idiosyncratic singer who 'outed' her second husband Kenny Everett, but not before he was best man at her next wedding

When Audrey Bradshaw fell in love with Alex Wharton, an aspiring rock star, she had a steady job at the Sheffield Empire. She was also married to a local footballer, Alan Bradshaw. This being the impulsive Sixties, she gave up job and husband to follow Wharton to London, where he formed the band the Most Brothers and produced the Moody Blues' second single. He also promptly abandoned her.

Bradshaw, a petite, charismatic blonde with a zest for life, was undeterred. She found a job singing in the 2i's Coffee Bar in Soho, where Cliff Richard had been discovered. There she was spotted and signed up by Larry Parnes. One of the original pop music impresarios, Parnes liked to give stage names to all his acts, including Tommy Steele, Vince Eager and Marty Wilde. He named his new signing Lady Lee. Only Joe Brown stood his ground, after Parnes attempted to change his name to Elmer Twitch.

With her new name came a recording contract and in 1964 Lady Lee released three singles, including *I'm Into Something Good*, later made famous, much to her annoyance, by Herman's Hermits. None was a hit but she nevertheless got a taste of fame as the girlfriend of another of the acts in Parnes's stable: Billy Fury.

They moved into a big house in Surrey together, with a menagerie of animals including a Great Dane and several cockatoos. But by 1967 Fury was no longer troubling the charts and Lee, deciding it was time to move on, headed back to Soho.

"In the country she'd been in jeans, sweaters and wellies," the music executive Tony King recalled. "Now she was in a miniskirt and white boots." She was still hoping for a career in showbusiness but few auditions came her way. At one she was shocked to be asked to take her bra off. The venue where she was auditioning turned out to be Raymond Revuebar, a strip club. She kept her clothes on and was shown the door.

Soon afterwards she met Kenny Everett, who after a spell on pirate radio had become one of the first DJs employed by the BBC on the newly created Radio 1. The two hit it off immediately. "They were heady, wild, euphoric days," she recalled. "Drug-taking was routine. We tripped a lot on LSD. John Lennon used to get it for us."

They married in 1969 at Chelsea register office, with King as best man. Lee, an accomplished needlewoman, made her own wedding dress out of a tablecloth from Harrods. "I organised an open carriage pulled by two grey horses but unfortunately we had the reception before the wedding," King recalled, "so everybody was completely legless. Lee's mum had to be held up."

As well as being fearless, irreverent and unpredictable, Everett also had a discerning ear. He championed records he liked and, when he moved to Capital, was largely responsible for the early success of Queen's *Bohemian Rhapsody,* which had been deemed too long, at six minutes, for the radio. Freddie Mercury became a close friend of both Everett and Lee. "Kenny would not have been Kenny without her," according to the music manager Vicki Wickham. "She was a one-woman extravaganza. They were a formidable duo."

Yet the Everetts were to separate in 1979, when Kenny finally came to terms with his sexuality. The breakup was amicable and Lee even introduced her ex to his first boyfriend, a waiter called Dave.

Lee's next relationship was with the American tennis player Shari

Barman, but she soon met the man who was to be her next husband, the actor John Alkin (DS Tom Daniels in *The Sweeney*). "We bumped into each other at a party thrown by Richard Branson at his Manor studios," Alkin recalled. "My marriage was breaking down, her relationship with Shari wasn't going well and we just gave each other this great bear hug. She flew back to America but returned and started looking for me."

When the couple married in 1985 Kenny Everett was their best man, Elton John was among the guests and instead of a bouquet of flowers Lee clung to her pet chihuahua throughout.

Alkin, Everett and Lee then embarked on something of a ménage à trois. The newlyweds moved to London and Everett moved into a flat across the road from them. Everett would pop in and ask what was for dinner and Lee would have to remind him that they were divorced.

Audrey Valentine Middleton was born in 1937 in Sheffield, where her mother was a cutler and her father was a fireman. Possibly because her father was trained to give first aid, the young Audrey became convinced that she too had an ability to "heal", calling on an array of unlikely powers, including psychic.

Elton John's manager, John Reid, became one who shared her belief in these powers, after she helped to nurse his broken feet after a fall. "It was remarkable," he said. "And I'm not into all that."

Encouraged by Alkin, Lee developed an interest in past life regression therapy. They opened a spiritual healing centre, the House of Spirit, in Bayswater and her clients there included Billie Jean King and Dusty Springfield, who would later bequeath her cat to Lee in her will, along with a lengthy list of instructions on how to feed and care for it.

Lee's healing powers were to prove unequal to the task of mending relations with Kenny Everett after she published her 1987 autobiography, *Kinds of Loving*. He accused her of publicly outing him as gay in the book and the two became estranged. He died of HIV/Aids in 1995 and his life story was made into a film in 2012, with the actress Katherine Kelly playing Lee.

Alkin and Lee, meanwhile, moved to Berkshire, where they ran a boatyard. A keen cook, Lee replicated a chilli jelly she had tasted in Florida. It became so popular with her friends that she launched it under the brand name Chilliqueen and it grew from a cottage industry to a mass-produced product. Poignantly, "Chilliqueen" was Everett's nickname for her.

Lee Everett Alkin was born on February 14, 1937. She died of cancer on February 24, 2022, aged 85

IRVING KANAREK

●

Lawyer whose defence of Charles Manson was one of the most bizarre in legal history, with 200 objections in three days

Irving Kanarek (left) escorting Charles Manson from a Santa Monica courthouse following a hearing in the Gary Hinman murder case.

Less than three days into the trial of Charles Manson, his lawyer, Irving Kanarek, had already broken court records by registering more than 200 objections. Nine of them came in the prosecution's opening statement and Kanarek kept up his belligerent barrage of interruptions until the end of the trial nine months later – another record at the time as the longest trial conducted in an American court.

Kanarek's brief was an impossible one, for the evidence against his client was overwhelming and gruesome. Manson was charged with ordering his band of hippy followers, known as the Manson Family, to visit an address in the wealthy Beverly Hills enclave of Los Angeles on August 9, 1969, and butcher everyone they found.

The house was the home of the actress Sharon Tate and her husband, the director Roman Polanski, who was away in London working on a film. In the carnage that ensued, more than 100 stab wounds were inflicted on Tate, who was pregnant, and three of her friends. A chance visitor was shot dead in the driveway. The following night Manson was alleged to have dispatched his followers again and Leno LaBianca, the owner of a chain of grocery stores, and his wife, Rosemary, died in a similarly frenzied knife attack.

Although Manson had not been present on either occasion, his guilt seemed beyond doubt and Kanarek called no defence witnesses. Instead he set about interrupting witnesses, disorienting the prosecution and confusing the jury with a torrent of disruptive objections and bizarre motions.

When Linda Kasabian, the prosecution's star witness who had kept watch outside the Tate property during the slaughter, and was given immunity in exchange for her testimony against Manson, was being sworn in, Kanarek began by objecting on the grounds that "this witness is not competent and she is insane".

When that failed, he picked up on her admission during her evidence that she had taken 50 LSD trips. In forensic but entirely irrelevant fashion he asked her to "describe what happened on trip number 23". He kept up his cross-examination in similar fashion for seven relentless days.

Inevitably he fell foul of Judge Charles Older, presiding over the case. "You seem to have some sort of physical infirmity or mental disability that causes you to interrupt and disrupt testimony," the judge told him.

On four occasions he found Kanarek guilty of contempt of court and twice sentenced him to spend a night in the county jail. Towards the end of the trial, Older told Kanarek that he was "without scruples, ethics, and professional responsibility" and described his summation, which took a week and a half, as "not an argument but a filibuster".

Manson was sentenced in April 1971 to die in a gas chamber, later commuted to life imprisonment when the California Supreme Court abolished the death penalty. He died in prison in 2017.

Despite Kanarek's dogged defence efforts his client was not particularly grateful. At one point Manson attacked his lawyer in court and on several occasions undermined his case by saying that he was going to instruct his followers to kill Kanarek.

Yet Kanarek was not, as many defence lawyers have done, defending the indefensible to enhance his legal career and reputation. He genuinely held that Manson was not guilty, on the grounds that he had not been present during the killings and all else was hearsay. "No question he was legally innocent," he said. "There was no evidence connecting him to those murders. Charlie wasn't a monster. When you look at the admissible evidence, you come to a very different conclusion."

He remained faithful to his infamous client even after he had ceased to practise. "Manson was a personable guy," he told the *Los Angeles Times* in 1998. "The people who testified against him are all criminals."

Vincent Bugliosi, the prosecution attorney, dubbed Kanarek "the Toscanini of Tedium" but despite exasperation at his antics, he also had a begrudging respect for his opponent's tenacity. In *Helter Skelter*, his book about the Manson murders, Bugliosi hailed Kanarek's ability to draw out cases as "legendary" and admitted that he had feared the Manson trial could drag on for years. "The press focused on his bombast and missed his effectiveness," he wrote. "He frequently scored points."

"I don't know if I was legendary," Kanarek responded. "In the atmosphere of a courtroom, there is an adversary process. And where you have the adversary process, blood flows."

His marriage to Sally Nava ended adversarially in divorce. He is survived by their two daughters.

Irving Allen Kanarek was born in Seattle in 1920, the son of Beatrice (née Prupis) and Meyer Kanarek, an insurance salesman. Educated at Garfield High School and the University of Washington, he graduated in 1941 with a degree in chemistry and moved to California where he worked as an engineer on aerospace projects for North American Aviation.

At the height of McCarthyism he lost his security clearance and his job over accusations that he was a communist. He fought for his reinstatement and won. It was, in effect, his first case and it gave him a taste for the law. He retrained and was called to the California Bar in 1957.

His early caseload consisted of routine personal injury and damage claims but he established a reputation for tireless obstructionism. He stretched out a simple case involving a $100 theft, which should have taken a morning, to three months at a cost to the state of $130,000.

"You take interminable lengths of time in cross-examining on the most minute, unimportant details; you ramble back and forth with no chronology of events, to just totally confuse everybody in the courtroom," the judge chided him in another case.

He even became the subject of an urban myth, that he had once objected to a witness identifying himself on the grounds that he had first heard his name from his mother and therefore it was hearsay.

In 1963 when Kanarek defended Jimmy Lee Smith, who had murdered a Los Angeles police officer, he filed so many pre-trial motions that after a year and a half a jury still had not been selected. The case became a seven-year epic of "appeals, mistrials, reversals and reinstatements" before Smith was sentenced to life in prison.

Kanarek continued to practise until 1990, when he lost his licence after a breakdown that led to him being hospitalised for psychiatric evaluation. He spent his later years living on social security in motel rooms and still protesting Manson's innocence.

Faced with accusations that he had made a career out of obstructing the efficient and expeditious execution of the law, he had a curt response, saying: "One man's obstructionist is another man's hero."

Irving Kanarek, lawyer, was born on May 12, 1920. He died on September 2, 2020, aged 100

GORDON LIDDY

———————•———————

*Eccentric lawyer and mastermind of the Watergate burglaries who
proved his toughness by holding his hand over a flaming candle*

Of the many weird characters to emerge from the Watergate
scandal, G Gordon Liddy, the man who led the bungled Watergate
burglary, was easily the most flamboyant and eccentric. To enforce his
professional tough-guy image he would hold his hand over a flaming
candle. To overcome his fear of rats, he ate one for dinner.

A short, articulate, fastidious man with a prominent, bushy
moustache, he was a key figure in President Nixon's "dirty tricks unit".
He was also the sole Watergate conspirator never to break his oath of
silence or betray his superiors, despite serving nearly five years in prison.

Shortly before his arrest he told his boss, John Dean: "I was
commanding the aircraft carrier when it hit the reef ... if someone
wants to shoot me just tell me what corner to stand on."

Nixon's aides in the White House lived to rue the day in 1971 that
they recruited this extraordinary character for the top-secret Special
Investigations Unit, which became known as "the Plumbers", set up to
staunch a flood of leaks of administration secrets.

The leak that most infuriated Nixon was the publication in *The New York Times* of The Pentagon Papers, a top secret and damaging account of America's involvement in Vietnam. The papers were leaked by Daniel Ellsberg, a disillusioned former government employee. In an effort to discredit Ellsberg and suggest that he was mentally unbalanced, Nixon ordered a psychiatric profile from the CIA.

Failing to come up with anything damaging, the Plumbers, led by Liddy, recruited a group of anti-Castro Cubans to break into the office of Ellsberg's psychiatrist and seize Ellsberg's psychiatric files. They failed to find any files, wrecked the office to make it look like a botched burglary and beat a hasty retreat. The operation was the start of the White House criminal activities that led directly to Watergate.

While waiting for his next assignment, Liddy offered to assassinate the high-profile American newspaper correspondent Jack Anderson. As Liddy noted in his memoir, he had floated the idea of this murder to his colleague Howard Hunt, a White House aide. He justified it on the grounds that Anderson, so he believed, had in one of his articles cost the life of a CIA agent overseas. If ordered to kill Anderson by a legitimate authority, Liddy reasoned it would be a "rational response" to the problem.

He wrote that he had discussed the idea with a CIA expert that Anderson should become the victim of a car crash or a Washington street crime. Nothing came of the proposal, however, and later that year, despite the psychiatrist office fiasco, Liddy was recruited for undercover work for Creep – the Committee to Re-elect the President. Shortly after this appointment Liddy arranged a meeting with John Mitchell, the Attorney General, and John Dean, the president's counsel, in which he proposed a breathtaking list of presidential election campaign dirty tricks.

Before an impassive, pipe-smoking Mitchell, Liddy set up charts for an intelligence plan code under the general name "Gemstone". These included "Diamond", a plan to counter anti-Vietnam war demonstrations scheduled for San Diego by kidnapping demonstration leaders, drugging them and holding them across the border in Mexico until the demonstrations were over. "Ruby" was a plan to infiltrate spies into Democrat campaigns. "Emerald" was for a "chase plane" to pursue Democratic nominees' airliners and buses and bug their radio communications. "Sapphire" was a plan to lease a houseboat on Miami Beach to which prostitutes would lure top Democrats and record their pillow talk.

The Attorney General sat in silence throughout Liddy's proposals of criminal acts and at the end told him that he was most interested in information gathering and protection against demonstrators. At the Senate inquiry into the Watergate scandal, Mitchell was asked how he could have listened to these bizarre plans, and responded bitterly, "I should have thrown Liddy out of the window."

A scaled-down version of Gemstone was finally agreed upon. Liddy was given a budget of $300,000 for his dirty tricks department, with bugging the Democratic National Committee headquarters at Watergate his first target. At the end of April 1972 Liddy received orders from Jeb Magruder, deputy director of the re-election campaign, to break into the Democratic headquarters, tap its phones and put a bug in the office of the committee chairman Lawrence O'Brien. "We want to know whatever is said in his office," Liddy was told. Their mission was also to search for salacious material including addresses of call girls thought to be having affairs with Democrats in order to discredit the Democratic election campaign.

In May Liddy gathered together his same band of inept Cubans and after two nights of unsuccessful attempts to pick the lock, finally broke in. Two phone bugs were installed and directed to a listening post in a room in the Howard Johnson Motel across the street which overlooked the Democrats' office in the Watergate building.

However, the O'Brien bug failed to work and a second break-in was decided upon to fix it. First a lock on a stairwell door leading to the Democratic offices was taped back in advance by the gang. But the tape was discovered and removed by a security guard, and when the break-in began in the early hours of June 17 the burglars found the door locked.

Instead of aborting the operation, the headstrong Liddy decided to go ahead. The lock was picked and re-taped and the burglars broke in. Making a later check, the guard, finding a new tape on the lock, called the police, who arrested the burglars at gunpoint.

Liddy, who was controlling the operation from the motel opposite, heard the last transmission from his entry team stating "they got us". A phone book belonging to one of the captured Cubans contained Liddy's office phone number and he was subsequently arrested.

On January 30, 1973 Liddy was found guilty by Judge John Sirica of charges including conspiracy, burglary and planting microphones. He was offered immunity but refused to testify either before a grand jury or Congress. He was later hauled back before a grand jury and took the Fifth Amendment more than 20 times. This earned him further sentences for contempt, but he refused to break.

George Gordon Battle Liddy was born in Brooklyn, New York, in 1930 to Sylvester Liddy, a lawyer, and Maria (née Abbaticchio). He was educated at St Benedict's School in Newark. As a sickly, asthmatic child, his first political hero was Adolf Hitler. The town he grew up in was full of ethnic Germans who idolised Hitler and Liddy learnt to salute the Stars and Stripes Nazi-style, with right arm raised high. When he listened to Hitler on the radio, he later told an interviewer, it "made me feel a strength inside I had never known before".

Following graduation from Fordham University he served for two years in the army before returning to the university to read law. After this he worked for the FBI for five years then found work as a lawyer before joining the Nixon administration in 1968.

In the wake of the Watergate scandal that led to the resignation of Nixon, Liddy was handed a 20-year prison sentence for "sordid, despicable and reprehensible" crimes. President Carter cut the sentence to eight years but he was finally paroled after 52 months – the longest time in jail for any Watergate felon.

He emerged from prison totally unrepentant. Not only did he claim to have no regrets, he said he would do it again. "When the prince approaches his lieutenant, the proper response of the lieutenant to the prince is, '*Fiat voluntas tua*'," he said, "Thy will be done."

Exploiting his notoriety and expertise as a former FBI agent, he set up an international security consulting agency in Florida – to "go anywhere and do just about anything" – specialising in VIP protection and hostage release.

Frances Liddy (née Purcell), a striking blonde he had married in 1957, stood by him through his trial, imprisonment and his subsequent enterprises when he became a folk hero of America's extreme right and a fanatical opponent of gun-control legislation. They had five children.

Liddy, the "silent man" of the Watergate scandal, made thousands of dollars a speech on the lecture circuit and even formed a double act with Timothy Leary, who had found fame in the 1960s as an LSD guru. The two men went way back. As a prosecutor in 1966 Liddy had joined a raid on a drug cult in which Leary was arrested.

By now in the realms of self-parody, Liddy agreed to play a role in *Miami Vice*. He also ran a radio talk show popular with right-wing Americans, even if he was condemned by them when he advised listeners to deal with agents of the Bureau of Alcohol and Firearms (an obsession of his) who broke into somebody's home, with "Head shots. Kill the sons of bitches. Get instructions on how to shoot straight." He advised listeners to use a cardboard cut-out of Hillary Clinton for target practice.

In retirement Liddy promoted nutritional supplements, sang lieder while he accompanied himself on a piano, and not only remained a keep-fit enthusiast but also took up motorbike riding and parachute jumping. He also retained a quirky sense of humour, driving around Washington DC in a Volvo with the licence plate H2O GATE.

Gordon Liddy, lawyer, was born on November 30, 1930. He died of complications from Parkinson's disease on March 30, 2021, aged 90

ANITA PALLENBERG

———————————•———————————

Actress and Rolling Stones muse who not only slept with the band, but also gave them a taste for drugs, fashion and hedonism

Anita Pallenberg was central to the myth of the Rolling Stones, not least because she slept with at least three of them. Much as their stint in Hamburg had rubbed some of the provincialism off the Beatles, so Pallenberg's bohemian ways and aloof, Teutonic intensity gave the Stones their sheen of sophistication. Her relationships first with Brian Jones and then with Keith Richards encouraged the band to dress more flamboyantly, to experiment with harder drugs, and to live a life of hedonistic excess that became the template for youthful rebellion the world over.

She became involved with Jones in September 1965 after seeing the group play a concert in Munich. That summer *Satisfaction* had become their first international hit, transforming their appeal, which previously had been limited to Britain. Although afterwards rather written out of their history, Jones at that stage still considered himself the Stones' leader. He was highly attractive to women – then 23 he had already fathered five children by different mothers. Like Pallenberg he spoke German, and took to her after she offered him some marijuana backstage. Experimental in her sexual tastes, she was soon introducing him to the vices associated with the Marquis de Sade, whips and manacles included, and, in her practical German way, she had their Chelsea pad soundproofed so as not disturb the neighbours.

As well as possessing a lithe, pantherine beauty, Pallenberg was alluring to the Stones because of the cosmopolitan circle in which she already mixed in London. She helped to introduce them to well-heeled young tastemakers such as the art dealer Robert Fraser (who suggested that Peter Blake do the cover for *Sgt Pepper*), Christopher Gibbs and the Ormsby-Gores. She had worked as a model and was also influential on Jones's dandyish fashion sense – including, presumably, the Nazi uniforms he was wont to wear – and later that of Richards (who wore her clothes for the album sleeve of *Their Satanic Majesties Request*).

More overtly sexy, strong and manipulative than Mick Jagger's muse of the time Marianne Faithfull (herself half-Austrian), Pallenberg came to fascinate Richards. She remained with Jones for two years, but as the pressure of fame and the effects of narcotics took its toll on him – especially the paranoia-inducing LSD to which she had introduced him – their relationship became increasingly abusive and violent. And it went both ways. When they fought Jones reportedly ended up as bandaged and bruised as she did. After one row in Torremolinos, where knives and glass were thrown by both, the pair were arrested.

In the summer of 1967, Pallenberg and Richards consummated their mutual attraction in the back of his chauffeured Bentley whilst being driven through Spain. According to Richards she made the first move and the chauffeur kept his eyes on the road. They were fleeing the publicity surrounding the notorious police drugs bust on Richards's house in West Sussex, Redlands, the one at which Marianne Faithfull, Jagger's girlfriend, had been wearing nothing but a fur rug. There were arrests. Jagger, Richards and then Jones were later imprisoned for drugs offences, prompting the editor of *The Times*, William Rees-Mogg to write his celebrated *Who Breaks a Butterfly on a Wheel?* leader. The sentences were later successfully appealed.

Richards and Pallenberg were to stay together for the next 12 years, but never married. With their status as rock outlaws established by the trials, they at first spent time in Rome, where she had grown up. There they were friendly with Paul and Talitha Getty, who had similar interests, in Morocco and in experimenting with drugs, and lived for a while at the Villa Medici, home to the painter Balthus, whose son Stanislaus Klossowski was one of the band's hangers-on.

Intelligent and with an enigmatic air about her, Pallenberg had done a little acting before meeting Jones, and her higher profile now led to offers of minor roles in films. During the filming of *Candy* (1968) she rejected the advances of her co-star Marlon Brando. "Brando whisked me off back to his country house and started to do his Brando-ish seduction and I got completely intimidated," she recalled. "He was lying in bed reading his poetry and I ran away." It was probably the only time that she was ever intimidated by anything or anyone.

Perhaps the most notable of her performances was as the Great Tyrant opposite Jane Fonda in *Barbarella* (1968), emblematic of her public image as a wicked seductress. Fonda herself fell for Richards around this time, but he did not return her feelings, and when she tried to visit him in Chelsea would not open the door to her. "He said that she reminded him of his aunt," Pallenberg revealed.

Intense as Pallenberg's relationship with Richards was – in 1969 she gave birth to their son Marlon – it was not exclusive. Richards wrote *Gimme Shelter* while waiting angrily for her to return from what he believed was an affair between her and Jagger. They were in the process of making *Performance* (1970), directed by another of Pallenberg's former lovers, Donald Cammell. It was claimed that little acting was involved as the cameras recorded one particular scene of lovemaking. For his part, Richards later admitted that in revenge he had slept with Faithfull, but he was philosophical about the state of affairs: "I mean, hey, I'd stolen Anita from Brian, and besides I was knocking Marianne."

Pallenberg later reflected that the Stones were chauvinists, as were the Beatles. She herself was never a great fan of the music or the bands of the era, and was somewhat shocked to see aristocratic hippies walking barefoot in the King's Road. In Italy, where she had grown up, only the poor did so. Nonetheless, in old age she also confessed to being bored by political correctness and having preferred the free ways of her youth.

By 1970 the focus of that had increasingly become heroin. It tinged the making of *Exile on Main Street*, recorded near Nice, and Pallenberg continued to take it while pregnant with their daughter, Angela. When she and Richards left France in 1972, they were pursued by police with warrants for their arrest.

They moved to Jamaica where Pallenberg (who had cultivated an interest in voodoo and went through a phase of wearing a string of garlic to bed to ward off vampires) became delusional and had to leave the island after being jailed. Back in London Richards would find constables waiting outside his house in Cheyne Walk, Chelsea, to search him for drugs. The couple spent much of the mid-1970s as addicts, during which time their infant son Tara died and their mood became self-destructive. Matters came to a head in 1977 when Richards was arrested in Toronto for possessing heroin, although it was Pallenberg whom the police had wanted.

"With Anita you knew you were taking on a Valkyrie, she who

decides who dies in battle," Richards said, "but she went right off the rails, became lethal ... she was unstoppably self-destructive."

Richards now began to break free of his habit, and gave Angela to his mother to be brought up (Marlon did not start school until he was eight, and his father's habit of sleeping all day instead of helping her with him added to Pallenberg's depressed state). Marlon is now a gallery curator, Angela runs a riding school.

Pallenberg remained trapped, however, by heroin and in 1979, when living apart from Richards, was embroiled in more scandal after her 17-year-old boyfriend Scott Cantrell shot himself in her bedroom in New York while seemingly playing Russian roulette.

This was too much even for Richards, who parted from her, and in 1983 married the model Patti Hansen. It would take Pallenberg another 25 years to fully sober up, but although they never quite managed a full reconciliation, Richards acknowledged in his autobiography *Life* (2010) the debt of inspiration that he and the band owed to her, and described how "Anita and I can now sit around at Christmas with our grandchildren and give each other a bemused smile, 'Hey you silly old cow, how you doing?' She's become a benign spirit. She's a marvellous granny. She's survived."

Anita Pallenberg was born in Rome in 1944. Her father, who was Italian, ran a travel agency but had artistic leanings and was a frustrated composer. Her mother, who worked as a secretary, was German, and after growing up a sporty child largely in the house of her prosperous grandfather Anita was sent to a German boarding school where she exhibited "challenging behaviour". She was duly expelled when she was 16 years old.

She returned to Rome, ostensibly to study at art school, but was soon offered modelling work – with her agency pitching her as "too beautiful to get out of bed". Her interest in acting and her ability to make useful contacts quickly brought her within the circle of the film-makers of the *Dolce Vita* era, Federico Fellini and Luchino Visconti. By the early 1960s she had moved on to New York, where she hung out with the beat poets Allen Ginsberg and William Burroughs, as well as Andy Warhol at his Factory – and from there she went to live in Paris. By this time she had become something of a linguist and would joke that she could say "fuck off" in six languages.

After her break-up with Richards, Pallenberg became increasingly isolated. She returned to America and lived with Marlon and Richards's father, Bert, in a series of Gatsby-style mansions on Long Island, occasionally bringing back new friends made at the Mudd Club in New York, such as the painter Jean-Michel Basquiat.

Her consumption of drink and drugs heightened her paranoia, as well as spoiling her looks, and in the early 1980s she spent a month locked in a room at the Grosvenor House hotel, London. Her sister managed to get her into a rehabilitation clinic in 1987, and by 1994 she had mastered herself sufficiently to complete a degree in fashion and textiles at Central Saint Martins. One wag described her graduation show as a "triumph of style over substance abuse". Throughout all this her own wit had never deserted her. Asked by the singer Courtney Love whether she would consider getting plastic surgery, she answered: "Darling, I was the most beautiful woman in 17 countries. I *like* being ugly!"

Clothes that she showed were well-received, but she disliked the business of fashion, and preferred to spend time in India researching fabrics. She then devoted herself to caring for her elderly mother, and by 2004 had begun drinking heavily again.

Several hip operations, which left her with a limp, helped her to take responsibility for herself once more, and by the end of the decade she had found a new tranquillity, aided by a passion for gardening. As well as maintaining a house south of Rome, and tending to Richards's garden in Jamaica in the winters, she continued to live in Chelsea, in a luxurious flat said to have been provided for her by Richards. From there she would bicycle to Chiswick to tend her vegetable allotment. She regularly refused entreaties from publishers to write her memoirs. In her early seventies, however, she did say this by way of reflection upon her colourful and quixotic life: "I honestly didn't think that I'd live beyond 40."

Anita Pallenberg, muse to the Rolling Stones, was born on January 25, 1944. She died on June 13, 2017, aged 73

PETER FARRER

●

*Tax inspector who loved taffeta skirts and became an authority on the
history of cross-dressing*

Peter Farrer enjoyed a long career as a senior tax inspector, but
when, towards the end of his life, he featured in the "Liverpool
Homotopia" season, it had nothing to do with fiscal matters. The
season's highlight was the exhibition *Transformation: One Man's Cross-
Dressing Wardrobe* at the Walker Art Gallery in the city, which showed a
small part of his collection of dresses, many of them made from taffeta.
It was the culmination for Farrer of 75 years of wearing women's
clothes.

"I longed to experience for myself the sensation of wearing a dress
of rustling taffeta," he wrote. "Dressing in a taffeta frock did not make
me want to be a girl, but it certainly made me understand how much
pleasure girls and women get from their party frocks and intensified
my interest in fashion and in the history of costume."

Farrer would cross-dress mostly at home, when his wife was out –
she was happy for him to pursue his inclinations, but felt
uncomfortable about being around when he was doing it. After-hours

visitors to the tax office might have been startled to come across Farrer in his full regalia.

Was he deliberately playing a dangerous game? Pauline Rushton, a senior curator at National Museums Liverpool, who staged the *Transformation* exhibition, knew Farrer for many years. "I asked him if deep down he wanted to be caught – was the danger the thrill?" she recalled. "He said, no, he'd have been horrified for anyone to know that he was doing it. It wasn't a cry for help. Peter wasn't transitioning, and he wasn't doing it because he wanted to perform. His main reason was simply that he had a sexual fetish for taffeta, the tactile nature of it, and the noise it makes, rustling as it moves."

Farrer first became interested in women's clothes when he was 14 and tried on a ballgown belonging to his mother, Lilian. He had been born in Surrey in 1926, along with a twin sister, Sarah. His father, William, was a teacher and vicar, and the family moved several times. During the Second World War his father had a parish on the Isle of Man, and the twins attended King William's College, where Peter was head of the cadet force and captain of rugby.

He did his National Service in Trieste – "records show that he spent most of his time pursuing Italian women," his son, Jonathan, said – then studied philosophy, politics and economics at St John's College, Oxford. After graduation he went into the Civil Service, where he remained for the rest of his career as a tax inspector. It was a career that, although pursued zealously, Jonathan said, "was really only a way of funding his interests".

He began dance lessons, and his teacher was Joan Winster, the daughter of a Preston ice-cream maker. In 1952 they were married by Farrer's father, and they had their only child, Jonathan. In the early 1960s the family lived in London, Barnsley and Kenya, when Farrer was seconded to the newly independent government to help to set up its inland revenue system. They eventually settled in Formby, near Liverpool, where Farrer was a senior tax inspector, dealing with large businesses such as the Littlewoods pools company.

Jonathan – who went on to set up a firm selling furniture – recalled his father's passion for collecting. "At my primary school in Barnsley my class was asked to collect and press as many local wildflowers as possible and a prize was offered. After two weekends, and miles of walking, he helped me to amass 135 species." Not surprisingly, Jonathan won – the runner-up had collected 15.

Farrer managed to keep his cross-dressing hidden from Jonathan, although his son did recall, "As a teenager I became aware of his slightly strange library in his study. In my twenties I had a fairly good idea of what he was up to, and when he remarried in 1982 he showed us his collections of dresses, but wouldn't admit to dressing up – although the size 12 gold slingbacks were a clue."

Farrer's life was blighted in the 1970s by the decline and death of Joan from early-onset Alzheimer's disease. He coped in part by turning to his love of women's clothing from the mid-19th and early 20th centuries, when the fashion for taffeta was at its height. He bought by mail order or in department stores, where he felt no pressure to explain that the clothes were for him.

He would visit Liverpool Museum in his lunch breaks to study Victorian dresses and corsetry, and joined the Costume Society and the Northern Society of Costume and Textiles. Through the Costume Society he met Anne Brogden, a lecturer in art and fashion – "a brilliant woman, far too good for him," according to Jonathan.

They married in 1982 and bought a house in south Liverpool, which they filled with their dress collections, textiles, books and magazines, fashion plates, illustrations and photographs.

When Farrer retired his serious collecting began. As well as his rapidly expanding collection of dresses and underwear, Farrer acquired complete runs of magazines such as *Vogue, Queen, The Englishwoman's Domestic Magazine*, other 19th-and 20th-century publications and more than 8,000 books. He began producing his own books – 13 in all – drawing on his magazine collections, and he set up Karn Publications, which he ran from home (Karn had been his mother's maiden name).

There were such titles as *Confidential Correspondence on Cross-Dressing, 1911–1915, Cross-Dressing Between the Wars: Selections from London Life, 1923–1933* and *Men in Petticoats: a Selection of Letters from Victorian Newspapers.*

When Anne died in 2014 Farrer, who was approaching 90, began to think about what would happen to his collections. Rushton arranged to take many of his clothes, and with his books and magazines they will go to make up a permanent exhibition devoted to the culture of cross-dressing. In his final years, he and Jonathan were finally able to discuss his predilection. "I began to appreciate the guilt and the pressure that he must have suffered carrying his secret," said Jonathan.

The *Transformation* exhibition ran at the Walker until February 2017, then transferred to Sudley House in Aigburth, where it will run until next year. At the Walker show, Post-it Notes were left on the wall. "So happy to see I'm not the only tranny in the world," one read, while another said, "We need more people like him, because there's not enough fun these days."

Peter Farrer, tax inspector, fashion historian and collector, was born on May 20, 1926. He died on February 10, 2017, aged 90

APRIL ASHLEY

Model, socialite and transgender rights campaigner whose reassignment surgery was part of a rollercoaster life of lovers and high drama

As George Jamieson lay on the operating table, the last words he heard the French surgeon say before administering the anaesthetic were "Au revoir, monsieur".

Seven hours later Jamieson had become April Ashley and as she came round she was greeted with the words "Bonjour, mademoiselle".

At the time of her operation in 1960, Ashley was one of the first Britons to undergo reassignment surgery and thought to be only the ninth person in the world. Although the 2004 act which legally recognised transitioning was still decades away, the British authorities accepted her change of identity and issued her with a driving licence and a passport as a woman. Under her new name – April for her birthday and Ashley after Leslie Howard's character in *Gone With the Wind* – she went on to become Britain's most celebrated transgender rights campaigner.

An inveterate socialite, she numbered among her friends such diverse personalities as Pablo Picasso, John Prescott and Elvis Presley who danced with her at a nightclub in Paris in 1959 before she had the operation and for a time afterwards sent her gifts, including bottles of champagne. John Lennon was another famous encounter. She would adopt a Liverpool accent when she talked about him: "John would say 'Here comes the fucking duchess'. I became quite good friends with him in the end."

Strikingly beautiful and blessed with an innate style, she became one of the world's leading fashion models, photographed by David Bailey, Terence Donovan and Lord Lichfield and appearing on the cover of magazines such as *Vogue*. She endured numerous scandals, was rarely out of the news and was subjected to violence, prejudice, mockery and abuse. She braved it all with good grace and faced the world with an extraordinary dignity. "I decided I was never going to hide who I was," she said.

In a rollercoaster life of high drama she survived suicide attempts, spells in mental institutions, bankruptcy and three heart attacks. Her 1963 marriage to the Hon Arthur Corbett (the future Lord Rowallan) caused a sensation when, in 1970, her husband sought to have the marriage annulled on the grounds Ashley had been born a man.

"I started life out as a boy," she said. "As I grew up, I turned into a feminine-looking boy. Perhaps I should have accepted my androgynous nature – most feminine-looking boys do. But I couldn't accept it because I felt myself to be essentially female. The feeling went as deep as feelings could go."

She was eventually appointed MBE in 2012 for services to transgender equality but over the years the pressure of fame and intense disapproval from sections of the media took its toll. She became a heavy drinker and admitted that in the 1970s when she was running a Knightsbridge restaurant she could knock back 32 dry martinis in a night. On one occasion she was introduced to Princess Margaret but was unable to shake the royal hand as she was swigging from a champagne glass in one hand and a whisky tumbler in the other.

April Ashley was born George Jamieson in Liverpool in 1935, one of nine children, three of whom did not survive. Her father, Fred, was a drunken but amiable cook in the Merchant Navy and her mother, Ada, worn down by nine pregnancies, was violent and short-tempered, regularly beating her son. After one brutal thrashing a doctor had to be summoned; he warned George's parents that if such an assault was ever repeated, he would have Ada arrested.

From as early as Ashley could remember, she did not feel like a "George" and by the age of 15 she knew she wanted to be a girl. "I never grew up as I was supposed to," she said. "I was emaciated and very shy. I felt like a total freak. There were no whiskers, my voice didn't break and I sprouted breasts. I hated myself and there was no one I could look to."

As a teenager, George was bullied at school and beaten up on the streets of Liverpool before following his father into the Merchant Navy as a 15-year-old cabin boy. After he was raped by a roommate he attempted suicide and was committed to a psychiatric hospital, where he underwent electroconvulsive therapy and his effeminacy was treated with male hormone injections.

Various jobs followed, including working at the Quo Vadis restaurant in Soho, where he encountered Albert Einstein, who remarked on his long eyelashes. "Why do you keep calling me Madame Butterfly, Mr Einstein?" the young man asked.

Working at a hotel in Wales, he met Prescott, who was training as a sous-chef. "So handsome, like a young Marlon Brando," Ashley recalled. (They remained friends and in 2005, with the Gender Recognition Act in effect, Prescott, then deputy prime minister, helped her to get a new birth certificate.)

In 1956 George moved to Paris where he performed in a drag act – "all feather boas and sequinned dresses" – at Le Carrousel nightclub. There he met Ernest Hemingway, Jean-Paul Sartre, Bob Hope and Presley, on weekend leave from the US army.

After four years in Paris, where he underwent a course of oestrogen injections to help develop his breasts and hips, he flew to Casablanca at the age of 24 and underwent expensive reassignment surgery. The process was excruciating and the side-effects of dizziness and nausea persisted for years.

As April Ashley she epitomised the freewheeling spirit of Swinging Sixties London. She became queen of the catwalk, had an affair with Omar Sharif and was close to Peter O'Toole, whom she was fond of calling "No Tool", though he always insisted their relationship was platonic. She shared a flat with Kenneth Tynan and turned down Picasso and Dalí because they seemed too lecherous. No Chelsea party seemed complete without her. "I was exquisite, darling," she recalled.

Few were aware that she had been born male until a friend sold her story to the *Sunday People* which ran an exposé under the headline "The Extraordinary Case of Top Model April Ashley – Her Secret is Out!" Overnight she found her bookings were cancelled and even the credit for a small part in the Bob Hope and Bing Crosby film *The Road to Hong Kong* was removed.

She never worked as a model again and when she was recognised in the street, strangers attacked her. "The most extraordinary moment was in Sloane Square," she recalled. "I saw this elegant woman coming straight at me. She slapped me so hard I had her finger marks on my face for three days. She didn't say a word, just kept on walking."

However, the revelation did not deter Corbett, a married nightclub owner with four children and a penchant for cross-dressing himself (according to Ashley, "at Sandhurst he used to ride side saddle"). The Eton-educated first son of Lord Rowallan, the former governor general of Tasmania, Corbett was heir to a Victorian castle and 7,000 acres in Scotland, but when his affair with Ashley became public, his furious father disinherited him.

He married Ashley in Gibraltar in 1963 and they opened a nightclub, the Jacaranda in Marbella. The union was stormy from the outset. Corbett indulged in numerous extra-marital affairs and within a fortnight of their marriage, Ashley had also strayed. "I ran off with the heir to the Duke del Infantado to his palace in Seville. I told Arthur, 'I'm going to see my lover in Spain,' and he took me to the airport with seven suitcases and a Great Dane." In Spain, she said, she and the duke "made love under the Goyas and Velázquezes. It was wonderful."

In 1970 Corbett sued for an annulment on the grounds that Ashley was "a person of the male sex". The case made headlines when Mr Justice Ormrod declared that the marriage had "little or nothing to do with any heterosexual relationship which I can recall hearing about" and ruled that Ashley was "not a woman for the purposes of marriage, but is a biological male and has been since birth". Ashley was devastated by the ruling. "It was just petty discrimination."

The case led to a nervous breakdown. Left without funds, she was reduced to performing in working men's clubs as "The Most Talked About Woman in the World". Undeterred, she found backers to open a restaurant near Harrods called AD8. On the opening night 2,000 people turned up.

Later she moved to Ibiza, where she enjoyed the hedonistic lifestyle and camaraderie of expats such as Terry Thomas and Robin Maugham but in the late 1970s suffered the first of three heart attacks, brought on by alcoholism and drug abuse. She retreated to Hay-on-Wye, where she lived for 11 years, before moving to California, where she worked for Greenpeace and married Jeffrey West. The marriage ended in divorce, but they remained friends. Back in Europe in the early eighties she had a one-night stand with Michael Hutchence, who at the time was just finding pop fame with INXS. "When I came downstairs in the morning, swinging my knickers around my finger, my friend said, 'Do you know who you have just been to bed with?'

I didn't. I'd never heard of INXS."

Her extraordinary life was chronicled in two memoirs, *April Ashley's Odyssey* (1982) and *The First Lady* (2006). Her final homes were a small villa in the south of France and a pied-à-terre in west London. In old age she resembled an aristocratic grande dame from another era, her beauty fading but still immaculately coiffured as she held court in the Chelsea Arts Club telling her self-mocking stories in a velvety husk. As one interviewer noted, "She will tilt her head back and raise her eyebrows to emphasise an ironic or catty observation; she will make warm, sweeping, off-the-shoulder gestures one moment and tuck her lips into cold little pouts of disapproval the next. Her anecdotes are polished and seemingly inexhaustible. They are well animated, too: she will give precious little claps of her hands, for instance, when imitating the sound of Kenneth Tynan being spanked."

She advised Eddie Redmayne on playing a trans woman in the 2015 film *The Danish Girl* and treated 21st-century controversies over transitioning with disdain. However, when the writer Julie Burchill called trans people "bed wetters in bad wigs" it was an insult too far. "I don't know where Miss Burchill goes to see people with crappy wigs on their heads," she responded. "All the transsexuals I know are very smart looking and I do not wear a wig."

Reflecting on her life, "I had to be brazen," she reasoned. "I was notorious and it was left to me only to exploit my personality. I was forced to become an artist of life."

April Ashley MBE, model and trans pioneer, was born on April 25, 1935. She died of unknown causes on December 27, 2021, aged 86

SAM LEACH

The hapless Beatles tour manager before Brian Epstein

After hearing an unknown group called the Beatles perform in Liverpool on a damp and foggy January night in 1961, Sam Leach went backstage and told John Lennon and Paul McCartney they were destined to be "bigger than Elvis". Lennon turned to McCartney and said, "We've got a right nutter here, Paul."

McCartney was more diplomatic. Aware that Leach was a well-known local club owner and sniffing the prospect of lucrative bookings, he offered the Beatles' services.

Leach became the group's agent and over the next two years organised and promoted almost 50 Beatles gigs, including a series of concerts at the New Brighton Tower Ballroom, which attracted audiences of 4,000 and more and played a crucial part in expanding the group's appeal beyond the regulars who packed into the Cavern.

His role in helping to launch the group's early career was recognised when the Beatles, who included the Latin standard *Besame Mucho* in their setlist, affectionately changed the song's title to "Be-Sammy Leacho".

However, Leach's bid to become the group's full-time manager collapsed in ruins on the night of December 9, 1961, the date he had booked the Beatles to appear at the Palais Ballroom in Aldershot. It was the first time the Beatles had played in southern England and was intended to be an important career milestone. "The idea was to get the London agents to come see them," Leach explained. In the event the night turned into perhaps the biggest disaster of the Beatles' career.

First, Tito Burns, who was the most important booking agent in London, with clients including Cliff Richard and the Shadows, refused the invitation. "Sam, they've got 5,000 groups in London. Who needs a group with a stupid name like the Beatles?" he told Leach.

It was to get worse. When the local paper refused to accept Leach's cheque, the advertisement for the concert failed to appear. Without publicity, there was a queue of six people waiting to see the Beatles when the Palais's doors opened. "We had to go around the pubs and coffee bars inviting people to come to a free dance," Leach recalled. In the end we managed to get 18 people."

Leach, whose powers of concentration were limited, had also failed to book his young charges anywhere to stay for the night. The Beatles were unimpressed and, after the show, staged a mock funeral for Leach before driving back to Liverpool in the back of a van. Five days later the group signed a management contract with Brian Epstein.

"Paul and John had left an urgent message for me to meet them at the Grapes pub in Liverpool's Mathew Street, round the corner from Brian's headquarters," Leach recalled. "When I strolled in, Paul and John looked a little uneasy. Stammering, Paul told me, 'Sam there's this guy wants to manage us. We know we have a handshake agreement with you, but he's a millionaire.'"

Leach acted as agent on several more gigs into 1962, but by August that year had been eased out of any further part in the Beatles' career by Epstein. Along with the unfortunate Dick Rowe, the Decca executive who in 1962 rejected the Beatles on the ground that "guitar groups are on the way out", Leach went down in Beatles folklore as the reddest face in the Fab Four's story; the man who could muster only 18 people to watch a group on the threshold of becoming "bigger than Elvis". That he was also the first to have predicted that the Beatles would one day eclipse Presley only added to the irony.

A 2016 documentary film, titled *The Sixth Beatle,* told Leach's story sympathetically and featured him talking at length about his "two-and-a-half-year rollercoaster ride through rock history". The film focused heavily on the rivalry between Epstein, cast as the "fifth Beatle", and Leach, who accused his successor of a calculated slight by writing him out of the group's history.

For a short while after Epstein took over, however, there was an uneasy truce between the two men, with Epstein even attending Leach's wedding to Joan McEvoy in 1962. They had four children. The marriage was later dissolved, but they remained on friendly terms.

Leach was born in Liverpool in 1935. His father, Stanley, was a clerk working on the city docks, and his mother, Pauline, a Canadian émigrée. On leaving school, he briefly worked as an apprentice for the English Electric Company, but his entrepreneurial spirit soon led him to set up several businesses of his own, including a hair salon.

He started promoting rock'n'roll shows in Liverpool in the late 1950s with regular nights at the Casanova Club. "I was looking for bands to appear at the Casanova and I'd heard about a new group called the Beatles, who had just returned from Hamburg," he recalled. "It was a dirty, rough place, a miserable little dance hall on the outskirts of Liverpool. There were fights breaking out all over the place."

In later years Leach made a modest living out of his Beatles connection. When the group led the "British invasion" of the American charts in 1964, he produced a cash-in magazine titled *Beatles on Broadway*, which sold almost a million copies. He wrote a memoir and for a while managed a tribute band.

"I've no regrets at all," he insisted. "I did my part and I was an important stepping stone. Even in 100 years I'll still be talked about, thanks to the Beatles."

Sam Leach, Beatles agent, was born on December 16, 1935. He died of cancer on December 21, 2016, aged 81

Sam Leach, bottom, with George Harrison and John Lennon.

MAURIZIO 'ZANZA' ZANFANTI

Courtly Italian lothario who claimed to have bedded 6,000 women, many of whom were German and Scandinavian tourists

Part Casanova, part Conan the Barbarian, and all man, Maurizio Zanfanti was God's gift to women, but not just in his own eyes. By the time a last, fatal tryst with an admirer 40 years his junior terminated his long chevauchée of love, he could claim 6,000 conquests.

It was a tally that made him for decades a proud symbol of Italian virility and of the fun to be had in Rimini, the Adriatic resort where Zanza, as he was known, plied his trade working for nightclubs favoured by German and Scandinavian tourists in the sexually liberated 1970s and 1980s.

One could perhaps question the precise numbers. "Frankly," admitted Zanza, "I've lost count." One could also wonder what compulsion drove such behaviour. Yet, in all the worldwide coverage of his career (if that is the word wanted) after his death, little was said about what underpinned his evident appeal to women.

For Zanza – Italian slang for "mosquito" – was not a mere lothario, attested many of those to whom he had been (if briefly) catnip. His trademark was a perhaps paradoxical courtliness, and an absence of vulgarity. He was not, recalled one former acquaintance, the kind of man who would be eyeing up other passing beauties when you were at the beach with him.

Zanza believed that gentleness was the key. "I loved them all," he said, "and for each had a kind thought, or a small present." This was of a part with his reputation locally of not hesitating to help someone in need, be it with a job, a meal or a place to stay.

Perhaps the only person who was not happy with how he carried on was his mother. Zanza lived above her, and the comings and goings at all hours of the night got on her nerves.

One of three children, Maurizio Zanfanti was born in 1955. His parents were fishmongers. His father kept ducks and hens, and grew grapes and vegetables. Zanza started work as a bottlewasher at 11 years old and by his late teens had graduated to working as a waiter in nightspots.

Impressed by his ability to strike up conversation, and his having mastered English and Swedish, the owner of a popular club, Blow Up, offered Zanza a job when he finished his military service. Rimini was then changing from the city of the director Federico Fellini's childhood, when it had been a provincial centre catering in summer to well-heeled Italians, to a magnet for mass tourism. Rimini's miles of sand and hundreds of newly built hotels made it the Benidorm of Italy, or a slightly racier version of Blackpool and it drew daily flights from sun-starved Sweden, Norway and Germany. These were palmy days when people thought nothing of leaving their clothes unattended while going for a midnight swim and Scandinavian women wore no tops to their bikinis. Many would arrive clutching Zanza's telephone number.

Based in the beachfront suburb of Bellariva, Zanza worked at distributing flyers to clients of agencies such as Club 33, which only flew holidaymakers under that age. This later evolved into showing them – more broadly – a good time.

He reckoned that at his peak he was sleeping with four women a day, one in the afternoon and three through the night. He attributed his strength to a diet of meat and salad. He also said that persistence was key. One in three of any potential haul would turn him down, but he would still reel in about 200 women every summer. These included a French reporter sent to interview him, who later wrote up their encounter.

In the early 1980s, *Bild*, the German publication, claimed Zanza bedded 312 women in three summer months, although the AIDS crisis later reduced his success rate. Zanza carried a doctor's certificate of health in his wallet, though like an MOT certificate it was probably only any good for the day of issue.

Much of his allure came from his style of dress – shirts slashed to the navel, high boots, flares when they were in fashion, and chunky chains and rings. Many of his outfits were tailored for him. During the winters, Zanza would go to Sweden to drum up business for the following year – a wax statue in his honour had been erected in one town by a former lover – and there he would dress just the same.

Zanza eschewed drugs and alcohol – milk and mint was his tipple – and gave up smoking. He claimed never to have honed his physique other than in bed. Later in life, he ran a nightclub in winter in Cortina and worked in a bar in Rimini. When his mother, Gina, had problems with her fish business, however, he unhesitatingly went to help her out, pulling the shutters down himself.

Although in recent years Zanza had a lengthy relationship, he never married and, officially at least, had no children. He died in harness, suffering a heart attack after entertaining a 23-year-old Romanian girl that he had known for some years in his car.

Maurizio Zanfanti, ladies' man, was born on October 20, 1955. He died on September 26, 2018, aged 62

DICKIE JEEPS

England scrum half and captain known for his practical jokes and colourful private life who went on to become president of the RFU

Once, when bored at a post-match banquet in Paris, Dickie Jeeps crawled under the top table and set off a firework under the feet of the president of the French Rugby Federation. He was wont to describe himself as "a water pistol man", and the sporting establishment had reason to be wary of his antic unpredictability and keen sense of mischief. With his small stature – he was 5ft 7in – enormous strength and ferocious competitiveness, there was something of the terrier about him, and these attributes made him an ideal scrum half. Between 1956 and 1962, when he won 24 caps for England and captained the side 13 times, he became arguably the greatest scrum half in the world.

Even New Zealanders admired his grittiness and apparent indestructibility when he toured with the 1959 British and Irish Lions. His ability to deliver decent possession from any unpromising angle led them to describe him as "the India rubber man".

His forceful character was evident both as a captain of England and, 24 years after his final international, as president of the Rugby Football Union. Jeff Butterfield, a team-mate, called him "the toughest, hardest player around. He was relentless in pursuing a win. He didn't just play for fun. Part of his essential gear contained a catapult: he was a grown-up Just William."

Jeeps, a fruit farmer from Cambridgeshire, did not care much for convention. As a player he understood the need for preparation at a time when the game's administrators considered that tantamount to professionalism. As president he offered leadership rather than emollience and his honesty with colleagues was sometimes a little too refreshing.

As a private individual he showed generosity and self-indulgence in like measure – and he could be an over-enthusiastic curator of his own mythology. According to one story he nearly drowned during an England trial on a flooded pitch at Taunton. He became trapped face down at the bottom of a ruck and had to be dragged to the touchline where Ron Jacobs, the four-square England prop, pumped the water from his lungs. According to Jeeps, he then stood up, shook himself and proceeded to put the ball into the next scrum.

He was one of those rare individuals who played rugby for the Lions before winning his first England cap and his views were shaped by hard-won experience on tour with the Lions in South Africa and Australasia. That he played 13 out of 14 tests on those tours is testament to his ability.

Richard Eric Gautrey Jeeps was born in Chesterton in 1931 to a family of fruit farmers. He was educated at Bedford Modern School, where he displayed an aptitude for cricket which carried him as far as the minor counties competition as a right-handed batsman with Cambridgeshire. He preferred rugby though and signed for Cambridge City and then Northampton. Between 1952 and 1962 he made 273 appearances for the club, but he always believed it was from an invitation game that his international breakthrough came.

He found himself partnering Cliff Morgan, the Wales fly half, on a visit to Cornwall: "I think Cliff got me into the [1955 Lions] party because he liked my service," Jeeps said. For his part, Morgan observed: "He served you like a dog, he was tough and he knew the game." Jeeps was third-choice scrum half behind Johnny Williams (England) and Trevor Lloyd (Wales) in the Lions squad but, once more, Morgan's influence with the tour selectors worked in his favour. The compact Englishman, who could take a battering from opposition forwards and still come up smiling, was named against the Springboks in all four matches in a series shared 2–2.

Jeeps was named for his first England cap four months later, one of nine debutants against a Wales side led by Morgan. England lost and Jeeps was dropped for the rest of the Five Nations championship. But thereafter, with the exception of the 1959 season, he was there to stay.

He was not a running halfback, like Williams, but his durability, defensive strengths and passing earned him 24 caps over six years. He was a significant ingredient in the England side that won the grand slam in 1957 and went unbeaten the following season.

England recalled him the next year for the first of 13 successive matches as captain. In 1976, at the age of 44, he became one of the youngest RFU presidents.

Though he was known as "a cocky little man" and a slightly tiresome practical joker who liked provoking people – he was a pusher into swimming pools and a placer of eggs in pockets – he also had a sense of fair play. When an English crowd started booing a South Africa team at Twickenham, Jeeps, as England captain, marched up to the stand and told them in no uncertain terms to desist. Away from rugby he was something of a boy racer who switched between an Audi, a Mercedes and his favourite, an Alfa Romeo Alfetta, which he would park nose outwards on his drive for a faster start to the day.

A forthright man of clear views but narrow horizons, the ruddy-cheeked Jeeps preferred the company of his own set and was not universally popular in the role of RFU president. For his part he felt it was "bloody difficult to get things through [the RFU's] big committee". Instead, Jeeps accepted the post of chairman of the Sports Council and was responsible for the noted "Sport For All" slogan. He brought an instinctive approach to the role but no great knowledge of sport across the board. His sympathies for apartheid South Africa led to him being sacked from that job in 1985.

His private life, meanwhile, had crossed from complicated into chaotic. His 30-year-marriage to Jean Levitt begat three daughters – Deborah, Caroline and Louise – before an extramarital liaison led to divorce. In 1984, at the age of 53, he married Janet Thurston, who was 36, but their honeymoon in blacklisted South Africa earned him a rebuke from the minister for sport. That marriage also ended in divorce, with his wife citing his alleged "unreasonable behaviour". Known for his voracious appetites, he is believed to have been married and divorced a third time, though there is no mention of this union in his *Who's Who* entry.

However, it is for his extraordinary prowess on the rugby field, not his extracurricular activities off it, that Jeeps will be remembered. He never had one of those handsome-looking long passes, but what he did have was the courage to put in a hard tackle and grab a rolling ball no matter how many All Blacks were descending on it, and him. His philosophy on the subject was typically curt. "There is a lot of cock talked about good and bad balls, and only being able to run a good ball," he said. For him a good ball was whatever got you over the line.

Dickie Jeeps CBE, rugby player and sports administrator, was born on November 25, 1931. He died of Alzheimer's disease on October 8, 2016, aged 84

LORD DENHAM

Popular and mildly eccentric Lords chief whip who liked to quote his cousin Nancy Mitford and stand his ground with Mrs Thatcher

Until his retirement in 2021 at the age of 93, Lord Denham was the longest-serving peer, having sat in the upper house since 1949. Such was his longevity, he was also the last man alive to have served in Harold Macmillan's government. He was not one for hogging the debates, though. The last time he spoke in parliament was six years earlier, and that was to tell off another peer for droning on too long.

Denham's long silence in recent years echoed the start of his political career. He waited six years before his maiden speech, in which, perhaps surprisingly, he opposed a ban on heroin. If this might have seemed quite a progressive, even libertarian, position for a Tory peer to hold, he countered it with his views on baronesses, warning in 1957 that women should not become peers because "the atmosphere will be altered, possibly for the worse".

The agreeable vein of eccentricity in his personality might have made him seem like a character from PG Wodehouse, especially as he was universally known as Bertie and had a penchant for snuff, but the mischievous Nancy Mitford would have been closer to the mark, not least because she was his first cousin and he was much given to quoting her.

Unlike many peers, Denham had no country estate or business to manage, only a small village shop. This meant he was able to spend a great deal of time in the House of Lords, relishing all aspects of its traditions and procedures, of which he was a staunch guardian. Changes that seriously affronted constitutional practice caused him considerable anguish. In particular, he deplored the removal of most of the hereditary peers by Tony Blair in 1999. He himself was one of the 92 hereditaries who stayed on. The House responded to this champion of its customs and heritage by making clear its affection for him across party lines. It even seemed to regard him as its resident "character".

Uninterested in striving for departmental office and a Cabinet seat, Denham achieved the summit of his ambition under Margaret Thatcher. Appointed Lords chief whip in 1979, he was her only senior colleague to keep the same post throughout her 11-year premiership. On one occasion, when she struggled to win a vote in the Lords, she summoned him and gave him a savaging for not securing the votes. "Prime Minister," Denham retorted, "even you should know better than to expect me to find you a majority during [Cheltenham] Gold Cup week."

Sir Bertram Stanley Mitford Bowyer Bt, was born in 1927 in Weston Underwood, Buckinghamshire. He succeeded as 2nd Baron Denham in 1948 on the death of his father, a long-serving Conservative MP and junior minister whose peerage had been preceded by a baronetcy to which Bertie Denham added a second, inherited from a kinsman. His mother was the Hon Daphne Freeman-Mitford, daughter of the first Baron Redesdale.

He was educated at Eton where he was a King's Scholar, and at King's College, Cambridge, where he read English literature. After the end of the Second World War, in 1945, he served briefly in the Grenadier Guards and subsequently as a lieutenant in the Oxford and Buckinghamshire Light Infantry between 1946 and 1948 as part of his National Service.

In 1956 he married Jean, daughter of Major Kenneth McCorquodale and sister of Alastair McCorquodale, who represented Britain at the 1948 Olympic Games. They had four children.

At the start of his career the Tories relied almost entirely on young hereditary peers to do most of their frontbench work in the Lords. Denham received his party's summons at the age of 34. In 1961, six years after his pro-heroin maiden speech, he was made a lord in waiting, one of a group of three junior whips on whom the main burden of expounding the benefits of Tory legislation fell.

He remained a member of the group, in government and in opposition, growing steadily in prominence until the Edward Heath years in the early 1970s, when he became deputy chief whip, an appointment that carried with it the ancient sinecure post of Captain of the Yeomen of the Guard, complete with a fine, elaborate uniform and a black silk cocked hat which he wore with aplomb. Another sinecure post accompanied the job, the captaincy of the Gentlemen-at-Arms, the monarch's "nearest guard", and he duly acquired another resplendent uniform, this time with a plumed helmet that he found rather cumbersome.

During the Thatcher years he worked with six different leaders of the House, not all of them personally congenial to him, as part of the duopoly that has always had charge of the business of the Lords in conjunction with its senior officials. His was the role that mattered above all to Thatcher. On him depended the progress of her government's legislation through the upper house. Since much of that legislation was controversial and unpopular among Tory peers, political skill was required, and Denham possessed it in abundance. He was invaluable to her and later confessed to feeling a little hurt that she had made no reference to him or to his efforts on her behalf when she came to write her memoirs.

That reflected in part their lack of common interests. He was a countryman to the core, in love with the traditional pursuits and sports of rural England, which he turned to good effect in writing the four thrillers that he published between 1979 and 1997. Thatcher was bored by the countryside, and the only thrillers she read were by Dick Francis.

Even at times of great political crisis Denham was often to be found in his office, calmly typing one of his novels on a portable

Remington. All four have as their chief protagonist a decent, if lustful, Lords whip, Viscount Thyrde (pronounced third), but his character lacks interest and depth. The books deal far more satisfactorily with events and places, such as White's club and country houses, than with people. There is, however, a fine vignette of the author. At one point Thyrde calls on his chief whip. "I found him sitting down, his lank form drooped over his desk, engaged in a rhythmic transfer of papers from his in-tray to his out, with only the formality of adding a ritual and hieroglyphic initial to each, as it passed in between." This was how Denham treated his own papers, to his private secretary's despair.

As well as not reading his novels, Thatcher also failed to appreciate the extent of the difficulties Denham faced in the Lords. Defeats, in some number, could not be avoided. The task that Denham set himself was to ensure that the government's principal measures passed the Lords without being emasculated by hostile amendments. Sometimes that meant keeping recalcitrant peers away from the House.

One June, a tight vote was anticipated. Thatcher spoke to Denham about it on the telephone. He told her he was at Ascot with a group of Tory peers. "But of course you will all be back tomorrow in good time for the division." "No, Prime Minister," he replied, "I am keeping them down here so they cannot vote against the government."

At other times the avoidance of defeat involved bringing in those rarely seen in the Lords, the backwoodsmen. He enticed them with the prospect of alcohol from his abundant supplies, which always included the finest whisky and brandy. The Cabinet Office once queried a monthly drinks bill of £400. "I have saved the government £40 million by getting its legislation through," he replied loftily.

In 1984 he got a much-disliked bill paving the way for the abolition of the Greater London Council through by 237 to 217, the largest turnout since the vote to join the EEC. Over the poll tax in 1988, he exerted his guile to secure the biggest attendance since the Lloyd George budget of 1909. The second reading was carried by 317 to 183. He thought it best if peers avoided listening to the speeches made in the chamber. "If you listen to the arguments, you should vote with your conscience," he was fond of saying. "If you have not listened to them, you should vote with the government."

Willie Whitelaw saw much of all this at first hand when he was leader of the Lords from 1983 to 1988. In his memoirs he paid tribute to the special skills that so often proved the government's salvation. Denham, he wrote, "must have been specially made for the job of chief whip ... He has an unerring instinct for the moods of the House and the likely attitude of its members day by day. What is more, he hides all these qualities and an extremely acute brain under a cloak of natural charm and a splendid sense of humour."

The humour was not always evident in Whitelaw's own case. According to one observer, "if Willie was making a mess of things, Bertie moved out to the middle of the chamber and glared at him until he shut up and sat down".

Sensing after Thatcher's resignation that his own days in office were numbered, Denham took the unprecedented step of announcing his departure some months in advance – and duly stepped down on May 22, 1991, chosen to avoid dismissal. Shortly afterwards he was appointed KBE.

He did not lose his love of uniforms. Invited to open the debate at the start of a new parliamentary session, he addressed the House in the scarlet full-dress uniform of a sergeant of the Honourable Artillery Company with three large chevrons on his sleeves. This was the last time a peer spoke in the House wearing uniform.

One of his favourite party pieces was to recite well-known poems such as Oscar Wilde's *The Ballad of Reading Gaol* to appreciative private audiences. After his retirement, three CDs were produced, with Joanna Lumley assisting in an advisory capacity. In his self-effacing way he described them as "moderately successful".

Lord Denham KBE, Conservative politician and author, was born on October 3, 1927. He died at home on December 1, 2021, aged 94

CLIVE NICHOLLS QC

Extradition expert who defended General Pinochet and was one of twin brothers who became QCs

The twins in the 1960s. Clive is on the left with the umbrella.

Throughout their lives Clive and Colin Nicholls were often mistaken for one another, with Clive being called Colin, and Colin Clive. It did not help matters that the identical twins had decided at the age of 14 to become barristers, despite there being no family connection to the profession. Like many teenage boys at the time they had been gripped by the trial of the acid bath murderer, John George Haigh, at Lewes Assizes, prosecuted by Sir Hartley Shawcross QC. They wanted to be "star silks" one day, like Shawcross.

They joined Gray's Inn as student members while still at school, obtained their law degrees from Trinity College Dublin, sat their Bar exams together and entered the same set of chambers on the same day. The parallel lives went further. Both became leading advocates in the same field, extradition law.

There were stories that they used to take each other's places, although they said that these were apocryphal, mostly. On one occasion, at Kent Quarter Sessions, Clive was halfway through his submission when the court rose. He was unable to attend the next day, so the defendant agreed to Colin continuing the submission. On arrival at court Colin told the prosecutor what was happening and sent a message to the judge. When he concluded, the judge said in open court: "If I had not been told, I would never have known." Only four people – the defendant, the chairman, the prosecutor and the court clerk – knew to what the judge was referring.

Born in 1932, Clive was the elder of the twins by 40 minutes. Their mother was Lilian Nicholls (née May), their father Alfred Nicholls, a civil servant with the ministry of local government. The boys were schooled at Brighton College before heading to Dublin. In terms of their education, their first divergence came when Clive went to do a master's degree at Sidney Sussex College, Cambridge, while Colin stayed on at Trinity for a year as auditor of the College Historical Society. They met up again to do their Bar exams in 1957. Both did their pupillage with James Burge, who went on to defend Stephen Ward in the Profumo case.

Clive appeared for the only member of the Kray gang to be acquitted in the first Old Bailey trial and later, in 1968, he defended Brian Jones of the Rolling Stones on charges of possessing cannabis. Jones, who was on probation, said the drugs had been left by previous tenants of his flat. The jury found him guilty. Instead of jailing Jones, the judge fined him £50 and told him: "For goodness sake, don't get into trouble again or it really will be serious."

On one occasion the twins appeared against each other at the Old Bailey. According to Colin, "It was a tie – the charge was grievous bodily harm and the result was unlawful wounding. A compromise."

The extradition work started in the 1970s, when, as Clive explained, it had mushroomed "because of the increase in international crime". He was appointed Queen's Counsel in 1982 (a year after Colin) and a number of legal victories followed, most notably when he represented the government of Denmark in its attempt to have one of its nationals, Jan Bonde Nielsen, extradited in 1984. His work resulted in the House of Lords overturning more than 100 years of established extradition case law. According to Julian Knowles QC, "if anyone can claim to be the father of modern extradition law, Clive can".

His most high-profile case came in 1998, when he led the defence of Augusto Pinochet, the former president of Chile, when his extradition was sought by Spain on charges of crimes against humanity. The case involved an unprecedented three appeals to the House of Lords, the first having to be reheard because of the apparent bias of one of the original judges. It generated headlines and protests around the world. Clive navigated the contentious areas of the case with skill, securing the return of Pinochet to Chile at the end of the process.

Throughout this period the twins tried to avoid going head to head for cases, and that included deciding whether they should both apply to be head of chambers in 1994 – in the end Clive did and was elected in 1995.

Despite their efforts to avoid confusion at the Bar, the twins did once sit in adjoining courts as recorders at the Old Bailey. The *Financial Times* ran a cartoon showing two heads with one full-bottomed wig and the words "Double Jeopardy". They also advised on opposite sides on a case in the US (when they both had to write to their respective clients to explain why there was no conflict of interest). Perhaps most confusing of all they also appeared for appellants in a conjoined extradition appeal before the House of Lords. Colin was for John Gilligan, the notorious Irish gangmaster who was tried for the murder of the journalist Veronica Guerin. The brothers anticipated that the

Law Lords would set one of them up to defeat the other. When Lord Steyn asked Clive what he would say about Colin's written submission, Clive replied: "I would say it is unarguable, but no doubt my learned friend will try to persuade you otherwise." When Colin rose to reply, the podium he was leaning on collapsed. It was Clive's podium. Colin replied: "There's no doubt who this belongs to."

One year the Law Commission published a paper noting that Clive had spoken on the offence of misuse in public office when it had been Colin. A month later *Graya*, a magazine for members of Gray's Inn, published a picture of Colin presenting the Du Cann prize for advocacy and put Clive's name under it.

Even their wives admitted that they were hard to tell apart, from behind at least. Clive met Alison while at Trinity College Dublin. They married in 1960 and had six children.

The cases of mistaken identity continued in their private life. On Sunday evenings in the 1960s, after returning from the country to their house in Pimlico, central London, Clive and Alison would go to Choys, a restaurant in the Kings Road, for a meal while the au pair would put the children to bed. After they returned, Colin and the au pair would go for a meal at the same restaurant. The Chinese waiters were naturally perplexed by the strange Englishman who had successive meals with two women on the same evening.

The waiters in the Garrick Club, meanwhile, always knew the difference because of the signet ring Clive wore on the little finger of his left hand. On the subject of rings, Colin went into a jewellers in Piccadilly he had never been in before wanting to buy one. As he was leaving the assistant asked him whether he had found a solution to his watch problem.

In many ways to know one was to know the other, as both were tireless raconteurs who were amused, curious, and clubbable. They even sounded the same.

His wife and children survive him, with his brother Colin. The twins would call each other at 5pm every day and now, at that ritual time, Colin finds himself staring at the phone.

Clive Nicholls QC, was born on August 29, 1932. He died from pneumonia on February 9, 2017, aged 84

PROFESSOR JAMES CAMPBELL

—————— ● ——————

Absent-minded academic who inspired generations of students as the creative doyen of Anglo-Saxon history at Oxford University

James Campbell, aged 23, standing third from the right in 1957, at the end of his first year as fellow of Worcester College.

James Campbell had a propensity for losing paperwork that his fellow Oxford dons found maddening. His former students, too. One reported seeing his unmarked essay on the professor's floor many years after he had graduated.

Considered by many to be the "last of the old dons", the bespectacled Campbell once almost set himself on fire after forgetfully putting a lit pipe in his pocket, yet he was not eccentric so much as unconventional and unkempt, and his brilliance as a historian was never in doubt. He was, indeed, hailed as "the most consistently creative influence on the writing of Anglo-Saxon history today".

He was, moreover, responsible for a profound reassessment of the origins of the English state. Long regarded as "simply a barbarous prelude to better things", the six centuries preceding the Norman Conquest instead produced, he argued, not just a rich culture but also many of the institutions usually said to have emerged only 500 years later.

Where other scholars saw in the architecture of Tudor government innovation and improvement, Campbell read backwards from it to discern much earlier roots.

His magnum opus was *The Anglo-Saxons* (1982). It was intended for a general readership but 35 years on it remains, even for scholars, the best overview of a civilisation that Campbell held was as well organised as our own.

Perhaps his most far-reaching achievement, however, was to have taught a generation of historians of the period how to think. Where those who studied later eras were liable, he wrote in characteristically epigrammatic style, "to confuse the less interesting with the more plausible", he took a maximal approach to meagre sources.

Above all, Campbell revelled in conversation – debate rather than gossip – preferably with glass in hand. Though he liked a tipple "before, during and after a tutorial", his ability to defend a position was formidable, fuelled as it was by his wide-ranging knowledge (the names, for instance, of dreadnoughts sold to South American navies), the harvest of his needing little sleep.

He traced his ability to order information to his childhood collecting of cigarette cards. Unfashionably, Campbell thought it essential that historians had a solid command of facts, from which he believed understanding came. Similarly, he deplored the obligation on academics now to publish in order to justify their worth, rather than allowing them primarily to teach or simply to contemplate. "There is a national need for scientific research," he reasoned. "There is not a national need for historical periodicals."

An only child, James Campbell was born in 1935 in Cheltenham. His parents separated when he was young and he was raised in Suffolk, in modest circumstances, by his maternal grandparents.

They had been teachers, too, but he attributed his bent for history to having been surrounded by older folk who were a link to the past. Campbell's grandmother recalled growing up in the Suffolk town of Bungay, where there was so little for the young to do that they would pass the time by throwing clods of earth at strangers.

Although evacuated to Derbyshire during the Second World War,

Campbell spent his childhood in Lowestoft. At 10 he went to the town's grammar school and won an exhibition to Magdalen College, Oxford. There he was taught by the medievalists KB McFarlane and Karl Leyser, and by AJP Taylor, whom he remembered amusing himself by making up facts in tutorials, such as the names of admirals.

Campbell shared the university's history prize, the Gibbs, with Keith Thomas, the future historian of early modern England. The award helped to fund his doctoral thesis, as did work at a Birds Eye plant. He was not the most practical soul and was not a success as a quality controller of frozen raspberries.

Myopia exempted him from National Service – he always wore jam-jar glasses – and, at 22, he was appointed to a fellowship at Worcester College.

Campbell's work was distilled mostly as essays rather than as books, often appearing in out-of-the way journals, but this belied its originality and importance. East Anglia remained close to his heart and he wrote, for example, about its herring trade and on medieval Norwich. He was elected to the British Academy in 1984 and appointed a professor at Oxford in 1990.

From 1973 to '74, Campbell served as senior proctor, in charge of public order in the university. It was a period marked by considerable student unrest, led by the International Marxist Group and their supporters (among them the future cabinet minister Chris Huhne), which culminated in the occupation of university buildings.

Campbell's firmness of purpose helped to resolve the situation but his refusal to make concessions to the demonstrators led him to endure considerable provocation. He received threatening telephone calls and once found a severed pig's head on the steps of his office. In fact, his own youthful sympathies had been with the left, but later his politics became tinged with a patriotic romanticism.

For many years Campbell occupied an elegant set of rooms, desperately cold in winter, with French windows opening on to a hanging garden. In tutorials he would play distractedly with the drawers of his desk or bounce excitedly in his seat as he listened to an essay. Long draws on a cigarette would accompany the framing of a judicious rebuttal of what he had just heard. Nonetheless, he was a kindly, stimulating teacher, especially adept at drawing out overawed students at interview and at seeing how they reacted to a novel line of thinking.

Campbell retired in 1996 but remained active in college as fellow librarian until 2002. Four years later, having appeared to be a dedicated bachelor, he married Bärbel Brodt. Several decades his junior, and the daughter of a U-boat commander from a Prussian family, she had come to Worcester to research medieval East Anglia.

Slightly unworldy to the last, Campbell never learnt to drive or use a computer. However, not all the stories about him were true. The one about him circumventing the Worcester College rules on prohibited animals by proclaiming that his cat, Frideswide, was a dog, was nothing more than a well-founded rumour.

Professor James Campbell, historian, was born on January 26, 1935. He died on May 31, 2016, aged 81

BEATRICE DE CARDI

Intrepid archaeologist who made important finds in the Middle East and was thought to be the world's oldest practitioner

One of Beatrice de Cardi's first tasks in her distinguished archaeological career was to ruffle the hair of her boss, Dr Mortimer Wheeler, to aid his concentration while he worked at his desk in the London Museum.

That was in the mid-1930s when she was also sent to select and buy gifts for his mistress, and later second wife, Mavis de Vere Cole. Wheeler shared Mavis with Augustus John, both before and during the marriage, but de Cardi maintained a detached friendliness with all concerned.

Wheeler later encouraged de Cardi to lead field trips to Baluchistan, in present-day Pakistan, and Afghanistan and helped her to get funding. He teased her about always wearing bright red lipstick in the desert. Her sardonic response was that it stopped her from getting cracked lips.

Clad in khaki in full make-up and perfectly coiffured hair, she established herself as one of Britain's most intrepid and admired archaeologists, making important finds including pottery dating back to the 4th century BC.

The terrain could not have been more inhospitable. "We camped out sharing a water channel with a pack of wild dogs who raced past our tent to drink twice daily," she recalled of one expedition. "At night the howls of wolves in the adjacent hills served as a reminder that Baluchistan was a wild and dangerous place. The impression gained substance when we moved back to Surab and were not allowed to camp at Siah Damb on account of a djinn [spirit] greatly feared by our workmen. I suspected a more material power and accepted a revolver lent by the local official."

Imbued with an aristocratic hauteur that commanded respect wherever she fetched up, the indomitable de Cardi liked nothing better than traversing the desert in a Land Rover or surveying the landscape while hanging halfway out of a helicopter. Unbridled curiosity drove her on. "If I see another curve in the hillside I have to go around it."

In the 1960s she embarked on adventures in the southern Persian Gulf where little archaeology had been done, excavating the pre-Islamic history of the lower Arabian Gulf states such as Ras al-Khaimah and Oman, elucidating early trading routes. When Qatar opened a national museum in 1973 she was tasked with organising an exhibition in just ten weeks. She promptly presided over eight digs and found evidence of trade with Mesopotamia in the fifth millennium BC.

Many of the ruling sheikhs and emirs had never met such an imperious, independent-minded woman. She almost always gained their admiration and sometimes patronage. She would often come away with valuable, if rather incongruous presents. She once returned home with a large solid gold model of a dhow.

De Cardi was still doing fieldwork in the Middle East in her early nineties when she was thought to be the world's oldest practising archaeologist. She would have carried on but could no longer get the insurance. "She took a very dim view of that," said a friend.

Beatrice Eileen de Cardi was born in 1914 into an aristocratic family. Her father was Edwin, Count de Cardi and her American heiress mother was Christine Berbette Wurrflein. She grew up in privilege in a large townhouse overlooking Ealing Common. One of her earliest memories was of being taken down to the coal cellar because of Zeppelins flying over London during the First World War. "My mother, clad in an evening dress of black velvet trimmed with sable, clutched me. I wondered what on earth she was doing in that sort of dress and surrounded by coal."

Of her father, who was of Corsican descent, she recalled taking weekend trips in his Belsize tourer, sporting leather, goggles and "snuggling under a large opossum rug".

She was educated at St Paul's Girls' School and studied history and economics at University College London. The lectures of Mortimer Wheeler reignited a passion for archaeology that had first stirred when she had been told about the Palazzo de Cardi in Corsica and begged her parents to take her to old castles. She joined Wheeler on his excavation of Maiden Castle, the Iron Age hill fort in Dorset and became his secretary at the London Museum, where he was Keeper.

In 1944 she joined the Allied Supplies Executive of the War Cabinet in China. The role involved hazardous flights over the Himalayas in a rickety plane. Most of the passengers closed their eyes and prayed as the aircraft lurched above the peaks. De Cardi, a picture of insouciance, powdered her nose. After the war she worked for the Board of Trade in Delhi and was reunited with Wheeler, who was by now director-general of archaeology in India. He facilitated her first expeditions in Baluchistan by lending her a Jeep and an illiterate official, Sadar Din, who knew by memory where the archaeological sites were and might offer some protection from bandits.

From 1949 to 1973 she was secretary and administrative head of the Council for British Archaeology, which co-ordinated the activities of the country's amateur and professional societies. One of her greatest achievements was to encourage volunteers by publishing an annual calendar of digs in Britain.

De Cardi disarmingly served coffee at CBA committees and conferences. She was always "Miss de Cardi": although she never married, she had a lively appreciation of male pulchritude. However, she remained singleminded about archaeology. When one longstanding boyfriend, who had accompanied her on many expeditions, died suddenly in the field, she quietly arranged his funeral and then returned to the excavation.

On her 100th birthday the Society of Antiquaries conferred on her its highest award for scholarship, the Gold Medal. Professor Charles Thomas in the CBA's first Beatrice de Cardi Lecture in 1976, envisaged her sailing away "into the Arabian sunrise, stern mistress of some chartered dhow manned by properly subdued mariners".

She never lost her habit of making dramatic entrances to Society of Antiquaries events. At one, when de Cardi was in her late nineties, she arrived with a "gorgeous young man" on her arm. She introduced him as "my IT consultant".

Beatrice de Cardi OBE, archaeologist, was born on June 5, 1914. She died on July 5, 2016, aged 102

JORDAN MOONEY

———————•———————

*Punk muse known as 'the original Sex Pistol' who appeared on stage
with them, guided their 'look' and then became a veterinary nurse*

Before the Sex Pistols scandalised Britain in 1976, Jordan started
her own punk revolution on the 7.22am from Seaford to London.

Commuters first noticed the vertiginous peroxide hair, then the
racoon make-up. Closer inspection would cause alarm. Jordan might
be wearing a net skirt with tattered black stockings and suspenders
underneath, but be innocent of underwear. On days when she did
deign to wear some, they were often see-through or bore legends such
as "Vive le Rock".

As the train rattled through the Sussex countryside, reactions
ranged from emptying carriages to her being surrounded by furtive
bowler-hatted City gents stealing glances at her as they pretended to
read *The Times*. One day a baying mob tried to throw her off the train.
In the interests of public safety, British Rail reserved a carriage for her
in first class.

"People said I was brave, but it was nothing to do with bravery,"
Jordan recalled. "Quite the opposite. It was about feeling comfortable

and at one with yourself. I wasn't a typical rebel. I simply had this strong idea of how I wanted to look."

Safely unleashed in the capital, Jordan found her spiritual home at SEX, a boutique on the Kings Road run by a young fashion designer called Vivienne Westwood and her mercurial partner and jack of many trades, Malcolm McLaren. Amid fetishwear such as gimp masks, the shop sold Westwood's proto-punk designs, including bondage trousers and "tits T-shirts" (which speak for themselves).

Recognising a kindred iconoclast, the couple hired Jordan to work in the shop. One photograph that has earned its place in the punk pantheon shows Jordan leaning insouciantly against the doorway of SEX wearing a skimpy black leotard while a male onlooker stares at her with a mixture of incredulity and rage.

As a provocateur-in-chief who fancied himself as a modern-day Fagin, McLaren wisely harnessed Jordan's input to create a band of disaffected youngsters to be avatars of his and Westwood's anarchistic visions. With Britain seemingly in terminal decline and the Labour government heading to its Winter of Discontent, the time was ripe.

Jordan was propping up the jukebox when a snarling Johnny Rotten auditioned to Alice Cooper's *I'm Eighteen* and was recruited along with other habitués of the shop, Steve Jones, Paul Cook and Glen Matlock. Jones, an accomplished petty thief, provided instruments.

Jordan helped to shape their look of ripped T-shirts held together by safety pins, tatty mohair sweaters and black suede creepers.

In grainy footage of the band's chaotic early gigs, Jordan is regally intimidating amid the pogoing, spitting and beer-can throwing foot soldiers of punk. As the band played *Anarchy in the UK*, she was not averse to joining them on stage and baring her substantial breasts at the cameras, but often steered clear of the debauchery that came with the territory. "Men were confused by me," she told *The Guardian* in 2019. "They would wolf-whistle, shout all kinds of things, even offer me money, because they didn't understand why I looked like I did. I was running a gauntlet every day. People were scared of me. And the funny thing is, I was actually quite shy."

In August 1976 she appeared with the band on the ITV music show *So It Goes* wearing a swastika armband. When fellow guest Clive James took exception to the Nazi reference on air, Jordan called him a "baldy old Sheila".

By the end of 1976 the Sex Pistols were public enemy No 1, exemplified by their foul-mouthed appearance on the early evening *Today* show with Bill Grundy when the band's guitarist Jones called Grundy "a dirty fucking rotter" live on air.

With the band now signed to EMI, McLaren dreamt up the ultimate publicity stunt of hiring a boat on the Thames during the Silver Jubilee weekend in June 1977 on which the Sex Pistols performed their banned hit *God Save the Queen* ("the fascist regime"). By now, Jordan was growing weary of the notoriety. "The papers insisted on seeing punk as a political movement, but I hated all that spitting and violence. To me, punk was a fashion statement and a rebellion against the mediocrity of the times."

By then she was living in a flat near Buckingham Palace ("a punk den at the heart of the British establishment") with, among others, Rotten, the Sex Pistols' new bassist Sid Vicious and his girlfriend Nancy Spungen, to whom Jordan became close. The murder of Spungen in October 1978, followed by the death of Vicious from a heroin overdose some months later after being charged with her murder, affected her deeply. Eventually, she feared that she would go the same way as her friends. For someone who had lost her power to shock, the "queen of punk" did the most shocking thing she could do at the age of 30 by moving back in with her parents in Seaford and spending the rest of her life living quietly as a veterinary nurse.

Pamela Rooke was born in Seaford, East Sussex, in 1955, one of three children, to Stanley Rooke, a Second World War veteran, and his wife, Linda, a seamstress.

The loving family home gave Pamela little to rebel against, but she recalled being quietly wilful about her fashion choices from the age of seven. The child was academically bright, captained the Seaford Head secondary school hockey team and was a keen ballet student; pictures of Margot Fonteyn and Rudolf Nureyev adorned her bedroom walls.

Being run over at the age of 14 and breaking her pelvis ended her dreams of becoming a ballerina, but it started what would become a metamorphosis in terms of her image and identity. First she changed her name to Jordan, after Jordan Baker, the androgynous female golf hustler in *The Great Gatsby*.

When she turned up at school with red hair, the headmaster called her "subversive" and forced her to wear a headscarf. Jordan, who had won a school debating competition, justified her look eloquently. She recalled simply being laughed at by her bemused schoolmates, but stayed on to pass six O-levels and two A-levels in English and law. Her mother instructed Jordan to walk ten paces behind her in Seaford.

From 1970 Jordan attended a "university of courage" by frequenting the underground gay clubs of Brighton and dodging the razor-blade wielding "bovver boys" down from London for the weekend to cause trouble.

Having first met McLaren and Westwood in 1973, it would be six months before she was offered a job. In the meantime, Jordan astonished her mother by securing work at Harrods.

When a vacancy arose at SEX, a more natural hinterland, she resigned from Harrods and established herself as a dominatrix-style saleswoman, wearing latex, brandishing a whip, and generally terrifying unsuspecting customers. "We tried to present a feeling that the shop was a place that, if you had the guts to walk in, you could just hang out," she recalled. "Like the coffee shops of the 1950s, or the cafés of Prague, where philosophers would go to chew things over."

If she did not think an item looked good on someone she refused to sell it to them. Anyone considered "uncool" or with a bad attitude was ejected, including Bianca Jagger. A young Boy George recalled being "corrected". The ITV newsreader Reginald Bosanquet, who bought fetishwear, was allowed in.

As a Pistol muse and early symbol of the movement, Jordan attracted attention from punk wannabes. One art school student called Stuart Goddard (aka Adam Ant) sent her letters with lipstick marks on them and asked her to manage his band. With the Sex Pistols close to their inevitable implosion in 1978, she started managing Adam and the Ants.

There was a hiatus when she appeared in Derek Jarman's seminal film about the punk scene *Jubilee*, playing Amyl Nitrate, complete with Britannia helmet, trident and little else. Jarman called her the "original Sex Pistol" and she accompanied the director to the Cannes Film Festival wearing a figure-hugging latex skirt that inadvertently became a live art installation as it melted in the heat.

She created Adam Ant's signature Native American-inspired

warpaint make-up. After their acclaimed 1980 album *Kings of the Wild Frontier*, the band prepared to hit the mainstream but Jordan jumped ship when she felt they were "selling out".

In 1981 she married the band's former bass player Kevin Mooney and they formed Wide Boy Awake. The group were signed to RCA but drugs wrecked the band and her marriage. She and Mooney separated after two years.

Her old teachers would bring their animals to the veterinary surgery in Seaford where Jordan later worked, saying how much they had loved her look back in the punk days. "A bit of history has been rewritten," said Jordan, who noted wryly how the punk movement had morphed into an exercise in warm nostalgia, so much at odds with its original icy mission. With her sister, she bred Burmese cats and twice won best in show at the Supreme Cat Show.

Despite finding contentment in a somewhat reclusive life on the south coast, Jordan continued to subvert the genteel East Sussex resort with her outré outfits. "I will always wear my tits T-shirt," she declared proudly. "I fill it out very nicely."

Jordan Mooney, punk muse and veterinary nurse, was born on June 23, 1955. She died of bile-duct cancer on April 3, 2022, aged 66

SIR ROGER SCRUTON

———————— ● ————————

Reliably controversial foxhunting philosopher, Wagnerian, scourge
of the left and author of 50 books

When Roger Scruton gave the inaugural lecture of the Royal
Institute of Philosophy at Durham University in 1989, he found
himself in competition with a choir practising in the next room. As
the choir grew louder and louder, his audience began biting on their
knuckles to avoid sniggering. But Scruton, a russet-haired man whose
pale, angular features always appeared part frozen, neither smiled nor
raised his voice. Instead he remained unperturbed, talking in a
measured and ponderous monotone and giving the impression that it
was, for him, an everyday occurrence to be accompanied by a heavenly
chorus.

Perhaps it amused him as well, for his sense of humour was dry.
Once, when asked what phrase he most overused, he replied, "the
transcendental unity of apperception". His favourite smell, he claimed,
was the French literature section of the London Library.

The scene with the choir seemed comical only because Scruton
always appeared, in public at least, to be so very serious. He was serious
about being an intellectual, serious about being an author (publishing
more than 50 books), and serious about his passions which were, in no
particular order, Wagner, the countryside, old-fashioned decency, the
appreciation of beauty, traditional values, architecture, law and
discipline, and, perhaps above all, conservatism.

He was one of the most outspoken and provocative conservative
thinkers of his generation and, for that reason, was one of the least
influential within the Conservative Party itself. His goal, however, was
vaguer and grander than shifting government policy, for he aimed to
change the intellectual climate and did not mind making enemies in
so doing – indeed he regarded the scars inflicted by his enemies as
badges of honour.

If he failed to rally many converts to his brand of Burkean Toryism,
his muscularly articulated critique of modernity and his sallies against
the icons of the liberal intelligentsia, from pop music to progressive

education, often succeeded in defining the field of public debate in Britain.

One of his most widely admired books was his clear and lively *Modern Philosophy* (1994), hailed in a *Times* leader as politically engaging without being polemical, "for those who would share the learning that has shaped our life, there are no better starts".

Scruton had an almost religious devotion to learning, and for him, high culture had a sacred quality. As a teacher he felt a priestly duty to safeguard this civilisation and ensure it passed safely to rising generations; as a public figure he saw for himself a proselytising role in persuading others of the transcendent importance of high culture in any account of the "good life". This may explain why the Cambridge don John Casey said that Scruton's philosophical armour-plating hid a quixotic, absurdist nature.

Scruton may have agreed, but he was under no illusions about where his philosophical and political beliefs had left him in the estimation of most of his fellow academics. "If you are a right-wing academic," he said, "your colleagues think that you are not a proper philosopher at all. My right-wing stance has always heavily compromised my career. If you criticise the whole idea of human equality, which is basically what I do, you are going against a prevalent quasi-religious orthodoxy."

His background always baffled his lefty critics, who lazily assumed that he was some kind of Tory toff. Yet Roger Vernon Scruton was born in 1944 in Buslingthorpe, Lincolnshire, and raised in Buckinghamshire with his two sisters in a pebble-dashed semi. His grandfather was a labourer and his father, Jack, a socialist primary school teacher and trade unionist who banned his children from reading Beatrix Potter on the grounds that it was bourgeois. Scruton said that Jeremy Corbyn reminded him of his father. His mother, Beryl was, by contrast, fond of romantic fiction and entertaining "blue-rinsed friends". He described her as "cherishing an ideal of gentlemanly conduct and social distinction that my father set out with considerable relish to destroy".

Young Roger was a precociously bright child who passed the 11-plus and in 1954 went to the Royal Grammar School, High Wycombe. He read widely and said that his schooldays transformed his life, even if he did have some scrapes along the way.

While at the school he was accused of riding on the London Underground without a ticket. The case was made rather more serious by the allegation that he had given a false name to the police. This was solemnly read out in court as John Stuart Mill. A rebellious, moody pupil, he was eventually expelled for putting on a play that ended up with "the stage on fire and a half-naked girl on it".

In 1962 he won an open scholarship to Jesus College, Cambridge, where he quickly switched from natural sciences to philosophy. When his girlfriend's clothes were discovered in his college room – where it was against the rules to entertain members of the opposite sex – he told his tutor the clothes were his and that he needed them because he was a transvestite. He graduated with a double first but was not keen to stay. "There weren't many women around, there was this mist of nostalgic pederasty that hung over it all." Instead he moved around Europe, attempting to write while discovering the counterculture.

He was in Paris in 1968 and the events of that May changed his life. As he watched the students rioting, erecting barricades and hurling cobblestones at police, and listened to his friends talk "Marxist gobbledegook" about revolution, "I suddenly realised that I was on the other side. What I saw was an unruly mob of self-indulgent middle-class hooligans. I was disgusted by it, and thought there must be a way back to the defence of western civilisation against these things. That's when I became a conservative. I knew I wanted to conserve things rather than pull them down."

He returned to Cambridge the following year to take up a research fellowship at Peterhouse and there he did a doctorate in aesthetics. In 1971 he became a lecturer in philosophy at Birkbeck College, London, becoming reader in 1979 and later professor of aesthetics.

Throughout the 1970s the "deviousness of Heath", the "dreariness of Old Labour" and the "decline of English institutions" encouraged him in the belief that Conservatives needed to think more. With the Tory MP Hugh Fraser, he founded the Conservative Philosophy Group and attracted the leading minds of the right – Friedrich Hayek, Milton Friedman and Michael Oakeshott among them – to their gatherings in Jonathan Aitken's house. Enoch Powell was often in attendance and Margaret Thatcher too, but the group made few converts among the party high command. "I've spent a quarter of a century trying to influence the Conservative Party," Scruton said in 2004. "I suppose I have to admit defeat."

Scruton's own vision of conservatism, with its emphasis on stability, authority and tradition, had little in common with the ideological radicalism that came to be known as Thatcherism. "Thatcher was completely indifferent to our kind of conservative philosophy," he said. "I'd never heard of her gurus – people like Alan Walters and Alfred Sherman."

Scruton was mistrustful of the free market and thought it should be subordinated to the social order, which he saw as the only real guarantor of happiness. Even freedom itself he did not endorse wholeheartedly, seeing it as the by-product, rather than the foundation, of a settled society.

Such views were developed in the book that made his name, *The Meaning of Conservatism* (1980), which saw him hailed as the right's new star. In this book, too, appeared the taste for arrestingly phrased overstatement that did much to ensure Scruton's prominence in the media but little to win over the uncommitted to the ideas he sought to promote. Democracy, for example, here stood condemned as a "contagion" that was "now raging so wildly that it is possible to mistake its high flush of fever for the light of health".

If an Oxford chair beckoned, it was off the cards once Scruton wrote that book. "It was ruled out that I would ever gain the highest of academic honours," he reflected. "Even if I deserved them. Which I didn't. But being free from the possibility of those ambitions enabled me to write rude and disgraceful things about the intellectual establishment. It meant I was free to say some really enjoyable and unpleasant things and thereby give pleasure to others."

But not to Professor Ted Honderich, of University College London, who called Scruton "the unthinking man's thinking man". Scruton retaliated by calling Honderich "the thinking man's unthinking man". He also concluded that: "Left-wing people find it very hard to get on with right-wing people because they believe that they are evil. Whereas I have no problem getting on with left-wing people because I simply believe that they are mistaken."

Throughout the 1980s Scruton lustily embroiled himself in the partisan conflicts of that era, not least through his column in *The*

Times, which he wrote from 1983 to 1987. The features editor who dealt with his copy said that no other articles had provoked more rage. Certainly his views were not for the faint of heart: generally, "punishment is a good thing. There should be more of it, and it should be more severe."

In 1982 he became editor of *The Salisbury Review,* a right-wing periodical with a tiny circulation but big ideas about "establishing a conservative dominance in intellectual life". He believed that the *Review* "helped a new generation of conservative intellectuals to emerge" – if only because it allowed them to claim that they were to the left of it.

The magazine's most controversial moment came in 1984 when it published an article by Ray Honeyford, a Bradford headmaster, arguing that it might not be a bad idea to integrate isolated Pakistani families through the education system, without overly accommodating their cultural differences. It attracted a storm of condemnation, through which Scruton offered Honeyford a stout defence. The article established Scruton in the public consciousness as the natural successor to that other inflammatory right-winger, Enoch Powell. Wherever Scruton went, demonstrators would be waiting. Some of his lectures had to be cancelled because city councils could not guarantee his safety. "It cost me many hours of paid labour, a hideous character assassination in *Private Eye,* three lawsuits, two interrogations, one expulsion, the loss of a university career in Britain, unendingly contemptuous reviews, Tory suspicion and the hatred of decent liberals everywhere," he said. "And it was worth it."

He went on the offensive the following year with *Education and Indoctrination,* in which he claimed that school lessons were becoming engines of left-wing propaganda, and *Thinkers of the New Left,* in which he attacked a series of prominent progressive intellectuals.

His magazine's most surprising success, though, was in Eastern Europe. A samizdat version began to appear in Prague in 1986 and was devoured by dissident groups. Scruton also taught there and Vaclav Havel, the first president of the Czech Republic, became one of his students. Scruton learnt Czech, helped to set up a resistance movement and found himself cast in the role of Scarlet Pimpernel – before eventually being arrested and expelled. Thereafter he was often followed by secret police on his regular visits to Poland.

In the 1970s he had studied for the Bar, and was called to it in 1978, but he could not afford to take an unpaid pupillage, and so remained at Birkbeck, where he claimed to be the only Conservative. He nursed a sense of grievance at the glittering academic prizes he believed were denied to him because of his uncompromising views.

As a philosopher he was, nevertheless, much admired and respected for his work on the meaning of aesthetic judgment, drawing on Kant and Wittgenstein, and his first book, *Art and Imagination* (1974) gave the imagination a central role in this process. His relentless criticism of modern architecture had its basis in this work, as did his studies on music. He composed two operas, *The Minister*, which was performed at Oxford, and *Violet*, performed at the Guildhall School of Music.

Frustrated by the left-wing atmosphere of academia, Scruton left Birkbeck in 1992, fleeing to the US, where he became a professor at Boston University. Although he did not think much of the students he encountered there, he enjoyed teaching the deeply religious ones. Scruton himself could not for most of his life bring himself to believe in God (although he later joined the Church of England and played the organ at his local church), but he was a strong supporter of the social role of religion. He echoed and amplified religious teaching on sexual desire, particularly, with its talk of vows and commitment, instead of liberation and contract.

Scruton left academia altogether in 1995 and made a living from journalism for a broad range of publications, including a wine column for *The New Statesman*, and a consultancy. This led to controversy in 2002, when an e-mail to Japan Tobacco International, offering to place pro-smoking stories in the national press, was printed by *The Guardian*. Scruton argued that he had never actually tried to put this plan into effect but he was dropped by the *FT* and *The Wall Street Journal* for not declaring his interest.

At home on his 100-acre farm in Wiltshire, surrounded by horses, labradors and ducks, he settled into a place and a community. He also threw himself, at the age of 45, into foxhunting; he wrote lyrically of its appeal and threatened demise in the autobiographical *On Hunting* (1998). In its traditions, Scruton found the practical expression of his conservative principles; a way of life that was in tune with both nature and English rural tradition, "not a means but an end, not work but leisure, not idle fun but active communion". It also seemed to have pleased him that he had found a pastime for which socialists would hate him.

It was said that he had been persuaded to take up foxhunting by Enoch Powell, because to do so was every true Conservative's duty. This may have been an exaggeration but it was true that Powell sold Scruton his hunting gear. "I happened to be sitting next to him at a dinner when he said he was giving up," he said in an interview in 1995. "I was a bit poor at the time so I offered to buy his second-hand clothes. I've still got his jacket but it never was quite big enough for me. It split down the seams."

Scruton met Danielle Laffitte when he was teaching in France and they lived together in Cambridge before marrying in 1973; they divorced in 1979. In 1996 he married Sophie Jeffreys, who was 28 years his junior. They met, naturally enough, out hunting. She is a descendant of "Hanging" Judge Jeffreys. They had two children and Scruton declared that they would not enjoy their childhoods much but would be more enjoyable company as a consequence. They would not be allowed to watch television or listen to pop, instead they would hunt, speak Latin and Greek by the age of six, as John Stuart Mill had, and learn the viola, "because it is not much fun to play".

Of his contempt for television, Scruton said: "I don't watch television at all and until I got married and had children it had never even occurred to me. I just didn't have time – there are all those books to read."

In 2016 the contrary don appeared to have been embraced, finally, by the establishment when he was knighted. He was even allowed to present *A Point of View* on Radio 4 and, most shocking of all, given his dislike of the medium, he presented a documentary on aesthetics on BBC Two. His bucolic life, meanwhile, was celebrated in his slightly self-mocking Scrutopia Summer School, which he set up through the Royal Agricultural University in Cirencester Park, delivering ten days of "intoxicating eccentricity in the Gloucestershire countryside".

Controversial until the end, in 2019 Scruton was fired from his post as chairman of the government's Building Better, Building

Beautiful commission after an interview he had given to George Eaton, the deputy editor of *The New Statesman*, that alleged he had made racist and antisemitic comments. Eaton posted a private Instagram post (later deleted) of himself drinking champagne, accompanied by the caption: "The feeling when you get right-wing racist and homophobe Roger Scruton sacked." Then a transcript surfaced and it became clear that Scruton's words had been misrepresented. The magazine printed an apology and Scruton was reappointed to the committee as co-chairman. "There's a general recognition that I was traduced by this wretched interviewer," Scruton said in an interview with *The Times*.

But he had by then perhaps come to expect such treatment. In *How to Be a Conservative* (2014) which was part polemic, part elegy, he wrote about how he thought the British had "surrendered education to the socialists and our sovereignty to Europe". While mostly serious, he was amusing in this book about what it felt like to be part of a conservative counterculture. "In intellectual circles, conservatives move quietly and discreetly," he wrote, "catching each other's eyes across the room like the homosexuals in Proust."

Sir Roger Scruton FBA, FRSL, philosopher, was born on February 27, 1944. He died of cancer on January 12, 2020, aged 75

BARRIE STACEY

———————•———————

Maverick theatrical agent, self-styled 'sandwich maker to the stars'
and author of 'the worst showbiz memoir ever written'

With his high-pitched, forceful laugh, loud floral shirts and effete manner, Barrie Stacey seemed to have stepped from the pages of a Ronald Firbank novel. A maverick yet almost permanent fixture in London's theatreland for more than 50 years, he worked variously as a theatrical agent, producer, occasional actor and playwright and, for over a decade, a self-styled "sandwich maker to the stars".

Although he produced variety shows with Frankie Howerd, Bob Monkhouse, John Hanson and an elderly Jessie Matthews, Stacey was probably best known as the proprietor of a sixties bohemian café, The As You Like It in Monmouth Street, Covent Garden.

He opened the café after an accident in 1962, in which he fell out of the back of a grocery van in Knightsbridge and received £1,000 compensation, and it became popular with drop-outs, would-be actors, eccentrics and Tin Pan Alley musicians. The raucous Countess De Vesmes was a regular, as was the strongwoman of variety Joan Rhodes and the up-and-coming writer Bernard Kops. While Stacey served bowls of Hungarian goulash and doorstep sandwiches a young George Jamieson (who became the transgender model April Ashley, obituary, page 226) cleared tables.

With his acid wit and caustic banter, Stacey was the star attraction, but he met his match in one of the café's most enduring patrons, Quentin Crisp, who found fame with the memoir *The Naked Civil Servant.* Crisp dropped in for coffee every day. "He always chose for his entrance a cool pair of linen trousers, shirt tied in a bow at his navel and high platform shoes," recalled Stacey. "His hair was electric with mauve tints. I was envious."

Barrie Edwin Stacey was born in Boscombe, Bournemouth, in 1926, the oldest of four sons. His mother, Phyllis, was a receptionist at the Vale Royal Hotel, Bournemouth, where she met and married Edwin Oswald Stacey, the hotel handyman.

On his own admission "stage-struck and precocious from an

early age", Stacey began singing in local concerts when he was five. His formal education was interrupted by the war and he left school aged 16. He did his National Service working as a military clerk and taught himself to type. In the late fifties he went to London, where he typed up theatrical scripts and had small acting roles. He wrote several unproduced plays and got a job as the manager at The Coffee House, a popular bistro in the Haymarket, where Lindsay Kemp, the performer, and Jeremy Wolfenden, the journalist, waited on tables.

"The bistro built up a gay reputation," Stacey recalled, "which was not at all surprising since it employed several workers of a camp nature. Eventually the bosses put a notice in the window asking 'undesirables' to go elsewhere." The "undesirables" and the rest of the West End's bohemia flocked to The As You Like It. "It was usually called 'The As' by its habitués who were too lazy to utter five consecutive words at any one time," recalled Crisp.

As the café's fame spread Stacey began to operate a personal sandwich delivery service to the casts of numerous London theatres and he became a familiar figure as he swept down Shaftesbury Avenue wearing red silk trousers and carrying a giant wicker shopping basket. "The most popular sandwiches for dancers are banana," he enthused. "Dame Beryl Grey can't get enough of them."

Eventually Stacey sold the premises to the Shaftesbury Hotel. With his contacts he set up a theatrical agency and production company. He represented an extraordinary number of unknown actors (including a young Rupert Everett and the astrologer Russell Grant) but he rarely held on to talent and frequently turned down future stars, notably Lewis Collins of *The Professionals* fame ("He'll never get anywhere, dear") and Mike Reid ("No talent at all"). One exception was Keith Hopkins, Stacey's partner of 56 years who survives him. They met when Hopkins first arrived in London as a young actor and Stacey became his manager.

Stacey's own productions were never noted for high acting or production standards. Unrehearsed actors fluffed their lines, scenery was dodgy and by the 1980s he had earned the unfortunate nickname in showbusiness of "the Queen of Tat".

In 1987 he self-published what was generally considered to be one of the worst showbusiness autobiographies ever written, *A Ticket to the*

Carnival, a mish-mash of name dropping ("I once saw Betty Grable in the street") and camp banter which was panned by critics. The normally restrained trade paper *The Stage* described the book as "one that once you put down you can't pick up".

Undeterred, Stacey began writing a sequel. To his credit he did successfully tour his old mentor Crisp for several years in a one-man show.

No one doubted Stacey's indefatigable energy and optimism but even his closest friends were aghast when in 2001 he had plans to tour "Mad" Frankie Fraser's one-man show, which had run in London under another management. The former gangster, who had once had a reputation for pulling out his torture victims' teeth using pliers, had spent more than 40 years in prison. He was summoned to Stacey's office and offered cheese and wine and contract terms. Confronted by the eccentric Stacey, Mad Frankie seemed startled. "You see, dear," said Stacey, "what we need with this show is a bit of camp. That's what theatre's all about, Frank. Pure camp." Fraser left the room stone-faced.

"I can't understand it," said Stacey, "most people love working for me."

Barrie Stacey, theatrical agent, was born on October 24, 1926. He died on January 1, 2022, aged 95

CHARLES BURNETT III

—————•—————

Flamboyant multimillionaire businessman and philanthropist who set a
land-speed record in 2009 and died in a helicopter crash

Charles Burnett III did not really care what vehicle he drove as long as it was either fast or powerful. At Newtown Park, his country pile near Lymington, Hampshire, classic roadsters shared parking spaces with Chieftain tanks and other military vehicles, which Burnett would drive along the country lanes close to his estate – much to the surprise of passers-by.

Scion of the Garfield Weston family, one of the wealthiest in Canada, Burnett also kept a collection of historical aircraft, including a Harvard military trainer, which could take off from a Second World War airstrip that he had restored in the grounds of his home.

In this multimillionaire's playground Burnett would bring his "toys" out to play during lavish parties. He once staged re-enactments of battles on his grounds, complete with mock air raids and tank attacks. Party guests were required to turn up in military uniforms, some of which were in questionable taste. "Some people are so busy trying to make money that they never get time to enjoy it," said Burnett. "I decided early on that this was not for me." A man of his word, he was said to have spent £100,000 on his own 40th birthday party.

Local opinion was divided about his war games party in 2007 – between anger and cold annoyance. Some of his neighbours were quoted as saying that he had brought "the Blitz" to their sleepy corner of Hampshire, with explosions shaking their windows. He managed to mollify some by inviting them to another party at which the Red Arrows gave a private demonstration.

The well-built, loud-shirted, Stetson-wearing Burnett always stood out at such events. Yet at closer quarters he was surprisingly shy, well-mannered and softly spoken. While his guests were having fun, he sometimes locked himself away, a Gatsbyesque figure working at his desk. He was wary of strangers, especially if he suspected they wanted money, but his generosity to causes he cared about was notable.

Like Gatsby he tended to see the world in different colours, and he was at his happiest when he was making mischief – one of his parties featured a row of confessionals where guests were required to reveal their sins before gaining entry to a room called "Heaven".

Although Burnett had an American father and Canadian mother, he was born in Britain and, when breaking world speed records, he liked to wrap himself in the Union flag. It featured prominently when he celebrated breaking one of the stranger land-speed records – for a steam-powered vehicle. In 2009 Burnett drove the *Inspiration*, which became known as the "fastest kettle in the world", at an average of 139.8mph at Edwards Air Force base in California.

The day after breaking the record he turned to his test driver, Don Wales, grandson of the former land-speed record holder Sir Malcolm Campbell, and invited him to set a new one. He took Wales and his team to a Beach Boys concert, then assembled them at Edwards Air Base the next morning. After turning off some of the safety equipment Wales took *Inspiration* to a top speed of 160mph and an average speed of 148.3mph, beating Burnett's record. "He prided himself on bringing joy to those around him," said Colin Stocker, a friend.

Although his extravagance knew no bounds – he had three aircraft hangars on his estate, one filled with cars, another with aircraft and a third with boats – he was also a lover of nature, and became the main sponsor of Tiggywinkles wildlife hospital in Buckinghamshire. He took a particular interest in the plight of the hedgehog, but his largesse extended to domestic pets. One friend recalled being with him on the Isle of Man when he found an injured cat. He chartered a private plane to fly it back to England for treatment.

Charles Ryland Burnett III was born in London in 1956, the only child of Charles Burnett Jr, a businessman from Richmond, Virginia, and Miriam Weston Burnett. His mother was the eldest of nine children of Willard Garfield Weston, who was the founder of Associated British Foods, a conglomerate with retail interests including Primark and Kingsmill. Charles spent a good deal of his childhood travelling between family homes in England, Bermuda and South Africa.

After his father was incapacitated by encephalitis, Burnett had to spend much of his childhood surrounded by nurses and carers and he later spoke of missing a father figure. He attended Pine Crest school in Fort Lauderdale, then studied science at Rice University in Houston and at the University of Richmond, Virginia.

He started his career in business by opening a nightclub in Houston. "I'm not an early riser, so I guessed this would be an intelligent choice," he said. He moved to London in the mid-1980s and launched Los Locos in Covent Garden, one of the first Tex-Mex eateries in the capital, featuring "tequila girls" selling shots. It made money and he opened a second restaurant.

A man who marched to the beat of his own drum, and was notoriously late for everything, Burnett turned his attention to reducing car fumes in London. He formed a venture to convert black cabs to run on greener fuels, but found that London taxi drivers, conservative by nature, were not ready for a green-fuel revolution. Undeterred, Burnett bought a company in the Netherlands called Prins and developed the first gaseous injection system for passenger cars that would let them run on liquid petroleum gas (LPG) and compressed natural gas (CNG). He claimed that the cost of converting a vehicle could be recovered in 18 months.

His "need for speed" first manifested itself on the water. Through his company Vulture Ventures he won the Class 2 offshore powerboat world championship for four years running between 1993 and 1996 in a sleek two-pronged powerboat, *Cultured Vulture.*

His interest in steam-powered vehicles started when his friend Lord Montagu of Beaulieu introduced him to a student steam-car project at the University of Southampton. He decided that their theoretical plans deserved to be turned into reality and his pursuit of the record became a passion.

The British-built vehicle consisted of 7.7m of lightweight carbon fibre and aluminium bodywork, which enclosed 12 boilers that could generate steam at 400°C to power the turbines, as well as 3km of steel tubing. Developing a vehicle that was lightweight, safe and capable of generating such heat took a decade.

After the death of his mother in 2008, Burnett inherited her share of the Garfield Weston family fortune. Until then he had subsisted on an annual allowance of about £25 million.

Burnett never married, but over the years he rested his head on many a perfumed pillow. He is survived by his girlfriend, Andra Cobb, a mother of two who was the sole survivor of the helicopter crash, near to Burnett's 12,000-acre ranch in New Mexico, in which he died.

At the time of his death he was developing another steam-powered vehicle in the hope of breaking the record again. His first vehicle, *Inspiration,* is displayed at the National Motor Museum in Hampshire. "While his death was premature," said Lord Montagu, "he went in the way that he might well have chosen – at speed."

Charles Burnett III, businessman and philanthropist, was born on May 31, 1956. He died in a helicopter crash on January 17, 2018, aged 61

Charles Burnett III

IGOR AND GRICHKA
BOGDANOFF

●

*French television star twins who were known for their popular science
shows, outlandish looks and habit of plagiarising*

In the 1980s, younger television audiences in France eagerly tuned
in each week to *Temps X* on the TF1 channel to see what the future
would be like. Their guides, the heirs to the traditions of Jules Verne,
were two striking-looking identical twins, Igor and Grichka Bogdanoff.

The programme, presented from a set resembling a spaceship,
showcased foreign science-fiction series, such as *Space: 1999*, *Star Trek* and
Doctor Who. It also, like the BBC's *Tomorrow's World*, introduced viewers to
exciting technological advances, prototypes of mobile telephones and
websites. Yet the journey of the Bogdanoffs on planet Earth would
become more outlandish than even they could have predicted.

They were born Igor and Grégoire Bogdanoff in 1949, in the
village of Saint-Lary, in Gascony. Igor was older by 40 minutes. Their
father was a Russian painter, Yuri Osten-Sacken-Bogdanoff, whose
ancestors included Baltic German and Tatar nobility. The twins had
three sisters but were raised largely at a castle by their maternal

grandmother, Countess Bertha Kolowrat-Krakowska; herself a member of an aristocratic family from Bohemia, she had been married to an Austrian nobleman, Hieronymus von Colloredo.

In 1925, however, she had had an affair with a classical singer who was among the first African-Americans to win renown in that field, the tenor Roland Hayes. Their daughter, Maya, born quietly in Switzerland, would become the twins' mother. Yet the scandal cost Bertha her marriage, access to her elder children, and her place in society in Berlin and Prague. She was exiled to France.

The boys would later attribute their interest in subjects such as astronomy to having had the run of her library as children. Despite possessing such an exotic background – they learnt to fly aircraft as teenagers – they were nonetheless also suspected of having embellished details of their upbringing. The two attended school in Auch and claimed to have attained the baccalaureate at 14.

Igor stated that at 11, tests had revealed their IQ as being 190. Last year, he said they had also been assessed as having the form of autism previously known as Asperger's syndrome.

The pair studied applied mathematics in Paris and in 1976 published their first book, *The Keys to Science Fiction*. They persuaded no less a figure than the philosopher Roland Barthes to contribute a preface and began to make appearances on television as popularisers of science. *Temps X* may now be regarded as somewhat kitsch, but it ran for a decade from 1979 and made them television heartthrobs and celebrities.

There was always an undercurrent to *Temps X* of the sensational, or at least of a less than sceptical tolerance of the outer reaches of science. Alongside interviews with guests such as Jean-Michel Jarre, who had composed for the ill-fated space shuttle Challenger, the first piece to be played in zero gravity, there ran segments on UFOs and alien astronauts.

When the programme was cancelled, the Bogdanoffs turned to print in an effort to emulate the popular success of the likes of Stephen Hawking. In 1991, they published a bestseller, *God and Science*, which incorporated interviews with the Roman Catholic philosopher Jean Guitton.

This came to the attention of a professor of astronomy in America, Trinh Xuan Thuan, who claimed it plagiarised a book of his, *The Secret Melody*. The case was settled out of court but exposed to scrutiny claims in the blurb of the Bogdanoffs' book that they had doctorates. They did not, and set about remedying this.

By 2002, they had both been awarded the higher degree by the University of Burgundy at Dijon. Grichka's was in mathematics and Igor's in theoretical physics, although both were given the lowest possible grade and Igor's was blocked for three years until he had published several articles in heavyweight scientific journals.

These, however, on such subjects as "topological field theory of the initial singularity of spacetime", quickly attracted more controversy. Scientists queued up to criticise the intellectual credibility of their content, with some, such as the physicist Max Niedermaier, asserting they must be spoofs (using "delightfully meaningless combinations of buzzwords").

A supervisor of their doctorates said his task had been "like teaching My Fair Lady to speak with an Oxford accent" and the matter periodically erupted into clamorous if somewhat abstruse brouhaha over the next 15 years, in what became known as "the Bogdanoff affair". It spawned several lawsuits for defamation and breach of copyright, as well as much Gallic musing on the role of peer review in academic circles. One official report from France's National Centre for Scientific Research stated of the brothers' theses: "Rarely have we seen a hollow work dressed with such sophistication."

If the fuss prevented the Bogdanoffs from attaining the standing in the scientific community that they thought their due, it did not stop them writing several other successful books, such as *Before the Big Bang* (2004).

In 2002, they reappeared on French television with the series *Rayons X;* the music was composed by their friend Pierre Sarkozy, the son of the former president. Then, three years later, they were appointed to the chair of cosmology at Megatrend University in Belgrade, Serbia. In 2014, however, the institution's founder, Mica Jovanovic, stepped down as rector after it emerged he had falsely claimed to have a doctorate from the London School of Economics.

By then, the twins had become best known in France for their rapidly changing appearance, as their chins, lips and foreheads became steadily more pronounced. When they trod the red carpet at the 2010 Cannes film festival their cheekbones were "so high and bulbous as to appear to threaten their owners' vision", remarked one commentator.

Their new look drew comparisons with the "Bride of Wildenstein", the socialite Jocelyn Wildenstein, known for her fondness for plastic surgery. It was said that the same plastic surgeon who did not perform plastic surgery on Michael Jackson, also did not perform plastic surgery on the Bogdanoffs. They denied having had procedures or Botox, although they liked to hint that they were part of a secret experiment "with protocols".

Despite appearing ever more grotesque beast than beauty, in 2015 Igor began dating a student 45 years his junior, Julie Jardon. Grichka never married – the twins confessed that sometimes they fell in love with the same person – but Igor had a son by a relationship with the actress Geneviève Gard. He had three more children by his marriage to Countess Ludmilla d'Oultremont, which ended in divorce in 1994. Between 2009 and 2018 he was married to Amélie de Bourbon-Parma, a writer and the daughter of a French war hero; they had two sons.

In 2017, Igor was fined for breaking into Jardon's apartment when their relationship ended. Matters took a still more serious turn the next year. Igor had been charged with forgery in 2014 after logging flying time in aircraft he had not flown, including ambulances, and in 2018 both brothers became involved with a rich hotelier-turned-producer, Cyrille Pien, then in a fragile mental state. Over the course of several months, Pien was said to have made over to the twins substantial sums, amounting to €800,000, for projects which included the relaunch of *Temps X* online and the purchase of a house for Igor. Pien was then classed as vulnerable by the police and the Bogdanoffs were banned from contacting him. He subsequently committed suicide. With four others, the pair were due in court in a fortnight to answer charges of aggravated fraud.

The Bogdanoffs had chosen not to be vaccinated against the coronavirus, stating that their health was such that the virus was no risk to them.

E pur si muove, as Galileo might have told them.

Igor and Grichka Bogdanoff, popularisers of science, were born on August 29, 1949. They died of Covid-19 on January 3, 2022, and December 28, 2021, respectively, aged 72

JACKIE STALLONE

———————— ● ————————

Much-married astrologer to the stars, Big Brother *contestant, ladies' wrestling manager and mother of Sylvester Stallone*

British television viewers were unsure what to expect from the third series of *Celebrity Big Brother* in 2005. Among the contestants were the feminist Germaine Greer, the Old Harrovian racing pundit John McCririck, and the Danish actress Brigitte Nielsen who was also the ex-wife of Sylvester Stallone.

On day five the housemates were instructed to dress in pseudo-medieval clothing before being told: "All rise to meet your queen mother." To Nielsen's horror in walked Jackie Stallone, an interestingly preserved octogenarian astrologer, female wrestling impresario and outspoken critic of her towering former daughter-in-law, whom she had vociferously branded a gold-digger.

The frisson lasted for four days before Stallone was the first contestant to be voted off, Greer having earlier walked out. During that time Nielsen was humiliatingly ordered to warm up her former mother-in-law's bed and lavatory seat. Stallone was billed as being 71, which would have meant that she gave birth to Sylvester at the improbable age of 13; in fact 83 was closer to reality.

She had been a little-known quantity until Sylvester found fame with films such as *Rocky* (1976), which he wrote and which won two Oscars, but then there was no stopping her. In a 1982 interview headlined "The mother behind Rocky" she offered an insight into her son's world, including how his English was so bad that he "couldn't even write a postcard". When she complained that his security guards were cramping her style, in terms of her romantic liaisons, he advised her to date one of them instead: "Ma, just pick out one that you like." On another occasion she told *The Sunday Times* of fighting with Sylvester over his choice of women: "I couldn't stand the bitches. None of them were good enough."

Her line in astrology, which she practised for 50 years, brought an assorted list of friends, some, such as Princess Diana and Michael Jackson, less surprising than others, such as Nelson Mandela. In 1989 she published *Starpower: An Astrological Guide to Super Success*, which left the reader "privy to delicious revelations about the rich and celebrated" including Jack Kennedy (Gemini), John Lennon (Libra) and Warren Beatty (Aries).

Not content with running her own psychic hotline, she claimed to have invented "rumpology", which involves divining an individual's future through the lines and crevices of their buttocks: the left cheek is their past, the right is their future and the dividing line their destiny. She claimed to keep an imprint of Mikhail Gorbachev's derriere.

If rear ends failed to give an accurate prediction of the future, she would consult a pair of psychic miniature pinschers that she dressed in tiny, glitter-covered jackets while they danced and snarled their predictions.

Just when it seemed she could go no further Stallone, whose lips were rarely sealed, claimed to have been in Qatar where she overheard the Duchess of York musing aloud about slimming pills. She intervened to recommend that the duchess marry a rich sheikh, adding: "There are all these men dressed alike, all very rich and with no underwear. Perfect for a single girl."

Jacqueline Frances Labofish was born in Washington DC in 1921, the daughter of John Labofish, a wealthy lawyer who wanted his daughter to go to law school, and Jeanne Clerec, a Frenchwoman who once swam the Channel and walked out when her daughter was ten. According to their daughter, the family lived with the bodybuilder Charles Atlas, who provided them with training.

She ran away at 15, becoming a trapeze artist in the Flying Wallendas act with Barnum & Bailey. "I stayed with the circus for two years and then got work on Broadway," she said, adding that she was also a chorus girl in a nightclub and a hairdresser. By the Fifties she had opened Barbella's, a women's gym in Washington, and had an exercise slot on local television.

In 1945 she had married Frank Stallone, a cobbler from Italy. They had two sons, Sylvester and Frank Jr, a singer. The family was evicted from their apartment in south Philadelphia after the boys attacked the elegant canvases in the lobby with their bows and arrows. "We tried to deny it, but it didn't work," she said. They also threw stink bombs in lifts and snakes in the pool "when two old ladies were swimming".

The marriage was dissolved in 1957. Two years later she married Anthony Filiti, "another greaseball", she said, who worked in a pizza parlour. They had a daughter, Toni D'Alto, an actress who died of lung cancer in 2012, six weeks after Sylvester's son, Sage, died of a heart attack.

At the age of 40 Stallone had returned to high school to finish her education before studying chemistry at an unnamed university. In the Eighties she was the mastermind behind *GLOW: Gorgeous Ladies of Wrestling*, an American television programme that attracted a cult following. She played the manager in the bizarre show, which was part women's pro wrestling, part beautiful madness. In recent years it has been the subject of a drama series on Netflix.

By then Stallone's second marriage had been dissolved and in 1977 she married Francis Maschek, who owned a nursing home in Florida for wealthy patients recovering from plastic surgery. "The first time I was married I wore white, and it ended in divorce," she said. "The second time, I wore pink, and that one didn't last either. This time I wore black. And if this one doesn't work out, I can wear it to my funeral." They divorced after four years because "he embarrassed me".

Her fourth husband was Stephen Levine, a Los Angeles neurosurgeon whom she married in 1998, and who survives her. In 1984 he had been accused of murdering his first wife by supplying her with a lethal dose of a painkiller but admitted involuntary manslaughter in a plea bargain.

Despite three heart attacks Stallone remained active into her nineties, describing the secret to her longevity as "a bag of spinach a day", adding: "Every morning for breakfast I steam a bowl of it and boil an egg on it." She was rarely seen without theatrical false eyelashes, an outrageously short skirt and a star-spangled headband, her dangling earrings scraping the floor.

She continued to work out while defying both age and gravity thanks to a succession of plastic surgeries. Eventually she called a halt. "I look like I've got a mouthful of nuts," she said in 2013.

Perhaps it was no wonder that in 2000 Sylvester sighed to a *Los Angeles Times* interviewer, "And people wonder why I'm odd."

Jackie Stallone, celebrity astrologer, was born on November 29, 1921. She died on September 21, 2020, aged 98

JAMES CROWDEN

———————•———————

Wodehousian figure who coached the Cambridge Boat Race team for 40
years and later became the Lord Lieutenant of the county

In his Pembroke bags and light-blue cap, James Crowden cut an
instantly recognisable figure around the towpaths of Cambridgeshire.
He could usually be seen on his bike, megaphone in hand, enjoining
the Cambridge Boat Race crew to greater effort. Having been an
Olympic rower himself he did not lack for authority as a coach, but his
gentleman amateur style and Wodehousian way with words earned
him a certain affection as well as respect.

No one could have mistaken Crowden's devotion to his university.
Even in nearby Wisbech, where he lived in a National Trust house, he
would walk the streets in his light blue tie, pink socks and Cambridge
boater and bags before putting on his 1952 Helsinki Olympics sweater
to do battle with the tide on the Cam. For 40 years he employed an
individual he called his "batman" who would accompany him down
the river and through the kissing gates, picking up his megaphone
when he had crushed it under a bicycle that, being a man of stature,
was invariably too small for his sizeable frame.

Crowden rowed in the Boat Race in 1951 when Oxford sank and
umpired another, in 1978, when the same fate befell Cambridge. At the
1952 Olympics he represented Great Britain in the coxless fours with
Adrian Cadbury, who became chairman of the eponymous firm. They
finished fourth. He was no less fond of the county of Cambridgeshire,
which he represented as high sheriff and Lord Lieutenant, mingling
with the royal family and politicians. He was not one to be cowed by
their presence.

Cambridge University in the 1950s still attracted talented
sportsmen who were not necessarily academically gifted. Rowing, as
with other sports, was taken seriously, but there was a charm about the
approach of the undergraduates that became lost in later decades.
Crowden and his fellow 1951 crew members were able to take up an
invitation to race against Harvard University not only because they
won the Boat Race that year but also because Oxford turned down the

opportunity on account of the proposed visit to Boston clashing with a hunt ball.

Crowden, who was also a brilliant after-dinner speaker, soon became famed for his bon mots after he returned to Cambridge in 1953 to coach a succession of crews. Referring to a not particularly competent oarsman in the middle of the boat, he intoned through his megaphone: "It's a headwind, boys. My old friend at 'five' likes lots of time to take lovely, wholesome strokes, over the waves and behind the rigger and sit back, sit back, sit back." Or, "On my right a Charolais Friesian calf worth £30 taking one bladeful at a time, you do the same!" He memorably coined the phrase "Sweaty Betty" to describe one of his female rowers.

Remembering the names of his crews – partly because there were so many – was at times beyond him. "He always called me 'cox'," said Tony Elgood. "Even ten years after leaving Pembroke, he was still calling me that." A "rowing heavy" – a bone China statuette sold at Henley – was modelled on his 16-stone size. He loved the toast at Cambridge rowing dinners: "GDBO" – God Damn Bloody Oxford – and he would speak wittily at them.

"His skill with rhythmical speech was extraordinary," remarked Howard Jacobs, who was coached by Crowden. "'Off the toes, and off the toes again, now stride her.' I still remember a light four outing when we went from one end of the river to the other in one piece, moving from light to flat out all via James's voice. If he had a coaching failing it was to emphasise the collective sometimes to the detriment of the individual – he was too polite to tell someone that he was rowing like a drain."

James Gee Pascoe Crowden came from an East Anglian family of land agents. He was educated at Bedford School and Pembroke College, Cambridge, rowing at Henley for the first time in 1945 in the Hedsor Cup. In 1950 he took part in the Great Britain Bronze Medal VIII at the European Championships in Milan. After Cambridge's triumph in the Boat Race in 1951, they narrowly lost to Oxford in 1952, the year he served as president. He subsequently coached Cambridge from 1953 to 1975 and coached the Pembroke College boat for 40 years. He was a vice-president of the British Olympic Association and a steward at Henley Regatta.

After graduating, he became a chartered surveyor and was senior partner of Grounds & Co, East Anglian auctioneers, from 1974 to 1988. His so-called batman, Richard Barnwell, said: "I would have paid to work for him. He was an extraordinary man of the people."

Crowden became high sheriff of Cambridgeshire in 1970 and was Lord Lieutenant from 1992 to 2002. He was granted the Freedom of Peterborough in 2008. "James was a large man and fitting into the uniform of Lord Lieutenant on a hot summer's day could not have been too pleasant," his friend, Michael Kuczynski, said. Crowden's duties brought him into regular contact with the royal family. He lived in the servants quarters of his National Trust house on the river at Wisbech, the main rooms being open to the public, but this did not deter him from entertaining them there. When he acted as auctioneer for the British Olympic Appeal, he broke his only pair of spectacles and had to ask the Princess Royal to help him examine the bids.

His sunny disposition was severely affected by personal tragedies. His first wife, Kathleen, suffered and died from multiple sclerosis in 1989. His second, Margaret, known as "Mouse", was his brother's widow and she died of a heart attack in 2009. His only child, Richard, from his first marriage, had just graduated from Cambridge when he was killed in a car crash in 1982. "Yet he never had any self-pity," Barnwell said.

As an after-dinner speaker, Crowden was in considerable demand. He had a fund of sometimes gently coarse stories, including one concerning two swans flying over the Boat Race course. One asks: "Who is going to win?" The other replies: "I've put all I've got on Oxford." He then would elevate the tone by talking about Ely Cathedral, for which, along with Peterborough Cathedral, he would raise funds. "I am reminded of the story of the verger who said to the visiting bishop, about to preach: 'I would speak up my lord, the agnostics in here are terrible.'"

James Crowden CVO, rower, was born on November 14, 1927. He died on September 24, 2016, aged 88

LADY CHITTY

Eccentric biographer described as 'Virginia Woolf without the genius' whose formative years were as strange as fiction

Although Susan Chitty wrote lively and literate non-fiction books, she was never considered in the first rank of biographers. By temperament she was better suited to fiction, since she lacked the indefatigable curiosity, conscientiousness and care in dealing with evidence which biography demands. She was a great trader in what might now be called "alternative truth", which made her an amusing companion, a racy gossip, sometimes even the life and soul of the party, but hardly qualified her as a credible recorder of other people's lives.

Once described by a critic as "Virginia Woolf without the genius", she would inflate incidents in the lives of others, as well as their personality traits; and, like Woolf, she would have violent alternations of mood, ups and downs, depression and even insanity throughout her life. Both were quarrelsome yet charming. They even looked alike.

Chitty was born Susan Elspeth Hopkinson in 1929 to an unmarried mother, the writer Antonia White, remembered by the public for her novel *Frost in May*, based on her years at a convent school before the

First World War, and by her family for being someone best kept away from scissors.

Chitty's disadvantages were psychological as much as social. Her mother, not naturally maternal and herself subject to mental ill-health and violent temper, had wanted a boy, and for some months put her daughter into a children's home. From her early years, Chitty sensed there was something odd, even shaming, about herself. At Godolphin, an old-fashioned boarding school in Salisbury full of the daughters of clergymen, she was seen as an exotic plant, bohemian, unplaceable, enviably unlike the rest. Yet children prefer to fit in, and she suffered.

It was probably not the right setting for a child with an unconventional, chaotic past, without a settled home or background, uncertain of her own identity. Academically, though, she shone and went on to read modern history at Somerville College, Oxford, where she met the man she later married, Thomas Chitty.

So far she had been known as Susan Hopkinson, after her mother's third husband, Tom Hopkinson, editor of the *Picture Post*; her father was a civil engineer called Silas Glossop, with whom she was on friendly terms throughout her life, and occasionally she was known as Susan Glossop.

After her marriage, in 1951, she became Susan Chitty and when her husband, a novelist, inherited a baronetcy on his father's death in 1955 she became Lady Chitty, nearly always called Lady Susan Chitty in the popular press, causing further confusion. When she came to write her own books, she used her married name and thereafter remained Susan Chitty. Like her mother, she seemed to have a profusion of names and identities and, to add to the mix, her husband used the pen name of Thomas Hinde and occasionally also wrote under his real name.

They had a son and three daughters, and tried to give them the stability their own childhoods had lacked: informal cottage life in a Sussex village, pets, riding and homemade amusements. Their house was capacious but crumbling, its rooms eccentrically disordered. With money often tight the family would eat off newspapers when there were no tablecloths and indulge in squirrel pie if Thomas had been out shooting.

A serious mental breakdown had meant that Chitty took no degree at Oxford, but professionally it made little difference as she soon went into journalism through winning a *Vogue* talent contest which brought her a job on the magazine. Tall, fair and willowy, she also modelled once or twice for *Vogue* and wrote a series of pieces for *Punch* which were later collected to make the first of her books, a novel called *Diary of a Fashion Model* (1958). Two other novels followed and there were a number of miscellaneous books including *The Intelligent Woman's Guide to Good Taste* (1958).

With her husband she wrote *On Next to Nothing*, a handbook on how to live cheaply, and *The Great Donkey Walk*, an account of an 18-month trek from Santiago de Compostela to Greece, with two small children, on foot and donkey. A reluctant explorer, she remarked: "The only reason I went on that bloody journey was because it was better than Thomas's other idea of sailing round the world."

In the early seventies she found the genre she stuck to, biography. *The Woman Who Wrote Black Beauty*, published in 1972, was a life of Anna Sewell which reflected Chitty's own love of horses – she was often seen trotting around her village on horseback, in between heated disputes with her neighbours.

More ambitious books followed, each depending on inside knowledge, which gave them a scoop value. *The Beast and the Monk: A Life of Charles Kingsley* (1975), with much in it about Kingsley's sexuality, was written with the benefit of a cache of letters to his wife, closely guarded till then by a member of his family; *Gwen John* (1981) owed something to Antonia White's friendship with Jacques Maritain; and *Playing the Game: A Biography of Sir Henry Newbolt* (1997), with its revelations about Newbolt's ménage à trois with his wife and mistress, came from family knowledge and previously unseen papers, since Newbolt was Thomas Chitty's great-uncle.

The book explained how scrupulously Newbolt divided his sexual attention. He left a ledger showing columns of figures which, Susan Chitty wrote, "represent the number of times he slept with each of his women each month between 1904 and 1917, averaging as much as 12 per head per month".

The most startling biography was *And Now to My Mother* (1985), an account of her painful and bitter relationship with her mother, whose diaries she also edited. Reviewing it in *The Observer*, Hilary Spurling began, "Antonia White had a splendid story about Dylan Thomas squashing a fried egg between the pages of a rare book belonging to Augustus John. This memoir by her daughter produces a rather similar sensation of appalled and fascinated revulsion."

A long public disagreement with Chitty's half-sister Lyndall Hopkinson (Countess Passerini) was aired in the press and Hopkinson's own book, *Nothing to Forgive*, gave another slant, arguing that their mother was not, as characterised, "a vain, quasi-nymphomaniacal monster". This sisterly quarrel, which also embroiled Carmen Callil, the founder of Virago, went on for years.

Lady Chitty, biographer, was born on August 18, 1929. She died after a short illness on July 13, 2021, aged 91

'RAINBOW' GEORGE WEISS

---•---

'Dreamer and schemer' who lived on the fringes of politics and could reduce his friend Peter Cook to hysterical laughter

George Weiss, right, with Peter Cook in the 1980s.

Alongside "Rainbow" George Weiss, Screaming Lord Sutch was a political dilettante. As leader of the Official Monster Raving Loony Party, Sutch stood in 39 parliamentary elections between 1963 and 1997, but Weiss outdid him to set a record at the 2005 general election by standing in 13 constituencies simultaneously.

He polled a grand total of 1,289 votes, less than 100 for each seat in which he was a candidate.

Over the years the hopelessly optimistic Weiss fronted a variety of political parties, including the Make Politicians History Party. In many of them he was the only member. In his final shot at power in the 2017 general election, he formed a Rainbow Alliance between his Captain Rainbow's Universal Party and the remnants of Sutch's Monster Raving Loonies.

Weiss's political career owed its genesis partly to his friend and Hampstead neighbour, the late comedian Peter Cook. When Cook jokingly formed the fictitious What Party, he appointed his friend Ciara Parkes as minister for lifts, his mother as minister for ladders and Weiss as his minister for confusion.

Weiss's first genuine candidacy came soon after, when he stood against Michael Portillo in the 1984 Enfield Southgate by-election. He polled only 48 votes but was in his element and became an "election junkie".

Standing for the www.xat.org party in the 2003 Brent East by-election Weiss believed the 11 votes he mustered had set a record, but was crestfallen to discover that a candidate in Kensington some years earlier had polled an even more modest five votes. He was proud to seize back the record in 2005 when a candidate for his Vote For Yourself Rainbow Dream Ticket party in Cardiff North scored just a single vote.

His own idiosyncratic method of measuring his popularity involved telling the electorate not to vote for him and then counting the number of people who didn't vote and claiming them as his supporters.

His most successful election result came when he persuaded Ronnie Carroll, whose *Ring-a-Ding Girl* was Britain's entry in the 1962 Eurovision Song Contest, to stand for the Eurovisionary Party in Hampstead and Kilburn at the 2015 general election. With Weiss as his agent, Carroll secured 113 votes despite dying before polls opened. It was too late to take Carroll's name off the ballot paper and as a result, for the first time, Weiss's party got its deposit back. "Perhaps I should find more candidates at death's door," he observed drily.

In addition to Cook, other friends who were charmed by Weiss's bohemian eccentricity included the businessman and gallery owner Charles Saatchi, the comedian Russell Brand and the musician Ian Dury. A fanatical fan of Newcastle United, he also befriended Jackie Milburn, the club's most celebrated footballer, and persuaded him to stand for election for the Rainbow Party in the 1985 Tyne Bridge by-election. When the former striker pulled out at the last minute, Weiss stood himself, getting 38 votes.

In later years he funded his political career with the proceeds of the sale of a mews house in the cobbled Perrins Walk, Hampstead, three doors away from Cook. Weiss had taken up residence there in 1969 but stopped paying rent in 1984 after the roof caved in and many of his possessions were ruined. He sought compensation and demanded his landlord repair the roof but never heard from the owner of the property again. He remained there rent free until 2004 when he claimed squatter's rights and HM Land Registry awarded him possessory ownership.

He went on to make a profit of £710,000 from the sale of the house then squandered it not only on election deposits but on an array of madcap projects, including launching a referendum to rename Belfast Best City after George Best, chartering a plane on which to host a month-long party around the world, and hiring the Camden Palace for a concert that offered free admission but for which he charged £1 to leave.

He was also a compulsive gambler and in 2008 staked £333 at 3,000–1 on aliens arriving during the Olympics opening ceremony.

A self-styled "dreamer and schemer", his manifesto centred around an egalitarian form of universal income which he called The Wonder and which was philosophically based on the lyrics of John Lennon's *Imagine*. During the 2019 general election in which Boris Johnson stood on a "get Brexit done" ticket, he proposed a new European Union "that has no countries to support or governments to obey" and was "peaceful, harmonious, leisure-oriented and poverty-free".

"He wanted a world with no money, no boundaries, no borders," his friend Sebastian Wocker, editor of the *Hampstead Village Voice*, said. "He wanted everyone to be OK and no one to want for anything. But the way he went about it was too eccentric to cut any cheese with anyone."

He never married and after a number of failed relationships opted for the life of a "solitary mystic".

George Weiss was born in Hampstead in 1940 as London was under nightly bombardment from the Luftwaffe. The son of a Hatton Garden diamond merchant, he failed his 11-plus and on leaving school went to work for his father for 15 years.

In 1974 he found his unlikely soulmate when Cook moved into a house a few steps away from Weiss's Hampstead home. An *Observer* profile in 1999 noted that Weiss "could have been one of Cook's absurdist creations" and until shortly before Cook's death in 1995 they saw each other most days, often in the company of "Bronco", a Hampstead vagrant. Cook found Weiss "endlessly amusing", especially his conviction that political success was just around the corner.

"Peter enjoyed the spectacular nature of my failures really," Weiss reflected. "He got great fun and enjoyment out of them."

When George's mother said she would not let him have the £30,000 his late father had left him until he agreed to see a psychiatrist, Cook would delight in playing the part of a Teutonic psychiatrist in a series of rehearsals for the real thing. The money was duly inherited and quickly spent. He fielded 50 candidates for his Rainbow Party in the 1997 general election, giving them £500 each for their deposits. Nineteen of them absconded with the money.

Weiss watched television with Cook most nights, he with a spliff in his hand, Cook with a glass of wine or vodka. They would ramblingly debate what they would do if appointed God for a day and call radio phone-ins to share their anarchic conversations with the world, Cook often posing as Sven, a depressed Norwegian fisherman living in Swiss Cottage. Weiss recorded many of their conversations and after a long-running dispute with Cook's widow, Lin, over the rights, in 2002 he released *Over at Rainbow's*, a CD of excerpts from his hundreds of hours of tape.

His life was peppered with other chaotic incidents and bizarre happenings, such as his imprisonment in 1989 when he was caught in a tabloid sting at the Swiss Cottage Holiday Inn, where he was filmed exchanging 100 tabs of LSD for £150. To his great amusement he was described in the *News of the World* as "the master pusher behind the acid house craze".

Michael Palin, in his diaries, recalled Weiss complaining to him on another occasion about how hard it was to get publicity for his political campaigns and so he decided to get himself arrested by walking into Hampstead police station smoking a huge joint.

"Rainbow" George Weiss, dreamer and schemer, was born on October 13, 1940. He died in his sleep on December 1, 2021, aged 81

JAMES WHARRAM

—— • ——

*Free-spirited sailor and catamaran builder who studied ancient
Polynesian multihull design and crossed the Atlantic with his two lovers*

James Wharram was 28 when he sailed the 23ft 6in *Tangaroa*, a flimsy double canoe, or catamaran, from the Canary Islands to the Caribbean in the winter of 1956–57. He was accompanied by his two German lovers, Jutta and Ruth, and a small terrier dog called Pepe who helped to keep morale up when "things seemed really black". With no GPS, no chart plotter and no clothes, it might be seen as the ultimate hippies-at-sea dream come true.

The five-week crossing was a challenge, not least because of his seasickness and the steep Atlantic waves. "Twice I feared the boat might topple over completely," he recalled. "We just sat steering and waiting and holding on while the little *Tangaroa* rode up to the boiling crests of the waves, then slid sickeningly to the hollows. Often the waves broke right over us." Yet there were clearly some calmer nights and once in Trinidad, Jutta gave birth to their son, Hannes.

The *Tangaroa*, modelled on a simple Polynesian fishing boat and named after the Polynesian god of the fish and sea, made landfall on February 4, 1957. "From out of the thick tropical vegetation a tiny water stream flowed into the sea," he recalled. "At once the girls stripped and jumped joyously in for their first fresh-water bathe in six weeks. For myself, food was my first thought. Armed with a large knife, I went searching for coconuts."

Wharram soon began preparing his next catamaran, the marginally sturdier 40ft *Rongo*, named after the Polynesian god of war. "Under the shade of three giant mango trees near a beach in Trinidad, I built her with the aid of my two-girl crew and the occasional help of two native boat-builders," he said, adding that he built a raft house from bamboo for them to live in.

During the summer of 1959 they sailed to New York, where Wharram appeared on television with Sir Edmund Hillary. He and his fräuleins then sailed back to Britain through stormy seas, arriving 50 days later having completed the first west-to-east crossing of the north Atlantic by catamaran. "Though by no means a record voyage," he wrote, "ours has shown that a catamaran, if designed on the principles of the ancient Polynesians, is a safe ocean-cruising boat."

The achievement gained little recognition among sailing's elite, perhaps because of his outspoken remarks about fellow boat designers, his northern accent or his unconventional domestic arrangements.

"What really got 'them' was that 'my girls' were not only good at sailing and navigation, but very good at building boats too – and in addition, they looked beautiful," he wrote.

They certainly brought him publicity, with one newspaper headline reading "Love tangle on the raft". Wharram was unconcerned. "Many men are in need of two women in their lives, one to complement the other," he told the *Sunday Pictorial* in 1959. "Many are like myself and are capable of walking the tightrope of human relationship necessary to do it."

James Wharram was born in 1928 in Manchester, "quite a way from the sea", and raised in Wythenshawe. He was the only child of James Wharram, a builder, and his wife, Blanche (née Cook), who declared that her son's "only vice is reading". His introduction to sailing came at age 17 during a climbing trip on the Isle of Skye, when a boatman called MacDonald took him out on the water. He was immediately hooked. "I decided what I wanted to do was to sail the oceans," he said.

He spent countless hours in Manchester central library reading everything about boats he could get his hands on, especially the ancient Polynesian construction. Eric de Bisschop's *The Voyage of the Kaimiloa*, about a 1930s voyage from Hawaii across three oceans to France, caught his imagination. "It was not only his boat and his voyage that inspired me, but also his theories on the migrations of the Pacific islanders," he wrote.

Wharram "ran away" from technical college, where he had been chairman of the Labour Party youth group, and for his 19th birthday received a passport for a climbing holiday in Switzerland. "Within three weeks I was having my first love affair with a Swiss girl who was the same age as me to the day," he recalled. Pat, an American girlfriend, sent him a book called *Boat Building in Your Own Back Yard* as a farewell present, while Traubl, a young Viennese psychologist, "saw me as a wild, primitive sexual animal, which she enjoyed and tried to civilise".

He worked on a Thames barge, in the stores at Thornycroft boat builders and on a trawler off the west coast of Ireland but lost that job because he missed a sailing while seeing an actress girlfriend. In 1951 he was "bog trotting" around the Lake District when he met Ruth Merseburger, a German au pair who was seven years his senior. Three years later he collided with Jutta Schultze-Rhonhof while practising underwater techniques in a swimming pool. All three rejected the monogamous mores of the postwar years, instead forming a ménage à trois.

Wharram's first serious boat was a 20ft converted lifeboat with a junk rig named *Annie E Evans*. He built the *Tangaroa* in a barn near Manchester airport in 1955, paying his way by working on building sites, where he was known as "professor" because he wore glasses and read sailing books during breaks. Having sailed to Germany and back, he prepared *Tangaroa* for its Atlantic crossing at Falmouth, where experienced sailors looking down from their large yachts advised his companions to stick to coastal waters otherwise they would surely die.

They were wrong and, after successfully returning from New York, Wharram and his companions settled at Deganwy, near Conwy in north Wales. He prepared a boat design for a friend that was published, leading to a demand for more and the start of a successful self-build boat-design business that continues to this day.

Wharram and Jutta married in 1959, but she suffered a breakdown brought on by traumatic childhood experiences from when the Red Army entered Berlin at the end of the Second World War. She died in 1961 after falling from a building in Las Palmas, Canary Islands. Ruth, whom he married in 1964, encouraged him to record their transatlantic adventure in *Two Girls, Two Catamarans* (1969), its cover depicting a naked woman astride the bow of a catamaran.

By the late 1960s they had been joined both professionally and personally by Hanneke Boon, whom he had met when she was a teenager on a camping holiday with her Dutch parents in north Wales. They too had a son, Jamie. Over the years others came and went and in 1969 he was pictured with a group of young women under the headline "Jim's away with another all-girl crew", preparing to follow the clipper route to Australia via Cape Horn. Wharram, a tall, intense and charismatic man who in his prime lived with five women, insisted that it was never a "harem" in the sense of a man ruling his women, adding: "The girls also had the freedom to occasionally explore and expand their sexuality within our known group of friends."

This group subsequently moved to Devoran, on the Fal estuary in Cornwall. "When we first arrived, some were hostile to our arrangements, but now everyone is very accepting," he told an inteviewer in 2001. "Cornwall had everything to offer the boat builder, and I fitted in."

They went on to build *Spirit of Gaia*, a 63ft catamaran that from 1994 to 1998 he sailed around the world with Ruth and Hanneke. A decade later they undertook the Lapita voyage, following an ancient Pacific migration route on two double canoes, from the Philippines to the remote Polynesian islands of Anuta and Tikopia, reinforcing de Bisschop's theories of migration on canoe craft out of southeast Asia. "I was 80 when I made this voyage and it was the hardest I ever sailed and physically the most strenuous," he reported.

Ruth died in 2013 and Wharram is survived by Hanneke, whom he married in 2018, and by his two sons: Hannes, now known as Jonathan, is a GP in London, while Jamie flies light aircraft. Latterly Wharram was living with Alzheimer's disease. "He was very grieved to lose his mental abilities and struggled with his diminished existence," Hanneke wrote. "He couldn't face the prospect of further degradation and made the very difficult choice to end it himself."

One of Wharram's final achievements was *People of the Sea* (2020), a memoir that not only covered his designs and sailing, but also his philosophy and ideas as well as his relationship with the ocean and its "people of the sea", the Polynesians. Asked once why he sailed with an all-female crew, he replied it was because they were "easier to handle", adding: "They work together better than men and carry out instructions without hesitation. In any case, they work harder."

James Wharram, sailor and author, was born on May 15, 1928. He took his own life on December 14, 2021, aged 93

KEITH VAN ANDERSON

———————•———————

Long-serving Lord's steward and obsessive fan who became a cult figure at the home of cricket

Growing up in poverty in Guyana, Keith van Anderson climbed coconut trees to watch games of cricket. In the last years of his life he could be found in the members' enclosure at Lord's, dressed in Marylebone Cricket Club's natty livery. His bow tie, the handkerchief in the pocket of his blazer and the band around his panama hat all displayed the club's red and yellow.

To his fellow members he was known simply as "the Pipeman", on account of the implement that hung permanently from his mouth, even though he had long given up smoking it. His passion for the sport, together with this distinctive outfit, made him as cherished a part of the experience at the greatest of all cricket grounds as the Old Father Time weather vane and the futuristic media centre.

Van Anderson had the proud distinction of having attended every Test match at Lord's since watching his beloved West Indies thrash England by an innings and 226 runs in 1973. He was overjoyed to see them win further series in 1976, 1980, 1984 and 1988. Fired by the ferocious fast bowling of Michael Holding, Andy Roberts, Joel Garner and Malcolm Marshall, West Indies humbled England on every tour. His favourite memory was the Lord's Test of 1984, when England looked favourites to pull off an unlikely triumph, but on the final day West Indies bludgeoned 344 runs to snatch victory.

Van Anderson was usually a laconic man, but his bass West Indian accent would get louder as he waxed lyrical about the sport. Many players found that a chat with van Anderson, who was for many years steward at Lord's, helped to calm their nerves in the moments before the start of a Test. Hearing of his death, several players tweeted tributes. Stuart Broad, the England fast bowler, simply said, "Ahh no. Top man."

Keith van Anderson was born in the Caribbean country of Guyana in 1951. Money was so tight while he was growing up that eggs were a luxury – he got to eat one a week – and his parents moved to Britain in search of a better life.

His father, Charles, found work as a carpenter and his mother, Gwendolyn, née McGregor, as a machinist. Van Anderson arrived to join them on October 30, 1964, at the age of 13. It was a cold day and he recalled his wonderment at being able to see water vapour as he exhaled. "I thought it was smoke," he recalled. Other new experiences included seeing chimneys billowing smoke and White people doing menial work, sweeping the streets and serving on market stalls. Until then the only White people he had seen were the privileged colonial types he had glimpsed in Guyana.

The family settled in east London, where he attended Upton School in Clapton and showed some promise as an offspin bowler and top-order batsman. After leaving school he found a job with the Greater London Council, where he would remain for many years. He ended his career as a finance manager in charge of housing projects.

Although cricket was his passion, he could afford to attend only the occasional game, so at a friend's suggestion he became a steward. "To be able to watch free of charge was fantastic," he said. Not long afterwards he married Dolores Redman, a nurse. She survives him, as do his four children.

In the summer months he would leave the house early to catch a morning game, carrying a bag full of food that he had cooked the night before, along with a flask of tea and a bible. He would spend hours after a game bantering over several beers in Bowlers, the bar at Lord's. But back at home in east London any thoughts of square cuts, googlies, bouncers or cover drives were banished. When the door closed it was strictly family time.

Van Anderson would help to prepare the Lord's ground two days before a Test match, and also started to make friends with the players. Clive Lloyd, then captain of West Indies, became godfather to van Anderson's daughter, Karel. Lloyd also sponsored his friend's application to become a member of MCC in 1980. Van Anderson joined the waiting list and 18 years later finally received his membership card. He said that he valued it more than his passport, which is unsurprising, given that he spent all his available holidays at the ground.

His proud record of Test-match attendance was four times threatened by cancer. In 2003 he absconded from hospital so he could watch England play Zimbabwe at Lord's. In 2014, while being treated for oesophageal cancer, "I somehow got out of hospital on the third day".

An assortment of pills was added to his bag of supplies. After the first diagnosis of cancer he stopped smoking his pipe. However, his trademark remained firmly attached to his lips as he avidly watched many more Test matches at his spiritual home.

Keith "the Pipeman" van Anderson, cricket enthusiast, was born on June 7, 1951. He died of oesophageal cancer on May 15, 2019, aged 67

RUARAIDH HILLEARY

———————— ● ————————

Idiosyncratic Scottish adventurer and soldier

Paddling in a dug-out canoe down the Zambezi in 1948, Ruaraidh Hilleary and his companion found themselves menaced by herds of semi-submerged hippopotamuses. The animals threatened to swim under the canoe and tip them into waters where crocodiles lurked. As they neared each group, Hilleary discharged his Colt .45 into the water, not aiming at the beasts but hoping to discourage them. By the time they had reached their destination, five dead hippos had floated under the Kariba bridge and the authorities had been alerted. A policeman arrived to administer a large fine, only for the two travellers to throw him in the river and run.

Hilleary sold the skins of six crocodiles shot on the trip for £5 each in Livingstone. Back in London, his friend Algy Asprey said his luxury goods firm would have paid £1 per square inch for them. As a commercial venture, the expedition accurately prefaced his career, which was to be one of mixed fortunes in business but never lacking in enterprise, variety or adventure.

While in Africa, Hilleary heard that a girlfriend with whom he was besotted was to marry the brother of Rory Fraser, his Zambezi companion. He determined to return home to persuade her to join him in Rhodesia instead, where he hoped to farm. Waiting to embark on the pier at Cape Town, his resolution wavered when he fell into conversation with the skipper of a whaler, who offered him a job as a harpoon gunner. He was sorely tempted but the toss of a coin settled it and he sailed home. Alas for him, the voyage was too long and he was too late to scupper the wedding.

In London, Hilleary accepted a job from his uncle, who had started the White Heather Laundry. He soon realised he was not cut out to be a laundryman. In a moment of boredom, he climbed the imposing laundry chimney, supposedly an impossible feat, and balanced on top, to the consternation of onlookers. At that time he had become engaged to his eventual wife, Sheena Mackintosh. When his future mother-in-law remarked how nice it was that Hilleary had a job in the family firm, his father was forced to reply, "Well, I'm afraid he was sacked this morning."

Ruaraidh Hilleary was born in 1926 at Bridge of Allan, but his true home was the Isle of Skye. His mother's side of the family owned an estate and a mansion there, paid for by a fortune made selling whisky into prohibition America. His father, Iain, also worked in the whisky trade.

At his much-disliked prep school, Sandroyd, Hilleary engineered dismissal by breaking the nose of a prefect. At Eton, his unruliness led to him being thrashed almost fortnightly. He recalled his housemaster "Bloody Bill" Marsden as "probably a sadist but he saved my bacon because he used to beat me instead of sacking me". About this time Hilleary developed his guiding philosophy in life of "don't get caught".

He was commissioned into the Scots Guards in February 1945 but, to his chagrin, was "just too late to get a shot at the enemy". In 1950 he enlisted instead as a territorial in a regiment better suited to his temperament. Joining B Squadron 21 SAS, he was recommissioned a year later and in 1960 he helped to set up D Squadron 23 SAS at Invergowrie, Scotland's first SAS unit.

Hilleary's protean and buccaneering business career included running a caravan park at Lossiemouth with a nightclub in a cave; selling wine in the Highlands, insurance in London, cashmere in

Spain, cutlery in Rhodesia; and a game dealership. Family skiing holidays were financed by Hilleary driving a vanload of smoked salmon to sell to Alpine hotels. He made his first Cresta Run in St Moritz aged 54 when he broke the record for over-fifties.

In 1952 he married Mackintosh, an Olympic skier and the couple had four children.

As the owner of Edinbane, a 1,500-acre crofted estate on Skye, Hilleary engaged productively with the crofters, setting up the island's first wind farm. He served 45 years as honorary secretary of the Skye Gathering and one year arranged for a troop of Masai warriors to come and dance a foursome at it.

A man who swore by "a damn good grouse or lobster for supper and beer for breakfast", not much could rattle Hilleary, an irrepressible character with an ever-present twinkle in his eye. Taking his sons stalking on the Sleat peninsula, for example, he found himself marooned by a failed rendezvous with a boat. Instead, they spent an agreeable night inside the gralloched bodies of the stags that they had shot and cooked their livers for supper.

He was less amused when disaster struck during his Dance of the Sugar Plum Fairy at a theatrical revue staged for friends. With a rope attached to his substantial frame, Hilleary launched from a ladder and swooped across the stage. The rope was too short, however, and he swung awkwardly for some time, unable to touch down, and offering ample proof that under his tutu he was a true Scotsman.

Ruaraidh Hilleary, soldier and adventurer, was born on February 8, 1926. He died peacefully on February 16, 2021, aged 95

RICHARD COLE

———————•———————

Tour manager for Led Zeppelin and hell-raiser extraordinaire whose behaviour managed to be even more debauched than the band's

The Continental Hyatt House on Sunset Strip in Los Angeles came to be known in rock'n'roll mythology as "the Riot House". This was in no small measure due to the assiduous efforts of Richard Cole, Led Zeppelin's tour manager.

In 1973, for example, Cole drove a motorcycle through the hotel lobby and into the lift, taking the machine up to the ninth floor, where the band was partying hard. They spent the rest of the night racing it up and down the hotel's corridors. What guests on other floors thought about this, history does not relate.

Cole's problem was that he not only organised the hell-raising for his employers to enjoy, but was frequently its most enthusiastic participant. Instead of seeking to curb the band's destructive tendencies, which famously involved throwing television sets out of high-rise windows, he was instrumental in egging them on.

When the band was on tour in Japan, Cole bought two Samurai swords, which he and the drummer, John "Bonzo" Bonham, used to chop down the door of the bassist, John Paul Jones, at the Tokyo Hilton. They then carried the semicomatose Jones into the corridor and chopped everything in the room into splinters. As a result, the entire group was banned from the Hilton chain for life.

Rather than hiring private jets they travelled on the Starship, a Boeing 720B acquired for the band by Cole and customised with a waterbed and faux fur bedspread for entertaining.

While the band were on stage playing some of the most ferocious rock'n'roll ever created, Cole would be behind the scenes organising the after-show sex and drugs. As part of his roadie remit, it was his duty to procure the groupies for band members and keep them "nourished" with copious supplies of their favoured narcotics: marijuana, cocaine and later heroin. In this way, in the days before the #MeToo movement and government warnings about the need to avoid the "glamorisation" of drug use, Cole helped Led Zeppelin to acquire a reputation as perhaps the most debauched rock band of them all.

"We were hot and on our way up and nobody was watching too closely," he recalled. "All the Led Zeppelin depravity took place in an alcoholic fog. We found ourselves in a position to do almost anything we wanted and there seemed to be a tidal wave of free-spirited groupies who were always co-operative."

Cole was the ringleader in perhaps the most notorious tale in the annals of rock'n'roll folklore. It occurred when Led Zeppelin were playing in Seattle in 1969 and Cole and Bruce Wayne, road manager for the support act Vanilla Fudge, caught some mud sharks and red snappers while fishing from a waterfront room at the Edgewater Inn, where both groups were staying.

They brought their catch to Jones's room, where the Led Zeppelin bassist was hanging out with the Vanilla Fudge drummer Carmine Appice and a 17-year-old groupie named Jackie. Versions vary as to what indecorous things happened next, but most authorities agree that: the mud sharks and red snappers were involved; Jackie took off her clothes; events got out of hand.

"Things got pretty intense, so we went out into the hall, where Bonzo and his wife, Pat, joined us, and we watched the action through the door," Appice recalled in Bob Spitz's 2021 book *Led Zeppelin: The Biography.*

As events got even more bizarre, other voyeurs arrived. "We were invited to take a look but after a while we left because it was all a bit unsavoury," Robert Plant, the Led Zeppelin lead singer, recalled. The incident was later chronicled in a song by Frank Zappa.

It was also Cole who introduced members of the band to heroin. On a stopover in Hong Kong on the way back from a tour of Japan, he was instructed to score some cocaine for the group. When he could only get hold of some heroin, he didn't bother explaining the difference and several members of the group soon developed a taste for it. "No one ever talked about the possible risks," Cole later said. The heroin simply "seemed to make the time pass more quickly" during the long periods of ennui on tour.

In the end, Cole's own excesses grew too much even for the hard-living Led Zeppelin. "We were all out of control, including myself," he admitted.

By 1980 he had a ruinous heroin habit and Led Zeppelin's manager, Peter Grant, fired him. Sent to a rehabilitation centre in Italy, Cole was arrested on arrival on suspicion of being involved in a plot to blow up Bologna railway station and spent weeks in prison before his innocence was established. He was still in prison when he was given the news that Bonham, his partner in so many on-the-road crimes, had died. The coroner found he had drunk the equivalent of 40 measures of vodka.

Much of Led Zeppelin's excess might have remained secret had Cole not broken the cardinal rule of rock'n'roll that "what happens on tour, stays on tour".

Short of money, he was the main source for Stephen Davis's controversial 1985 biography *Hammer of the Gods* and his erstwhile employers made clear their sense of betrayal. "These stories would filter out from girls who'd supposedly been in my room when in fact they'd been in his," Plant complained to *Melody Maker*. "A lot of the time he wasn't completely well and so his view of things was permanently distorted."

In 1992 Cole followed with his own book, *Stairway to Heaven: Led Zeppelin Uncensored*, billed as a "close-up, down-and-dirty, no-holds-barred account". Jimmy Page, the band's lead guitarist, declared that he felt "completely ill" when he read extracts from it. However, much as some of Cole's taller tales were disputed, he was never sued. "It would be so painful that it wouldn't be worth it," Page reasoned.

There is also no doubt that when he was straight and sober, Cole was not only hugely loyal but a brilliant fixer. When Plant and his wife had a near-fatal car crash in Greece in 1975, it was Cole who organised to have them airlifted to London for surgery. Later when Plant received the news on tour that his five-year-old son Karac had died, it was again Cole to whom he turned and who took charge of the arrangements.

Ultimately such personal ties transcended the standard employer and employee relationship. Despite the bitterness caused by his revelations, in recent years Cole was invited as a VIP guest to official Led Zeppelin film and book launches and to the 2007 reunion concert at which the band performed in public for the first time since Live Aid. Plant also visited him in hospital towards the end of his life.

Richard Cole was born in 1946 in Kensal Rise, north London, the son of a Rolls-Royce engineer who was involved in the development of the Merlin engine, which powered the Royal Air Force in the Second World War.

He left school at 15 to work in a dairy, and used his earnings to buy a drum kit, inspired by the jazz recordings of Buddy Rich. A host of blue-collar jobs followed, including as a sheet-metal worker and a scaffolder.

A chance meeting in 1965 at a gig at the Marquee Club led to him becoming the road manager for Unit 4 + 2, who topped the charts with *Concrete and Clay*. He moved on to work with the New Vaudeville Band and the Who, recalling a road trip with the homemade-bomb-obsessed Keith Moon in which he went to fetch weedkiller and sugar.

By the time Led Zeppelin formed in late 1968 and undertook their first American tour, Cole had moved to Los Angeles and was an obvious choice when Grant was looking for a road manager.

Cole's taste for danger and his determination that "the show must go on" were evident from the outset. On Led Zeppelin's first tour, he drove the band from a gig in Oregon through blizzards in an attempt to reach Seattle to take a flight to Los Angeles. The weather grew so bad that the roads were officially closed; Cole was pulled over by state police and ordered to stop the journey. He drove on regardless, over treacherous mountain passes and swaying suspension bridges, and both Plant and Bonham were convinced they were going to die. His intrepidity was in vain: when they arrived in Seattle, the weather had shut the airport.

He later cleaned up his act and went on to work as a road manager for Black Sabbath, Eric Clapton and a number of other acts before retiring from the music business in 2003.

After the years of mayhem he learnt to value his privacy. He was thought to have married twice, once to Marilyn Woolhead, a "Bunny girl", in 1974, and eventually became a stable family man, dividing his time between London and Los Angeles. He is survived by his daughter Claire.

If he counted himself lucky to have been around Led Zeppelin in their pomp to enjoy rock'n'roll hedonism at its most rampant, he was even more grateful to have survived to tell his rambunctious tales.

Richard Cole, Led Zeppelin roadie, was born on January 2, 1946. He died after a long illness on December 2, 2021, aged 75

ARDESHIR ZAHEDI

Flamboyant Iranian ambassador to the US whose lavish, often decadent, soirées were popular with Washington's social elite

Ardeshir Zahedi, left, with Barbara Streisand and Jon Peters in 1975.

Flamboyant and charismatic, Ardeshir Zahedi was known in Washington's circles of power as "the playboy of the western world".

As the Shah's ambassador to the US, his parties at the Iranian embassy were as glittering as anything the capital had to offer. He entertained not only presidents, senators, diplomats and businessmen but the likes of Jacqueline Kennedy Onassis, Liza Minnelli, Barbra Streisand, Frank Sinatra, Andy Warhol and Elizabeth Taylor, with whom he had a whirlwind romance.

After Taylor had separated from her husband, Richard Burton, Zahedi moved her into the embassy's royal suite, escorted her to the premiere of her 1976 movie *The Blue Bird*, and invited her to join him on a holiday in Iran.

There were rumours of marriage but in the end the trip to Tehran was cancelled and the romance stalled. It was said that the Shah, who was not only Zahedi's boss but his former father-in-law, had objected to the prospect of his ambassador marrying a Jew, albeit a converted one.

The ambitious Zahedi was never going to disobey his ruler. His diplomatic papers, which are archived at Stanford University, show that he addressed the Shah as "the Shadow of my God" and habitually concluded his ambassador's reports by offering "to kiss your royal feet a thousand times".

Doris Lilly, who for many years wrote a high society gossip column for the *New York Post* and was a frequent guest at Zahedi's parties, called him "a terrific charmer" who "flirted outrageously with everyone".

In her memoirs, Barbara Walters wrote that Zahedi ran "the number one embassy when it came to extravagance", holding lavish soirées in a palatial, four-storey, 46-room Georgian-style brick mansion with terraced gardens on Massachusetts Avenue. The jewel in this architectural crown was the Persian Room, with an enormous domed ceiling "encrusted with a kaleidoscope of mirrored mosaics, glittering medallions and tendrils cascading 30ft down the walls".

In 1977 alone, the official record shows that Zahedi hosted more than 7,000 guests for social events at the embassy. *People* magazine called him "the Sun King of the capital social whirl". An invitation to one of his embassy bashes was "a mark of social acceptance in Washington", wrote Kitty Kelley, author of biographies of Nancy Reagan and Taylor. "Always there were music and feasts. Sometimes there were belly dancers, hashish and pornographic movies."

Sally Quinn of *The Washington Post* recalled "more caviar than you could eat" and "dancing on tables". There were also conga lines, kissing games and an endless flow of alcohol. His favourite tipple was Dom Pérignon and, after the overthrow of the Shah when representatives of the new Islamic republic under Ayatollah Khomeini occupied the building, they uncorked more than 43,000 bottles of champagne, Scotch, vodka, vermouth, gin and wine from the ambassadorial cellar, and in keeping with Iran's new prohibitions on alcohol, poured them down the drain of a fountain in the embassy's backyard. It reportedly took four hours to dispose of all the alcohol.

After the Shah's downfall in 1979, Zahedi was sentenced to death back home and fled into exile in Switzerland. He was also investigated by the FBI over improper gifts and payments to public officials and it was alleged that he had a slush fund of $25,000 a month with which he showered tins of beluga caviar and fine Persian rugs on those whose favours he sought.

He knew eight American presidents, from Truman to George Bush Sr, and on his watch Iran sold vast amounts of oil to the US and in return purchased billions of dollars' worth of arms to become America's largest customer for military equipment. Yet despite the allegations of corruption, Zahedi was never indicted.

He remained loyal to the Shah, tried to negotiate asylum for him variously in Panama, Mexico and Morocco, and was by his side when he died in Egypt in 1980. However, he was not entirely hostile to the new regime in Tehran and was a defender of the country's nuclear programme.

He lived the rest of his life in a villa in Montreux, making occasional political interventions to lament the breakdown of relations between Washington and Tehran. He was particularly critical of President Trump's threats against Iran, which he described as "a pressure tactic wrapped in bellicosity folded inside a chimera".

He is survived by his daughter, Princess Zahra Mahnaz Zahedi, from his marriage to Shahnaz Pahlavi, the Shah's daughter. They met in 1954 when she was 14, married three years later and divorced in 1964.

Ardeshir Zahedi was born in Tehran in 1928, the son of General Fazlollah Zahedi and Khadijeh Pirnia, whose father and brother both served as prime ministers of Iran.

His parents separated when he was a boy and his father was imprisoned during the Second World War by the British on suspicion of being a Nazi sympathiser. He later became prime minister of Iran in the British-and-American-backed coup of 1953, replacing Mohammad Mossadegh. After the war, Zahedi finished his education abroad, studying in Beirut and Utah State University, from where he graduated in 1950 with a degree in agricultural engineering.

He supported his father in the 1953 coup and having first met and befriended the Shah in America several years earlier, he was well placed to act as a courier between monarch and prime minister.

He was 32 when the Shah sent him to Washington as ambassador in 1960. When he protested that he had no understanding of diplomacy, the Shah reassured him. "I am personally in charge of foreign policy and since you have studied in America, you know America and the Americans quite well."

Zahedi proceeded to get into a war with US-based dissident Iranian students and fell out with the Kennedy administration. After two years he was reposted as ambassador to Britain, where he spent four years enjoying everything "swinging London" had to offer.

Back in Tehran he served as foreign minister to the Shah before he returned to Washington in 1973 to a warm welcome from President Nixon, whom he had known since the early 1950s.

Over the next six years he tore up the template of the discreet, buttoned-up diplomat, turning himself into a celebrity and Iran into a splashy luxury brand, which blinded President Carter's White House to the revolution that was fomenting back in Tehran.

The result was disastrous for US foreign policy and contributed to Carter's election defeat by Ronald Reagan, after militants took over the embassy in Tehran and held 52 US diplomats and citizens hostage.

For Zahedi the rupture between America and Iran was a shattering blow but he kept up his attempts to reconcile them until the end. "It is in their interest to pursue a new and constructive approach in their relations and prove their sincerity," he wrote shortly before his death.

Ardeshir Zahedi, diplomat, was born on October 16, 1928. He died after a prolonged illness that included Covid-19 and pneumonia on November 18, 2021, aged 93

SIR JEREMIAH HARMAN

Rude and erratic judge who kicked a taxi driver and had not heard of Gazza

Known in legal circles as "Harman the Horrible", Sir Jeremiah Harman had what psychologists might call "an unfortunate manner". He was one of the most unpopular judges of his day and several polls of the legal profession labelled him the worst judge on the High Court bench, his critics complaining that he was rude, lazy, short-tempered, unpredictable and completely out of touch.

Harman's infamy was by no means confined to the legal community. In 1990, months after Paul Gascoigne's tears in the World Cup finals had made the England footballer a national hero, Harman attracted headlines when he asked, "Who is Gazza?" In 1991 he refused to apologise for kicking a taxi driver in full view of TV and newspaper cameramen, an event that earned him the epithet "the kicking judge".

If his notoriety bothered him, Harman never showed it. He was not entirely lacking in self-awareness and seemed at times almost to relish his bad reputation. However, there was some criticism even he could not ignore and in 1998 he was left with little option but to resign after an unprecedented attack from the Court of Appeal over his delay in delivering a judgment.

Jeremiah LeRoy Harman was born in Kensington in 1930, the son of Helen LeRoy Harman (née Lewis) and Sir Charles Harman, a judge of the Court of Appeal. After attending Horris Hill School and Eton College, Harman joined the Coldstream Guards in 1948 then moved on to the Parachute Regiment. In 1954 he completed his legal studies and was called to the Bar. Specialising in Chancery work, he practised from 9 Old Square, Lincoln's Inn, the chambers that was also to produce Lord Hoffmann, one of the most popular and user-friendly judges for many years. In due course, Harman gained a reputation as an outstanding, but extremely aggressive, advocate who sometimes antagonised opponents through his win-at-all-costs attitude. This willingness to go for the jugular set Harman apart from most of his colleagues at the Chancery Bar, which to this day retains a reputation for gentlemanly behaviour. It also guaranteed him a steady flow of work.

After taking silk in 1968 Harman notched some notable successes. In *Re Bond Worth* (1980), a case that became an authority on retention of title in goods, he successfully imported Chancery concepts into the commercial arena. In *Birkett v James* (1978) he turned around a seemingly hopeless position and helped to create another seminal authority, this time that the court should not dismiss proceedings for want of prosecution (that a claimant had allowed an issued action to become dormant). In 1982 he followed his father on to the bench, joining the High Court's Chancery Division.

Harman was married to Helen Wharton between 1955 and 1958. In 1960 he married Erica, née Bridgeman. They divorced in 1986. He is survived by their three children: Sarah, a barrister; Charles, a garden designer; and Toby, who works in IT. In 1987 he married Kate Pulay, widow of the journalist George Pulay. Like her husband, she was a barrister with legal ancestry. Her father was Sir Eric Sachs, a judge in the Family Division of the High Court, and her grandfather was Lord Goddard, former lord chief justice. She died in 2002.

As a pillar of the legal establishment, Harman would not have enjoyed seeing details of his divorce and remarriage splashed across newspapers. Before long, however, the judge's increasingly bizarre behaviour left him wide open to attack from the press.

In 1988 Harman was challenged by *The Observer* to explain why he had taken more than two years to give judgment in a case involving the American oil company Union Texas. Not only did he fail to give a reason, but he could also not tell the newspaper when he planned to make his decision. Two years later Harman was asked to grant an injunction halting the publication of an unauthorised biography of Gascoigne entitled *Gazza*.

When Gascoigne's lawyer declared that his client was a very well-known footballer, Harman asked, "Rugby or association football?" Ever the eccentric, he later queried whether Gascoigne was more famous than the Duke of Wellington had been in 1815. In the end he refused to grant the injunction on the basis that the name "Gazza" was not sufficiently well known. He had initially thought Gazza was an opera. In later trials he admitted that he had never heard of Bruce Springsteen, UB40 or, at the height of their fame, Oasis.

A darker side to Harman's character was displayed in December 1991, when he was hearing an appeal by Kevin Maxwell against the confiscation of his passport. Annoyed by the presence of journalists outside his west London home, Harman lashed out, kicking a man in the groin. It transpired that the victim was the taxi driver who had come to collect him. Far from apologising, Harman insisted: "I would not recommend what I did to anyone, but it was necessary."

Harman made himself unpopular with many of the lawyers who used his court. Few relished appearing before a judge who sometimes displayed wild mood swings, quickly lost patience with junior barristers and showed little respect for solicitors and their clients. He seemed to enjoy making life as difficult as possible, often displaying a pedantic enthusiasm for rules.

Some said he could be a bully and was particularly hard on women, regularly admonishing female barristers for not tucking their hair completely behind their wigs. On one occasion, when a witness asked to be referred to as Ms, he proclaimed: "I've always thought there were only three kinds of women: wives, whores and mistresses. Which are you?"

Harman's erratic conduct caused many barristers and solicitors to lose confidence in him as a judge. Some complained that he leapt to conclusions long before he had heard all the evidence. Others protested that he would take a dislike to people because of their appearance or background. Certainly, some lawyers with foreign clients were extremely reluctant to have their cases heard by him.

The one criticism that was never made of Harman was that he lacked intellectual ability. Indeed, on his day Harman could be an outstanding judge. The trick was to give him a case that held his interest. All too often, however, he would get bored and fall back into bad habits. This was because Harman lacked one of the most important attributes of a good judge – patience – although his list of hobbies in *Who's Who* (fishing, birdwatching and reading) appeared to show him to be a man capable of that virtue.

Despite all the bad press Harman was never officially disciplined, successive Lord Chancellors maintaining the principle that the independence of the judiciary was sacrosanct. But it is possible he was given one or two private warnings.

However, in February 1998 Harman had no option but to fall on his sword after Lord Justice Gibson, Lord Justice Brooke and Lord Justice Mummery criticised his performance in *Goose v Wilson Sandford*, a negligence claim by a Lincolnshire farmer against a firm of accountants. Despite frequent requests from Goose's barrister, the parties had to wait 20 months for a judgment from Harman, who managed to lose his trial notes in the interim, though it later emerged that he had been undergoing medical treatment.

Ordering a retrial, the three Court of Appeal judges declared: "Conduct like this weakens public confidence in the whole judicial process. Left unchecked, it would be ultimately subversive of the rule of law. Delays on this scale cannot and will not be tolerated. A situation like this must never occur again." Given the senior judiciary's penchant for understatement, this was extremely strong criticism.

At a time when the rest of the senior judiciary was trying to improve the bench's public image, Harman had let the side down again and again. His unworldly ways, bad manners, and refusal to curb the worst excesses of his capricious personality had served to reinforce an image that has burdened the High Court's Chancery Division since the publication of Charles Dickens's *Bleak House*. The reign of "Harman the Horrible" was over.

Sir Jeremiah Harman, High Court judge, was born on April 13, 1930. He died of cancer on March 7, 2021, aged 90

NEXHMIJE HOXHA

———————•———————

*Formidable wife of the Albanian dictator who was known as Lady
Macbeth and insisted all foreigners shave their beards*

The world of Cold War communist dictatorships was overwhelmingly
male-dominated. Yet within some regimes were women who, often
married to the dictators themselves, played a significant role in their
countries' life. Examples including Madame Mao or Margot Honecker in
East Germany have received some attention. Elena Ceausescu,
meanwhile, was executed by firing squad next to her husband.

Yet almost completely unknown outside her hugely isolated
country was Nexhmije Hoxha, wife of Enver Hoxha who ruthlessly
ruled Albania for several decades.

Unlike some first ladies, Hoxha was not content to remain
unheard. She served in several key roles in the Albanian Communist
Party's dominant institutions. Some idealism was evident. She
promoted the cause of women's education in a terribly underdeveloped
country. Yet there was a menacing side to this chilly, twinset-wearing
woman with the scraped-back hair. Not for nothing was she known as
the "Lady Macbeth of Albania". Described as the only person her
famously paranoid husband could trust, she joined in the persecution
of his opponents through purges and show trials and attempted to
retain a grip on power after his death in 1985.

After the final overthrow of the communist regime in 1991 she
was convicted on charges of corruption and served several years in
prison. But she showed no sign of repentance for her actions nor for
the catastrophic effects of communist rule.

Hoxha's bond with her husband emerged from their shared
experience of wartime. She was born Nexhmije Xhuglini in 1921 in
Bitola, now part of North Macedonia, but later moved with her parents
to the Albanian capital, Tirana. While training as a schoolteacher she
had joined the Albanian Communists in 1941 and through them
became involved in resistance against the occupation of Albania, first
by Mussolini's Italy and later, after Italy's capitulation, by the Nazis.
The National Liberation Army in which she served was communist-led

and its backers included Special Operations Executive forces sent by Britain. As the war moved towards its end in 1945 she married another ambitious young member of the communist resistance, Enver Hoxha, and joined him in securing prominent positions in the party as it moved to monopolise political power.

She led the Albanian Women's League and by the mid-1960s had become head of the party's Institute of Marxist-Leninist Studies, a keeper of the flame of ideological purity and propaganda efforts. She was also a member of the party's centre of power, the central committee, for several decades.

That kind of career required considerable ideological flexibility as Albania moved through a bewilderingly varied set of international alliances. First there was adulation of the Stalinist Soviet Union and hostility towards the western powers seeking to depose the Hoxha regime in the early Cold War period. A break with Moscow came in the 1960s after which Albania aligned itself with China, seeking to emulate Mao's cultural revolution. Religion in Albania was officially banned, with one cathedral turned ostentatiously into a basketball court. Norman Wisdom's films were almost the only ones by western actors that were permitted, and the slapstick British comedian became, in consequence, revered as if he were a matinee idol. The bonkers behaviour did not end there: Mrs Hoxha decreed that all foreign men entering the country had to have their moustaches and beards shaved off by customs officials.

When relations with China soured after its rapprochement with President Nixon's America, the regime retreated into an extraordinary self-imposed isolation ruled by the elite around Hoxha and backed by the Sigurimi secret police. Its symbol was the building of hundreds of thousands of concrete bunkers in a country with a population of only about three million. The bunkers, many still visible today, were supposedly designed to protect against attack by what the regime saw as its many enemies. Yet the huge futile construction effort merely added to the dire state of the Albanian economy under isolationist communist rule.

For Hoxha and her family, however, there was little sense of poverty as they enjoyed life at the apex of a privileged elite with access to foreign goods never seen by most of Albania's population. The Hoxhas had three children: two sons, Ilir and Sokol, who were said to make a living characteristic of the elite mixing "business and politics", and a daughter, Pranvera, who trained as an architect and used her skills to design the Enver Hoxha Pyramid in Tirana, the county's capital city, of which Norman Wisdom had been granted the freedom.

The family's privileges extended to some 25 fridges and TV sets as well as access to American cigarettes, French wine, Italian salami and foreign doctors to treat Enver's poor health. He suffered a first heart attack in the 1970s and Hoxha took great care to control access to her ailing husband while attempting to plan a succession favourable to her own political ambitions. Potential rivals were purged and their families often persecuted too with Hoxha's active approval, a practice that continued after Enver's death in 1985. Nexhmije was seen at his huge state funeral stroking the golden letters around his memorial in the National Martyrs' Cemetery.

She was prominent among the Albanian Communist diehards who thought they could somehow defy the wave of popular hostility towards communism sweeping over eastern and central Europe from 1989. After the Albanian regime was finally toppled she was arrested and put on trial, not for her alleged involvement in human rights violations but on a lesser charge of corrupt use of public funds.

Unabashed by her reputation, after she was jailed in 1993 there was no contrition. "I am innocent. They are mistaken," she stated. "We wanted nothing but the wellbeing of the country." In prison she read voraciously but complained that her only international news source was BBC broadcasts in Albanian.

After her release she lived quietly with family members in a Tirana suburb. She supported a tiny party, the Enverists, which believed it could somehow revive the spirit of her husband's regime.

Ever keen to quarantine herself from unwelcome reality she insisted in a rare interview: "I do not regret anything, and there's nothing I should feel guilty for. I continue to have faith in the communist ideal that will never die."

Around her, meanwhile, Albania embarked on the long road to recovery from the condition that decades of Hoxha rule had left it in.

Nexhmije Hoxha, Albanian communist, was born on February 8, 1921. She died on February 26, 2020, aged 99

BRIGADIER CHARLES RITCHIE

———————— • ————————

Seemingly indestructible army officer who survived sharks, the IRA,
cyanide, the Stasi and even a duel with shotguns

Charles Ritchie's military career almost ended before it began when he challenged a fellow cadet at Sandhurst to a duel with shotguns. The cause of the Scotsman's ire was a friend's legerdemain in depriving him of an attractive woman's company at a party.

The cadets' agreement had been for the friend to collect two female guests before picking up Ritchie at his billet and going on to the party together, but when the friend's date cancelled, he told the other girl that Ritchie had become indisposed and took her to the party himself. Having waited, pacing up and down for several hours, dressed and primed for action, Ritchie's solitary pre-party drinks session turned sour, and he went to bed.

Roused at 2am by the raucous return of his friend, who hesitantly gave a full confession of his conduct, Ritchie said: "You contemptible bastard, I am challenging you to a duel! Firearms, at dawn, with seconds in attendance." The appointment was postponed until after lunch and it was decided that each party would take alternate shots, starting at a distance of 75 yards, advancing one yard after each shot, until blood was drawn. Tweed caps and bowed heads would offer some protection to the eyes. In the event the pair walked, shooting at each other in turn with pellets stinging their bare arms until at about 50 yards his opponent charged, yelling a war cry and shooting from the hip, drawing blood from Ritchie's arm. The friend claimed victory, but Ritchie was not satisfied, ambushing him and firing over his head as they returned to the lines. A company sergeant-major predicted their ejection from Sandhurst, but the duel resulted only in a dressing-down and a lasting reputation for being a swashbuckler.

The escapade characterised the luck and derring-do of an incident-prone life during which Ritchie survived encounters with sharks, tribesmen, the IRA and even his own men, as well as arrest by the Russians for espionage. It also showed the passion for drama of a frustrated actor who would go on to mobilise his extrovert's charm to defuse tensions in hostile environments ranging from Libya to the Edinburgh Military Tattoo. Living according to his motto that "laughter is the best weapon", the title of his posthumously published memoir, he was a fine raconteur in the military mould.

Soon after passing out from Sandhurst in the mid-1960s, Ritchie had two scrapes with death while serving with the Royal Scots in the Radfan campaign in South Yemen. One afternoon he was sitting on a radio battery out in the open while taking an early supper when he came under sniper fire. He collapsed to the floor, thinking that he had been hit. After the firing stopped, he realised that he had not been wounded but the battery had taken a direct round.

He had another brush with death while clearing an empty house of bugs so that it could be used for shelter for his mortar section. He ordered a young soldier to "flash-burn" it – meaning laying a trickle of petrol inside its walls and lighting it – but the subordinate poured a 20-litre jerrycan over the floor and dropped a lit match through a window as Ritchie entered to inspect it. The explosion blew him back 30 yards into a cattle ring.

Badly burnt and apparently lifeless, he was given the last rites by a padre as he was lifted into a helicopter. A letter of condolence was sent to his parents in Scotland. Medics then realised that an overdose of morphia had sent him into a coma. He was discharged from hospital a few weeks later without any obvious signs of lasting damage.

Charles David Maciver Ritchie, the elder son of Lieutenant-Colonel Bill Ritchie of the Royal Scots, was born into a military family at Inverness in 1941. At Wellington College he wanted to be an actor, but a friend persuaded him to join the army.

In 1962 Ritchie was posted to the 1st Battalion in Libya, where he gallantly survived poisoning from a bunch of grapes which local Italian farmers had sprayed with hydrogen cyanide as a pesticide. Not long afterwards he emerged without significant harm from a helicopter crash on Salisbury Plain and shot a wolf with which he came face to face at the entrance to his tent during winter warfare training in Arctic Canada. He also swam unperturbed among venomous sea snakes and saltwater crocodiles off the coast of East Timor and fought off a shark in the waters of Belize.

His memoir modestly glossed over the achievements of a

distinguished army career. He was appointed Operations Officer with the British commanders-in-chief mission to the Soviet Forces in Germany in 1978. Suited to the game of "gentleman spying", his many cat-and-mouse escapades with the East German Stasi ended when, having spent all night in a ditch to photograph previously unseen Russian military equipment, he was captured by members of the Spetznatz (Russian special forces) while making his escape. He was formally expelled from East Germany and appointed an MBE. He was later advanced to CBE.

While an instructor at the Joint Services Staff College at Greenwich in 1984 he married Araminta Luard, who with their son, Paul, survives him. Araminta would in time become a veteran of his bardic tale-telling.

In the 1980s he commanded 3rd Battalion The Ulster Defence Regiment in Northern Ireland and was promoted to brigadier in 1988 at a time when his regiment was subject to increasing terrorist attacks off duty and claims of misconduct on duty.

The remainder of his army career was marked by a series of senior appointments, including national military representative at Shape, the Nato command centre in Belgium, and chief of staff to the UN Protection Force in the former Yugoslavia during one of the most bitter periods of the conflict.

Towards the end of his soldiering life he was appointed colonel of the Royal Scots and an aide-de-camp to the Queen. His final military job, military attaché in Paris, coincided with the death of Diana, Princess of Wales, and he broke protocol by draping her coffin with the Royal Standard, not the Union Flag. He went with his heart, he said, not his head.

His sense of duty and generous spirit won him many admirers throughout his life – even among his enemies. Before his Russian captors had ejected him from East Germany, they held a farewell party out of respect for "the mad Scotsman".

Brigadier Charles Ritchie, CBE, was born on December 12, 1941. He died after a short illness on December 16, 2020, aged 79

EVE BABITZ

———————•———————

*Artist, author and muse who wrote steamy autobiographical exposés of
life in the fast lane with Hollywood's leading men*

Eve Babitz was furious. Walter Hopps, her married lover, was
curating the 1963 Marcel Duchamp retrospective at Pasadena Art
Museum. Knowing his wife would be there, Hopps had not invited
Babitz to the preview. Later, when Julian Wasser, a photographer with
Time magazine, asked her to pose playing chess with Duchamp, Babitz
took her revenge: she was naked; Duchamp was not. The black-and-
white image, depicting the sitter contemplating her next move, has
since achieved folkloric status.

Babitz, who designed memorable album covers for Linda Ronstadt,
the Byrds and Buffalo Springfield, was well known for her lovers.
Harrison Ford would have sex with nine people a day, she said of the
unreliable carpenter in his pre-Hans Solo days. "Warren Beatty could
only manage six."

Many of her adventures were recorded in *Eve's Hollywood* (1974),
a "confessional novel" in the form of semi-autobiographical vignettes.
It was followed by *Slow Days, Fast Company: The World, The Flesh, and LA*
(1977), another memoir-described-as-fiction offering a guide to the
world of film stars, writers and lovers of ambiguous sexuality. Later
came *Sex and Rage: Advice to Young Ladies Eager for a Good Time* (1979).

Babitz ate muffins with Andy Warhol, drank chartreuse with
Salvador Dalí, dressed Steve Martin in his white suit, listened to
Dennis Hopper droning on about the *Easy Rider* screenplay, and had
an affair with Jim Morrison, describing their nocturnal adventures as
"like being in bed with Michelangelo's David, only with blue eyes". Earl
McGrath, president of Rolling Stones Records, once declared that "in
every young man's life there is an Eve Babitz", adding, "It's usually Eve
Babitz."

Eve Babitz was born in Hollywood in 1943, the daughter of Sol
Babitz, a Russian-Jewish violinist who worked with Stravinsky on *The
Soldier's Tale*, and his French-Cajun wife Lily Mae (née Laviolette), an
artist; she had a younger sister, Miriam, known as Mirandi, a designer,

334

who had a fling with Ringo Starr in 1964, when the Beatles played the Hollywood Bowl during their first American tour.

Home was a perpetual artistic salon: Stravinsky was her godfather, passing glasses of whisky under the table and slipping rose petals down her top ("very low-necked white, of course") during her 16th birthday party; Charlie Chaplin, Greta Garbo and Bertrand Russell came on family picnics; and Arnold Schoenberg roared with laughter when she got stuck to her sister with bubble gum during one of his premieres.

Young Eve was presented with a violin but drove her father crazy by playing out of tune. "I was a sinister child, lazy and cynical," she observed. She was 14 when a "spectacularly handsome man" was driving her home from a party when she revealed her age. "Don't let guys pick you up like this, kid, you might get hurt," he advised. Two years later he was found dead in Lana Turner's bathroom. On the day she left Hollywood High School she lost her virginity to a "serious composer".

Babitz took acting lessons with Corey Allen, who appeared in *Rebel Without a Cause* (1955), and moved to Europe, where her father was doing research on baroque music. To pass the time she "indulged myself in the huge, new, unbelievably diverse world of men who wanted to sleep with me" and wrote her first novel, *Travel Broadens*. She wrote a fan letter to Joseph Heller, author of *Catch-22*, that read: "I am a stacked 18-year-old blonde on Sunset Boulevard. I am also a writer." Impressed, he sent her work to his editor, who turned it down.

After the Duchamp episode she moved briefly to New York, working as a secretary on Madison Avenue. At 23 she appeared before the Senate juvenile delinquency subcommittee to propose creating a national park as a launching pad for "trips" with LSD, policed by Zen Buddhist monks instead of park rangers. As for marijuana, she told the committee: "It's not fattening, you don't get a hangover, it's not addictive – and, well, it's nicer." She soon returned to LA.

By the end of the 1960s Babitz was suffering from what Lili Anolik, her biographer, described as "squalid overboogie". She turned to writing, landing a gig at *Rolling Stone* magazine with a piece about her schooling. Annie Leibovitz, another of her lovers, shot the cover depicting Babitz wearing only a black bra and a white feather boa.

Life in the fast lane ended abruptly in 1997. Babitz was driving home from a party in her Volkswagen Beetle and lit a cherry-flavoured Tiparillo cigar. Ash fell on her clothing, which ignited, causing her third-degree burns. She was uninsured and friends, family and former lovers rallied to her aid, donating cash and auctioning works of art to cover her medical bills. Told the identity of some of her benefactors, she lifted her head and muttered an explicatory: "Blow jobs." She stopped writing and became a recluse, with only her cat and right-wing radio stations for company.

Anolik, then an unpublished writer, discovered Babitz's work in the late 2000s and tracked her down. She sent postcards, telephoned and even slid a note under the door of her rundown West Hollywood apartment, but to no avail. She began calling Babitz's circle and was eventually granted an audience. Her story appeared in *Vanity Fair* in 2014, jump-starting a Babitz revival. By the time Anolik's book, *Hollywood's Eve: Eve Babitz and the Secret History of LA* (2019), was published, the 75-year-old former hedonist was smelling what she called the "stench of success".

Yet Babitz, who never married and had no children, remained her own person. As for the infamous Duchamp picture, she recalled her father's advice: "Take his queen."

Eve Babitz, artist, author and muse, was born on May 13, 1943. She died of complications from Huntington's disease on December 17, 2021, aged 78

JAN MORRIS

Travel writer known for her gender reassignment, as well as 'the scoop of the century' for The Times

On the morning of the Queen's coronation in 1953, James Morris, a journalist with *The Times*, produced one of the most dramatic scoops of the 20th century. Edmund Hillary and Sherpa Tenzing Norgay, he revealed, had conquered Everest.

Morris, an Oxford graduate who had served five years as an officer in the Queen's Royal Lancers, had been picked to cover the Himalayan expedition partly because of his physical fitness. *The Times* had exclusive rights to dispatches written by the expedition leader, Colonel John Hunt, and Morris, in addition to reporting events, was responsible for getting the dispatches out of the mountains and on to London.

He was camped at nearly 22,000ft when the two climbers who made the final ascent, Hillary and Tenzing, came back down from the peak on May 31. It was late afternoon. There had been fresh snow and a thaw, and in the dwindling daylight the markers on the path were hard to see. Once he had made his way down to base camp, Morris typed out the brief message and handed it to Sherpa runners. They set out at first light for the British embassy in Kathmandu. From there it would be cabled back to London.

More recognisable to the modern journalist than this antiquated method of communication would have been the fear of being scooped by the competition. Morris had to guard against skulduggery that might divert his news out of the hands of the Sherpas and into the columns of rival newspapers. To this end he sent home code that had been prearranged with his editor at *The Times*. If the mountain was successfully scaled, the triumphant message would start with the innocent phrase "snow conditions bad", followed by a form of words that would indicate which members of the expedition had got to the top. The code for Hillary was "advanced base abandoned" and Sherpa Tenzing was "awaiting improvement"; that way, if the radio operator were co-opted by another newspaper, the story would remain safe.

"The news from Everest was to be mine," Morris said, "and anyone who tried to steal it from me should look out for trouble."

That scoop turned Morris from a jobbing foreign correspondent into an international celebrity. "The effect on my ego was disastrous," he said later. "I was 26 and sufficiently pleased with myself already."

But Morris was not only a gutsy reporter he – later she – was also, as the author of more than 50 books, one of the finest prose stylists in the English language, described by Rebecca West, no less, as "perhaps the best descriptive writer of our time". In 2008, indeed, Morris was listed 15th in the *Times* top 50 postwar British writers.

Running in parallel with this glittering literary career was a private life hard to chronicle in conventional terms. Though he had married and fathered five children, Morris claimed that since childhood he had been convinced he was, by rights, a woman. After a much-publicised gender reassignment in 1972, James became Jan. After that Jan Morris liked to joke that news of her death would be greeted with the headline "Sex-change author dies".

While it is true that the best-known of her books was the candid and autobiographical *Conundrum* (1974), which covered her gender reassignment operation, she was so much more than a "sex-change author". *Conundrum* wasn't even her best book. That, arguably, would be one of her volumes about "places": Oxford, Venice or Trieste. (She did not think of herself as a travel writer but rather a writer about places.)

James Humphrey Morris was born into an Anglo-Welsh family in Somerset in 1926. His early education included several years at the Christ Church choir school in Oxford. The choir school was followed by public school, Lancing, which he found "frightening", and he left early to join the army. A "smart" cavalry regiment suited him better, and when he served in the Middle East it recognised him as a good intelligence officer. "I have always admired military values," Morris reflected in later life. "Courage, dash, loyalty, self-discipline and I like the look of soldiering."

Incredibly – but this was the chaotic period at the end of the war when delightfully incredible things sometimes happened – military duty at one point included being in charge of boats on the canals of Venice. This was another city he fell in love with, and *Venice*, published in 1960 and never out of print, made his name as a writer about great cities.

If James was following on a well-trodden path of English romanticism in being ensnared by the charms of Venice, he had already moved down a similar path as a young soldier in becoming fascinated by all things Arabian. When he left the army, while waiting to go up to Oxford to a delayed university education, he worked for the Arab News Agency and reported the first motor crossing of the Oman desert. Journalism provided the discipline which he knew, as a born writer, was required if there was to be shape to his effervescent style.

After Everest his next big scoop, this time for the *Manchester Guardian,* came in 1956 when he found evidence of French involvement in Suez. He also covered the Adolf Eichmann trial in 1961, capturing in print "the banality of evil". "With his hands in his lap, blinking frequently and moving his lips," he wrote, "Eichmann reminded me irresistibly of some elderly pinched housewife in a flowered pinafore, leaning back on her antimacassar and shifting her false teeth, as she listened to the railing gossip of a neighbour."

After this Morris started on his most substantial work, a trilogy under the overall title *Pax Britannica,* tracing the British imperial dream from the start of Victoria's reign until the death of Churchill. He hoped it might read like what might have been written by a literate centurion recording what it felt like to be watching, from the field, as the Roman Empire moved from glory to decline. Modestly he once described *Pax Britannica* as "one big swagger".

The period in the late 1960s, which saw the Morris reputation grow internationally, also marked the start of the long process of gender reassignment. With the support of his wife, Elizabeth, James started on years of drug treatment to alter the body's hormonal balance, followed by surgery, which took place in Casablanca.

Perhaps the whole experience was enjoyed as an adventure. "There was a spice to it, as there is in any undercover work," Jan Morris recalled. "For a time I was a member of two clubs in London, one as a man and one as a woman, and I would sometimes, literally, change my identity in a taxi between the two."

Upon returning for the first time after her operation to the male-only Travellers Club – in a skirt – she found it amusing to be harrumphed at by a Monsignor in a clerical frock.

The first book to appear under the authorship of Jan Morris was

Conundrum. Never before had there been such an articulate patient, able to discuss the problems – psychological, spiritual, social – with such skill and humour. Not that that saved her from the anger of some critics, including Germaine Greer, one of the best known women's liberationists of the time.

After her gender reassignment Morris found that she cried more easily and became "ludicrously susceptible to flattery".

She certainly got a lot of praise for her books. Most of her output consisted of her individual kind of travel writing, a phrase she in fact disliked: "The books," she once said, "have never tried to tell somebody what a city is like. All I do is say how I've felt about it."

At first there may have been a lot of derring-do in her books, but her technique matured into a highly personal descriptive style, giving the feel of a place. A Morris travel book typically provided the charm, and insight into human nature, of a collection of good short stories. Her writing was marked by an idiosyncratic mix of whimsy, impressionism, high subjectivity and irreverence.

One of her quirks was always giving the longitude and latitude whenever she entered a city. As Derek Johns, her agent, noted: "It was as though, having been almost everywhere, Jan always needed to situate precisely the place she now happened to be in."

"The first place I visit," she once said, explaining how she approached a new city, "is the law court, where you can see every kind of rapscallion and decent person too, and you can judge the temper of the city by the magistrates. Then the market. And the railway station, because it sets a city in its environment, political and historical – and because I'm thrilled by it."

As a writer about places, her dual techniques were "wandering aimlessly about" and innocently asking people the way, even when she knew it, simply to get into conversation. It was a style that appealed to transatlantic readers too. In 2001 she was touched when _The New York Times_ on the Sunday after the attack on the World Trade Center published a supplement containing essays about the city and wanted to include words from her. Under a picture of the now ruined area were lines from her 1987 book _Manhattan '45_: "The Manhattan skyline shimmered in the imaginations of all the nations, and people everywhere cherished the ambition, however unattainable, of landing one day upon that legendary foreshore."

Morris worried about a surfeit in her prose of "the instrumentals of fine writing – metaphor, simile and so on" and was anxious about being seen as a show-off. She nevertheless tried her hand at fiction, and was short-listed for the Booker Prize with *Last Letters from Hav* (1985). Increasingly she became interested in Welsh Nationalism and wrote a satirical novel, *Our First Leader*, about what might happen in an independent Wales. What she described as her last book, *Trieste and the Meaning of Nowhere*, appeared when she was 75.

Less of an extrovert in person than in her writing, she latterly lived in north Wales with Elizabeth; they had had to divorce at the time of Morris's gender reassignment but remained devoted to one another, and in 2008 they formalised their partnership once again by entering a civil union. Jan would describe herself as unofficial sister-in-law to Elizabeth, the woman that James married, and as aunt to his children. His life, and hers, was a conundrum to the end.

Behind her desk in her study was a gravestone that was ready made up, the idea being that she and Elizabeth would be buried together on an island in a stream near their home, beneath a stone bearing an inscription in both English and Welsh that reads: "Here lie two friends, at the end of one life."

Jan Morris CBE, writer, was born on October 2, 1926. She died on November 20, 2020, aged 94

Jan Morris

JOHN McAFEE

Sometimes dangerous, often strange, but always colourful and hard-living creator of the first antivirus computer software

A turning point in John McAfee's life came when two brothers in Pakistan created the first known computer virus aimed at PCs in 1986. They were not trying to destroy anything, but to see how far it could travel. They even included their names and telephone numbers in the coding, a bit like a message in a bottle. They called it Brain, after their computer services shop in Lahore. Within a year, angry PC users around the world were phoning the shop to demand action.

McAfee was a computer programmer at Lockheed in Sunnyvale, California, with a troubled background, though he had been sober for four years. He read about Brain in *The Mercury News* and found it terrifying because it reminded him of his childhood, when his alcoholic father would beat him and his mother for no reason. "I didn't know why he did it," he told *Wired* magazine. "I just knew a beating could happen any time."

In 1987, while still at Lockheed, he started McAfee Associates from his home in Santa Clara, creating antivirus software that could detect malicious software and remove it automatically. He was not expecting users to pay for the basic model; he simply wanted to impress on them the need to be protected from computer viruses.

Within five years half of America's Fortune 100 companies had installed McAfee software and were paying a licence fee for the full protection it purported to offer. By 1990 he was making $5 million a year. As a sideline he ran the American Institute for Safe Sex Practices: any member who paid him a fee and tested HIV-negative could have sex with other members for six months free from the risk of Aids.

McAfee's fortune, then, came from spreading fear, whether around human viruses or computer ones. He appeared on television in 1988 saying that some companies were "near collapse" because of viruses. In a book called *Computer Viruses, Worms, Data Diddlers, Killer Programs and Other Threats to Your System* (1989) he declared that "a major disaster seems inevitable", and in 1992 he warned that the newly discovered Michelangelo virus would destroy five million computers on March 6, the anniversary of the artist's birth. Don't run software sent to you unsolicited, was his warning, adding: "It's very much like safe sex." In reality, Michelangelo infected only a few thousand PCs, but McAfee's sales soared.

The company floated on the Nasdaq market that year, valuing McAfee's holding at $80 million. He left in 1994, sold his shares and dabbled in several ventures, some of them computer-related, others more esoteric, such as buying a 400-acre plot in Colorado and turning it into a yoga retreat. Pagans were employed to beat drums and employees allegedly competed to have sex in his office, while he wrote yoga manuals and dated teenage girls.

After a spell in New Mexico, where he indulged in aerotrekking – that is, flying unlicensed microlight aircraft at low altitude – he moved to Belize, the ideal place for a dotcom millionaire playboy with its white beaches, coral reefs and azure skies. There he kept a harem of seven women aged between 18 and 25, and set up a laboratory supposedly to carry out research on medicines derived from jungle plants, though there were later suggestions he was manufacturing methamphetamine. It was protected by 11 ferocious dogs and a small army of security guards.

He would have remained a rich man, albeit one with a penchant for drugs, guns and sexual promiscuity, but for the murder of his neighbour, Gregory Faull, who was found with a single gunshot wound to the head on the small island of Ambergris Caye, off Belize, in November 2012.

Faull, who owned a sports bar in Orlando, Florida, had taken a dislike to the constant barking of McAfee's dogs and had told their owner as much in forthright terms. Convinced that the police would frame him for the killing, McAfee, who always denied any involvement, dug a shallow trench in the sand and buried himself, pulling a cardboard box over his head. He remained there for several hours. "To put myself in their hands I think is lunacy," he told the media in a phone call while in hiding. Later he said that Faull's killing was a case of mistaken identity and the assailant had been looking for McAfee himself.

He went on the run with Samantha Vanegas, a 20-year-old girlfriend who was 47 years his junior, dyeing his hair and wearing fake dreadlocks and a multicoloured beanie hat. He rang NBC Television to offer 25,000 Belize dollars as a reward for information leading to Faull's killer, and his blog detailed the steps that he was taking to disguise himself, including shoving a tampon up one nostril to distort the shape of his nose. Dean Barrow, the prime minister of Belize, described him as "extremely paranoid, even bonkers".

Turning up in Guatemala, McAfee sought political asylum but was arrested for entering the country illegally and deported to the US, without Vanegas. On his first night there he picked up Janice Dyson, who was working as a prostitute in Miami Beach. They began a relationship and were married the following year. Dyson said that McAfee had rescued her from people traffickers.

The couple settled in Portland, Oregon, where McAfee seemed to calm down, although there were still occasional unorthodox interventions, such as when he offered to decrypt the iPhone used by the killers in the 2015 San Bernardino shooting, sparing Apple the need to build a back door.

Every so often he would poke fun at the company that still bore his name, producing a video in 2013 entitled *How to Uninstall McAfee Antivirus* in which he mocked the company's software while snorting white powder and being undressed by scantily clad women to a background of classical music.

He became chief executive officer of the technology company MGT Capital Investments, unsuccessfully sought selection as the presidential candidate for the Libertarian Party, and championed cryptocurrencies. In July 2017 he predicted that the price of one bitcoin would reach $500,000 within three years, adding that "if not, I will eat my own dick on national television".

Trouble was never far away. He was arrested in Tennessee for drink-driving and being in possession of a firearm. A lawsuit relating to Faull's death continued to plague him, and he was held on firearms offences on board a yacht in the Dominican Republic, but released after four days. However, it was McAfee's refusal to file tax returns that really irked the US authorities. He fled in 2019, and the following year claimed on social media to have been detained in Norway for refusing to replace a lace thong with a more effective Covid mask. He was later arrested at Barcelona airport at the request of the US Justice Department, which accused him of evading paying millions of dollars in taxes. He was about to board a flight to Istanbul.

John David McAfee was born in 1945 on a US army base at Cinderford, Gloucestershire, the son of Don McAfee, an American serviceman, and his English wife, Joan (née Williams). The family moved to Salem, Virginia, where his alcoholic father hoped to escape his creditors. McAfee Sr became a road surveyor, but shot himself dead when his son was 15. "Every day I wake up with him," McAfee told

Wired. "Every relationship I have, he's by my side; every mistrust, he is the negotiator of that mistrust. So my life is fucked."

He studied maths at Roanoke College, Salem, supporting himself by selling magazine subscriptions door to door, at which point he discovered that confidence was the only skill he needed. "I made a fortune," he said. Much of it was spent on drink, though at some point he followed the hippy trail through India and Nepal. He started a PhD at Northeast Louisiana State College, but was kicked out after sleeping with an undergraduate whom he subsequently married.

A job coding punch cards for the computer company Univac at Bristol, Tennessee, ended when he was arrested for buying marijuana, although he avoided a conviction. His next stop was Missouri Pacific Railroad in St Louis, which was trying to computerise its train timetables. He discovered LSD and other illicit substances, and at one point his computer was churning out schedules purporting to send trains to the moon.

His wife left him, he gave away his dog and, after being fired, he went to a therapist. "That's when life really began for me," he told *Wired* in 2012.

Eventually he was given security clearance to work at Lockheed and married his second wife, Judy, a former flight attendant at American Airlines. The marriage was dissolved in 2002 and he is survived by his third wife, who in a Father's Day message on Sunday described him as "father of many, loved by few".

Life locked inside a Spanish prison was "a fascinating adventure", McAfee told *The Independent* in November, adding that "the graffiti alone could fill a 1,000-page thriller", but he was determined never to return to the US.

John McAfee, computer programmer and antivirus manufacturer, was born on September 18, 1945. He killed himself on June 23, 2021, aged 75

PRINCESS EMMA GALITZINE

———————●———————

Much-married, free-spirited society hostess who seemed to have walked straight out of the pages of Evelyn Waugh's Vile Bodies

A young Princess Emma Galitzine, left, with a fellow debutante.

Emma Galitzine was said to have "the naughtiest face in London". It was a reputation that she lived up to with marriages to the gossip columnist Nigel Dempster, a Russian prince and a wealthy British businessman (twice).

Along the way this "society beauty", as *Tatler* was wont to describe her, who spoke several languages and was photographed by Lord Lichfield, was a horizontally generous woman who reciprocated the attentions of many a male admirer. Most of all she enjoyed making mischief, shocking people and having fun. Unfettered by rules or propriety, she rarely shrank from speaking her mind or acting upon her whims. She was a notable cook, for example, and after the main course at one of her dinner parties, she decided to change into skimpy riding gear, including thigh-length boots, before bringing out the pudding, jumping on the table with it and performing a dance.

Her great passion was for riding horses, which she kept at home in Oxfordshire, first at Caulcott and later at Great Tew. She was a memorable presence at the Heythrop and Bicester hunt balls, where her flirtatious manner and plunging décolletage made her unpopular with the wives, as did her enthusiasm for challenging the huntsmen to arm-wrestling contests.

Emma Magdalen de Bendern was born in London in 1950, the third child of Lady Patricia Douglas, daughter of the 11th Marquess of Queensberry, who was married to John de Forest, an English amateur golf champion who used the Liechtenstein title Count John de Bendern. They were divorced seven months after their daughter's birth and Emma once confided to a friend that her biological father was Herman "Marno" Hornak, a libidinous sculptor who became her mother's second husband.

Her siblings were Simon, who works in conservation with Madagascan lemurs, and Caroline, who achieved infamy in 1968 when she was photographed bare-breasted in a recreation of Delacroix's painting *Liberty Leading the People* and was subsequently disinherited by her wealthy grandfather.

Emma was schooled at home but considered her real education to have come from Beechwood Riding School in Surrey. She once took her pony up to her attic bedroom, but he was not keen to come down the stairs and the fire brigade had to be called to rescue him through the roof.

By her mid-teens she had fallen in with a cast of amoral characters that included John Bindon, an actor and gangster who claimed he once had a fling with Princess Margaret, and Bryan Walsh, a handsome criminal with a drug problem who did several spells in jail. He was something of a fixer on the fringes of high society. "It was just fun hanging out with these guys; smart little aristo me, all blissed out," Emma recalled. "It was quite a sexy atmosphere."

As a debutante she was at Queen Charlotte's Ball at the Dorchester Hotel when the leather-clad Walsh, who had a sideline as a getaway driver for bank robberies, rode up on his motorcycle. She hitched up her white dress, jumped on and rode pillion into the sunset. Two days before her 18th birthday she gave birth to their daughter, Atalanta, who has been a professional surfer.

In 1970 she met Dempster at a friend's wedding. "When he mentioned a horse he fancied for the next day – it was L'Escargot at Cheltenham – I wanted to show off so I gave him £20, which was a lot in those days, and asked him to put it on for me," she told his biographer. L'Escargot romped home and she rang Dempster to ask for her winnings. "You'll have to come out for dinner to collect them," he said. So began a whirlwind romance. They had a grand wedding with a reception at Les Ambassadeurs in Mayfair and, bizarrely, Emma's mother joined them in bed for the first night of their marriage.

Marriage did little to curb the new Mrs Dempster's enthusiasm for unorthodox liaisons. Six months after her nuptials she visited her brother's house in the south of France with John Hobbs, a louche antique dealer. Halfway through their holiday Hobbs was rumbled by his wife, Sonya, and rushed home without packing. Emma agreed to bring his clothes back, but the suitcase failed to arrive at Heathrow. When it surfaced the ground staff spotted the label reading "Mrs Nigel Dempster" and dispatched it to her husband's office at the *Daily Mail*. "Poor Nigel opened it in front of everyone, only to discover another man's underwear packed on top," she recalled.

Dempster demanded a meeting with Hobbs. Fisticuffs followed, a record player was broken and in 1974 he and Emma divorced. The next year she married Giles Trentham, a founder of the interiors company Fired Earth whose previous wife married John Cleese; they had a daughter, Amber, who is a screenwriter. That was dissolved and in 1986 she married Prince George Galitzine, an art director. They had a son, Dmitri, who is an artist. That marriage ended in 1992 and she remarried Trentham, who died ten weeks later. She spent 12 years with John Wickham, who works in shipping, and for the past eight years had been with Jeremy Walsh, a stockbroker.

A conventional career was never a priority for Emma, who was independently wealthy and managed her money astutely, but at various times she worked as an interior designer, a reflexologist, and as a volunteer at the Lighthouse Centre for people with HIV and AIDS.

Above all, Emma de Bendern / Dempster / Trentham / Galitzine never lost her free spirit. "Her fortunes varied enormously," her daughter Amber said. "But she followed her heart and her passions."

Princess Emma Galitzine, society hostess, was born on March 2, 1950. She died on January 28, 2021, after a fall aged 70

SIDNEY ALFORD

Maverick explosives expert who marched to the beat of his own drum

Sidney Alford took up skydiving in his fifties. He started learning Russian in his sixties, and German in his seventies. But his real passion, the one that he acquired as a schoolboy and pursued almost all his life, was blowing things up.

Self-taught, non-conformist and contemptuous of "pointless rules and regulations", he invented and developed, first in his garage and later in a Somerset quarry, all manner of explosive tools to destroy the mines, bombs and improvised explosive devices (IEDs) of terrorists and other enemies – tools rejoicing in names such as the BootBanger, the Bottler and Krakatoa.

A British establishment of which Alford was emphatically never a part did not always appreciate his creative (and destructive) genius, especially in the earlier years of this somewhat combustible character's career.

When he was 41, and just hitting his stride, the Royal Armament Research and Development Establishment refused to employ him on the grounds that he was too old to have original ideas. The Royal

Military College of Science blacklisted him for "teaching young officers things about explosives that they are not supposed to know". Yet as the decades passed Alford came to be seen for what he was: one of the world's leading experts in explosive engineering.

The British and US militaries employed him to find ways of neutralising IEDs planted by the Taliban in Afghanistan, and by Islamic jihadists in Iraq and Syria. Documentary makers turned to him to recreate events such as the Dambusters' raid, or the anniversary of the Gunpowder Plot (for the latter, he blew up a life-sized replica of the Palace of Westminster).

He carried on working well into his eighties, though by then he was fairly deaf from all those bangs. "I enjoy blowing things up too much to do otherwise," he said, not unreasonably.

Sidney Christopher Alford was born and raised in Ilford, Essex, in 1935, the son of a First World War veteran who then worked as a clerk for Shell for 45 years. His interest in things that exploded began during the Second World War. After a brief evacuation to Bournemouth, where he witnessed a Stuka strafing a shopping street, he would huddle under the stairs with his mother as the Germans bombed east London by night. By day he would visit the bomb sites and, if lucky, find unexploded magnesium alloy incendiary bombs from which he made fireworks. He once found a V1 flying bomb engine in Epping Forest.

After the war he developed a love of chemistry at Buckhurst Hill grammar school and was spanked for detonating rolls of toy caps in the locker room. He also put bangers made of nitrogen triiodide under his French teacher's chair.

Alford went on to Southampton University, but failed his first-year exams and instead did two years' National Service as a radar technician. Thereafter he enrolled for a general science course at South West Essex Technical College, but failed that too because he was poor at maths.

Despite that unpromising start he was offered a research job at the University of Paris after a chance meeting with a chemistry professor named Charles Mentzer in the early 1960s, and, with no first degree, ended up earning a doctorate on the chemistry of plant products.

Mentzer recommended Alford to a chemistry professor he knew at the University of Tokyo. Alford stayed there for a couple of years and added Japanese to his growing portfolio of languages. He also met Itsuko Suzuki, whom he married in 1970 and with whom he would later have two sons.

Back in Britain he struggled to find a proper job: he studied fatty acids in the brain at the Nuffield Institute and acted as an interpreter when Emperor Hirohito visited. It took the eruption of the Troubles in Northern Ireland to reignite his interest in explosives. Working in the garage of his house in suburban Ham, west London, he invented "water-lined shaped charges" – explosive charges that generated 3,000mph armour-piercing jets of water – to destroy Provisional IRA bombs.

He left his car running in the hope that neighbours would think it was backfiring whenever they heard bangs, but to no avail. He was soon visited by two gentlemen from the security services. He explained his work, and instead of arresting him they put him in touch with the Ministry of Defence. The MoD arranged for him to continue his testing at its Pirbright range in Surrey, and subsequently adopted his pioneering technology for a variety of highly classified projects.

In the late 1970s Alford designed underwater charges to sever the well heads of decommissioned North Sea oil rigs and blew up three old blast furnaces in Co Durham. He blasted away the old iron penstock gates at the Royal Dockyard in Portsmouth and assisted in an operation that recovered gold ingots from the wreck of a cruiser torpedoed by U-boats in 1942.

By 1985 he had had enough of working for others. He set up Alford Technologies in Trowbridge and he finally came into his own. One of his first jobs was to salvage supertankers sunk in the Gulf during the Iran–Iraq war. He invented a form of linear cutting charge that he called Dioplex ("Do-It-Oneself Plastic Explosive") to slice the ships in half while Iranian Revolutionary Guards watched from a distance.

Another early commission was to help Stanley Kubrick, the film director, to destroy an old industrial building in south London to create a set for his Vietnam film *Full Metal Jacket*.

Mostly, however, Alford invented devices for military use. He adapted his water-lined shaped charges for a variety of purposes, including the destruction of unexploded ordnance left in Cambodia and Laos after the Indochina wars, and in Kuwait after the Iraqi invasion of 1990.

Among his many other inventions were devices for destroying terrorist IEDs, limpet mines stuck to the sides of ships, the Bangalore Blade to blow holes in razor wire defences, the BootBanger for blowing open the boots of booby-trapped cars, and the Gatecrasher for punching holes in walls in hostage situations.

Army officers from around the world visited his quarry in the Mendip Hills to watch him demonstrate his devices or take his courses. "I teach dirty tricks so they don't get caught out by them," Alford told *The New Statesman*. The Americans were particularly keen on his services, the British a little less so because, said his son, he had "put a lot of noses out of joint" with his plain speaking.

Alford was disdainful of authority. In 1996 he was prosecuted for repeatedly refusing to install an expensive alarm on his store of ammonium nitrate. A judge at Swindon crown court fined him £750 but, perhaps sensing he was dealing with a useful maverick, ordered the police to return his licence.

Sidney Alford OBE, explosives expert, was born on January 11, 1935. He died of heart failure on January 27, 2021, aged 86

THEODORA DI MARCO

———————•———————

Carmelite nun with a rebellious streak who developed a penchant for
negronis and had a 60-a-day cigarette habit

With her dyed pink hair and taste for negronis, there was little
about Theo di Marco, at least on the surface, to suggest that she had
lived for 30 years as a Carmelite nun.

"I was not very obedient," di Marco would sheepishly recall at the
popular salons she held every Sunday evening in Notting Hill, west
London.

As a 27-year-old violist she had joined St Peter's convent in
Edinburgh, incurring the rancour of her father. The Carmelite Sisters
of Charity was an enclosed order, adhering to a strict rule of prayer
and silence: chatter was only permitted during daily recreation.

Di Marco's colourful tales of pre-convent life soon made an
impact. The mother superior drew her aside for a quiet word. "You
have known men," she observed, advising di Marco to tone down her
anecdotes lest they incite the envy of other novices.

In later years di Marco was tight-lipped on why she had joined the
convent: according to family lore, she had been jilted by a man who

subsequently became a priest. To Catholic friends, she intimated that she had been concerned for the soul of her agnostic identical twin, Norma.

Of the pair, the fiery Norma was the more dominant. A professional cellist and journalist, she was described in her *Times* obituary in 2009 as "a kind of composite rebel with CND leanings with challenging views embracing radical feminism, Marxism and Scottish Nationalism", and as someone who possessed "a gift for making enemies as well as friends".

Both twins enjoyed the reaction to their provocative remarks, such as "Are you the stupid one of the family?" to a cousin they had just met. Observing a relative prone to twin-sets, they said, "God! You look like something out of an M&S catalogue." The chastened Theo would subsequently apologise for any upset caused. Norma would not.

In 1983 St Peter's closed due to falling numbers in the community. Remaining nuns joined neighbouring convents. Di Marco was politely informed that no objections would be raised if she chose to leave religious life altogether. An older nun observed that after 30 years in the cloister di Marco was "still in a purgative state". Once she had placed some doughnuts just brought by Norma on the metal spikes of the grille in the convent parlour.

After leaving the convent di Marco embraced secular life with relish. She moved to London to live with Norma and developed a 60-a-day cigarette habit. Every Sunday a group of musicians, painters and poets would traipse up the stone steps to the blue door of the sisters' terraced house in Pembridge Road. Occasionally they included Ann Barr, co-author of *The Official Sloane Ranger Handbook*, the poet Michael Horovitz or the novelist JG Farrell.

Held in a book-lined room with a Bechstein grand piano, the salons were convivial and conversation would flow in what one saloniste described as "a creative cacophony", occasionally interrupted by the sisters performing on the viola and cello.

Theodora di Marco, known as Theo, was born in 1925 in Edinburgh. She was the youngest child of Antonietta (née Tartaglia) who came from an Italo-Scot clan in Glasgow, and Orace di Marco, who chose, given the anti-Italian prejudice then rife in Scotland, to be known as Horace.

After weathering several reversals of fortune, and a failed attempt to open one of the first vegetarian restaurants in Edinburgh, he enjoyed success as a restaurateur and confectioner, later diversifying into property.

By the time Theo was born, the family dwelt in a spacious apartment occupying half of a sandstone mansion house. Coloured ribbons were tied around the twins' wrists as babies to distinguish them. As children they delighted in swapping the distinctive jumpers they were dressed in to confuse relatives.

In 1879 Luigi, their paternal grandfather, had hitchhiked, allegedly bearing a hurdy-gurdy, to Scotland from the Abruzzi mountains in Italy. He came from Picinisco, a village that inspired DH Lawrence's novel, *The Lost Girl*. In a letter in 1919 Lawrence observed of its denizens: "The brigand men are by no means fierce; the women are the fierce half of the breed."

Di Marco's cousin Richard Demarco, the artist and arts promoter, said: "Theo's family kept at a great distance from the Italians in Edinburgh. All the twins' friends were non-Italian and they were educated."

Both obtained bachelor of arts degrees from Edinburgh University, after attending a boarding school in Aberdeenshire. Subsequently they taught in private schools in Oxford and Switzerland and in later years were assiduous in attending the Edinburgh Festival.

Demarco, who played a key role in the inception of the Edinburgh Fringe, recalled his cousin as "a remarkable, feisty character". They would discuss the Palladian influence on Edinburgh's architecture, Catholicism in a principally Presbyterian nation, Cop26 and Brexit. Conversing with her was akin to "playing ping-pong against a very vicious opponent. She knew how to sharpen you up."

For her part di Marco compared her conversational style to boxing. "I don't like priests with double-barrelled names," she once remarked on being told that an eminent Jesuit was a fellow guest at a friend's birthday party. When he asked how she prayed, "Read Anselm" was the brisk reply, referencing the medieval theologian known for his ontological proofs of God's existence.

This waspish exterior concealed reserves of tenderness: she cared devotedly for Norma as her health declined. Many of their friends assumed Norma's death in 2009 meant an end to the Sunday soirées, yet di Marco was soon on the phone summoning some of their 200-strong circle to the next gathering.

Her esprit did not waver: she sampled her first negroni at the age of 92. Always sprightly, she would appear at gatherings with streaks of scarlet, emerald or lavender in her grey hair.

She curated her soirées with all the thought of an 18th-century Parisienne aristocrat, alternating the guests for variety: some had just written books, others might be giving a concert or have just returned from a long sojourn in an exotic location.

What counted was not the simple fare or modest decor (guests perched around folding card tables) but the art of conversation: this ranged from music and art to burning political issues, recondite facts about 7th-century martyrs and ways to keep meat fresh in the Moroccan desert. Di Marco would reprove any guest who hogged the food – or the limelight.

To the last she retained a sharp wit, telling one habitué who recently visited to make her lunch, "If I'd known you made such good scrambled eggs, I'd have married you."

Theodora di Marco, Carmelite nun and salonnière, was born on October 14, 1925. She died in her sleep on August 17, 2021, aged 95

NANCIE COLLING

Indomitable champion bowls player of the 1950s, 1960s and 1970s who later became a respected, if somewhat feared, administrator

At a meeting of the English Women's Bowling Association (EWBA) council in 1993, it was decided to ditch the old-fashioned hats, which most bowlers felt were holding the game back.

It was thought that the hat-haters, of whom there were many, had waited until Nancie Colling, the indomitable EWBA secretary, was out of the country before pushing the proposal through. Mrs Colling, a stickler for standards, had previously managed to sabotage every attempt to get rid of "those hats", and this was the first AGM she had missed.

So, the wearing of hats became optional for the first time at the British women's home international series in Llandrindod Wells in 1994. In a memorable pep talk to the 24-strong English team, Mrs Colling rose to her full height and said: "I have to tell you you are not required to wear a hat ... but" at this point she lowered her voice to a menacing whisper "... you know how I feel." So forceful was her personality that only two out of the 24 team members, Mary Price and Norma May, dared to play hatless.

At the annual national championships at Victoria Park in Royal Leamington Spa, where she ruled with the flexibility of iron, grown women were reduced to tears as their dress code was inspected, and even spectators trembled as she bellowed instructions to them from the tournament office.

Even her best friends would not consider graciousness and an affable manner to be among her prominent qualities. In the 1980s, the bowls correspondent of *The Times* was startled to receive a brusque letter from the EWBA secretary on the association's headed official notepaper. It read, "If you are coming to Leamington this year, my Council request that, please, you do not wear your shorts. Yours sincerely, Nancie Colling (Secretary)."

Florence Nancie Whalley was born in Colwyn Bay, north Wales, in 1919. Her parents were Alice and Bertram, a printer. She had two brothers, Derek and Bertie, and went to school in Clacton, Essex, before the family moved to Somerset.

She first played bowls as a teenager at the Frome Selwood club in Somerset, and it was from there that she won her three national singles titles, under three different surnames. Her first success was in 1956, under her maiden name of Nancie Whalley, her second came two years later, after she married Harold Evans. A new chapter in her life started when Evans then died and she married the Rev Corrie Colling, so it was as Nancie Colling that she won the title for the third time, in 1970. This victory was all the more remarkable because she had been paralysed after a spinal injury four years earlier and had only begun playing again in 1969.

She played for England in 14 home international series between 1957 and 1978, and represented her country at the 1973 world outdoor championships in Wellington, New Zealand, where she won a silver medal in the women's fours.

John Bell, the incumbent president of World Bowls, said: "Nancie made a fantastic contribution to bowls worldwide, despite the strait-laced image which she liked to cultivate."

Nancie Colling MBE, bowling champion, was born on April 19, 1919. She died on July 1, 2020 aged 101

RUPERT CHETWYND

*Bohemian SAS soldier, advertising executive and adventurer who led
humanitarian missions into Soviet-occupied Afghanistan*

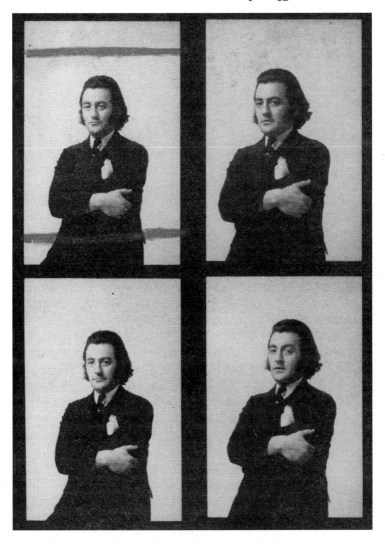

Rupert Chetwynd never drove a car, but he used to jump from those of friends before they had fully stopped. He believed that the saddest words in the English language were "too late" and he hated wasting time. There was so much to pack into a human lifespan, he felt, and being an old school romantic and dreamer, he was determined to do as much as he possibly could in his.

As well as being a soldier who broke his back twice, and his nose eight times, while parachuting from aircraft, he was also an advertising executive who made and lost a fortune. He led humanitarian missions into Soviet-occupied, and later Taliban-infested, Afghanistan. A resolver of conflicts and a hermit who would vanish into the wilds of Corsica for weeks on end, he combined all this with being a writer and a bit-part actor. He was, in short, one of a long line of eccentric and irrepressible British adventurers in the mould of men like Wilfred Thesiger, Richard Burton and TE Lawrence, Chetwynd's heroes all.

He disliked doctors and dentists, and once glued a tooth back in with Araldite adhesive. He was a military man, but also a bohemian rebel who believed that the trouble with possessions was that they possessed their owner. A mesmerising personality with at times a luxuriant moustache and bushy beard in later life, he never knowingly passed a mirror without pausing to appreciate his reflection and was as comfortable in a rudimentary Afghan tea house as he was in a smart London club and at ease wearing a tatty sarong, a traditional Afghan shalwar kameez or a pinstripe suit from Savile Row.

Aged 87, he spent the last day of his life wearing a T-shirt that proclaimed: "I caught crabs in Karachi."

Rupert Milo Talbot Chetwynd was born in Brighton in 1934 and doubtless inherited his divided personality from his parents. His father, Major Wentworth Randolph Chetwynd, was an army officer and his mother, Bridget (née Walsh), was a novelist who raised her son in Chelsea while consorting with Francis Bacon, Lucian Freud and other prominent members of the London arts scene. A carpet with burn holes from his home somehow ended up hanging on a wall in a Royal Academy exhibition.

Another early influence on his life was an aunt, Betty, who fought with the French resistance during the Second World War and regaled her impressionable young nephew with tales of derring-do.

Chetwynd was educated at Stowe, where he became an accomplished boxer. From there he joined the Grenadier Guards, his father's old regiment. A year later he joined the Guards Independent Parachute Company and, at some point, the SAS. His commanding officer in the Guards wrote on his discharge papers: "We have no problems with Rupert, but he seems to have joined the SAS without telling us."

Exactly what he got up to with the SAS is not known, but during his years in the military he saw active service in the Suez crisis, and fought a Greek-Cypriot terrorist organisation, the EOKA, that was seeking an end to British rule in Cyprus. After he broke his back in a parachute jump he was told by his doctors that he would never walk again. He swiftly proved them wrong.

In 1956 he married his first wife, Antonia Clark, though it was initially her mother who had caught his eye. They went on to have five children and lived in a large country house in Kent until it burned down. Their marriage ended in the 1960s when Antonia took the hippy trail to India.

By that time Chetwynd had joined the glamorous world of advertising, first with an agency called SH Benson (now part of Ogilvy, Benson and Mather), where he worked with JG Ballard before Ballard became a novelist, and later as head of his own agency, Chetwynd and Partners, in Red Lion Court off Fleet Street. His secretary Naomi Hall (Saldanha) recalled: "In the winter Rupert always wore a Victorian black suit with tails, and in the summer it was a three-piece cream suit. I had to make sure he always had a box of violet cream dark chocolates to hand. He hardly ever sat at his desk, rushing around all the time. I'd say, 'Where are you off to now?' and he would reply, 'Just ratting around the City.'" She would arrange lunches for him with City notables such as Mark Weinberg and Marmaduke Hussey. One day a PR man rang out of the blue to ask him to lunch and Chetwynd wondered why. "When he came back I asked, 'Well. What did he want?' Rupert replied, 'He wanted to admire me – so I let him.'"

For a while the business prospered, despite its offices being destroyed by another fire. Chetwynd became a millionaire. He lived in fashionable Campden Hill Square in Holland Park and in 1970 married Luciana Maria Arrighi, a former model and daughter of an Italian count whom he had met while they were helping to restore a mutual friend's château in Normandy. He had two more children with his second wife.

His advertising agency went bust in the mid-1970s and he lost his fortune. Undaunted, he moved with his family first to Hong Kong, and later Australia, to work as a security consultant for Boeing, before returning to Britain in the early 1980s. He and his family moved into the New Stables, a huge neo-Gothic edifice designed to house 50 horses that stands in the grounds of Ingestre Hall in Staffordshire, the family seat for several centuries until it was sold in the 1960s.

He did not sink into tranquil retirement. Soon he was making trips to Peshawar, on the ill-defined Afghanistan–Pakistan border, as a guide and troubleshooter for a group of volunteer doctors from Guilford, who went out to treat civilian victims of the Soviet occupation of Afghanistan each year. The role involved dodging militias and minefields to rescue casualties, but on occasion he would dress in a white three-piece suit.

Back in London his daughter-in-law, Anna, met a journalist recently returned from Afghanistan who described a bizarre spectacle he had witnessed while standing on a hilltop in the Panjshir Valley.

"Out of sight at first, the sound of patrician voices and rallying cries in English, could be heard across the valley. And bursting over the brow of the hill came a group of sunburnt octogenarians, bound up in headscarves and walking with sticks, with one shouting at the other to "get a move on, Chetwynd". 'My God,' I said when the tale was retold, 'that's my father-in-law!'"

Making few concessions to old age, he would take himself off to the wild, forested mountains of Corsica and live, hermit-like, in a tent for months at a time, sleeping on the ground, cooking on an open fire and gazing at stars in the night sky.

It is a moot point whether he actually died of pancreatic cancer, or a ruptured aorta, but either way he collapsed on the day he was supposed to attend the unveiling of a Grenadier Guards monument at the National Arboretum in Staffordshire.

As the doctors attended to him, he told them he had no time to spare and that he had a very important engagement that he could not miss.

Rupert Chetwynd, soldier, advertising executive and adventurer, was born on January 7, 1934. He died of pancreatic cancer, possibly, on April 26, 2021, aged 87

KATHERINE JOHNSON

———————•———————

Brilliant NASA mathematician known as 'the human computer' who plotted the trajectory of John Glenn's historic orbit of Earth

As he ran through a checklist two days before the launch that would set him on his way to becoming the first American to orbit Earth, John Glenn pored over computer-generated data and decided that the numbers warranted a second opinion. "Get the girl," he urged. "If she says they're good, then I'm ready to go."

The "girl" was Katherine Johnson, a 43-year-old mother of three whose mathematical brilliance helped her to defy sexism and racism to become the most trusted "human computer" at NASA, the American space agency.

Glenn wanted her to verify calculations of the trajectory of his Friendship 7 spacecraft. The plan was to lift off at Cape Canaveral, Florida, circle the planet and splash down near Bermuda. If Johnson's figures matched the computer's, he would feel confident enough to proceed.

Stacks of data sheets piled high on her desk, Johnson spent a day and a half recalculating the course of the entire voyage by hand, accounting for 11 potential variables and providing figures that went two decimal points beyond the numbers from the computer, which proved correct.

It was a high-risk mission filled with unknowns for NASA, which was desperate to catch up with the Soviet Union in the space race. "This was an enormous assignment, and I felt its weight upon my shoulders," Johnson recalled. "Then again, it was simply maths – and maths was my strong point."

Glenn launched on February 20, 1962. Despite malfunctions that complicated what proved to be a fiery re-entry, he survived and the flight was deemed a triumph. Johnson turned her attention to the moon.

She helped to calculate the trajectory of the lunar module and synchronise it with the command module for the return journey. Determining the appropriate positioning and angles to land a craft back on Earth at the correct place and time was no small matter. Calculations had to factor in data such as the speed of the rocket, when it should fire, the weight of the capsule and the rotation of Earth. Johnson tested formulae to an accuracy of many decimal places.

The mission's computers were programmed with her calculations when Apollo 11 launched in 1969. Johnson felt secure enough in her numbers to attend a sorority reunion in Pennsylvania where she watched Neil Armstrong's "one small step" on television.

"The nation might still have thought of our people as inferior, but a Black woman had performed the computations that had taken White male astronauts into outer space, landed them on the moon and brought them back safely to their families again," she wrote in her 2019 autobiography, *Reaching for the Moon.*

Creole Katherine Coleman was born in 1918 in White Sulphur Springs, in the Allegheny Mountains of West Virginia, the youngest of four children. Her mother, Joylette (née Lowe), was a teacher who made ends meet by doing laundry for White families; her father, Joshua, was a farmer and lumberjack. Though he left school at 11, which made him determined that his children would receive a better education, he had a gift for problem-solving. He could look at a tree and accurately estimate how many logs it would make once it was chopped down.

Johnson attended a segregated school. She was fascinated by numbers from a young age and counted everything she saw, from cracks in the pavement to steps in a staircase. In 1926 her parents moved the family across the state so the children could attend a school adjacent to what is now West Virginia State University, a historically Black college. She started high school aged ten and graduated three years later.

She took a summer job unpacking guests' luggage and babysitting children at the Greenbrier, a luxurious resort, and practised speaking French with the chef. She loved mathematics, she said, for "its simplicity, its elegance, how in a world rife with the dangers of racism and economic uncertainty, it provided clear-cut answers: either you were right or you were wrong".

Johnson graduated from West Virginia State aged 18 with a double major in French and mathematics and became a mathematics teacher in Virginia. She met Jimmie Goble, a relative of one of her students, when she recruited him to sing in a school play. They married in 1939. A science teacher, he died of a brain tumour in 1956. Two years later she met James Johnson, a postman, military veteran and substitute teacher, at a church service. They married in 1959; he died in 2019. She is survived by two daughters from her first marriage: Joylette, who worked as a NASA mathematician and as a computer analyst at Lockheed Martin; and Kathy, who worked in education. A third daughter, Constance, a schoolteacher, died in 2010.

Johnson briefly pursued graduate studies at what is now West Virginia University – she was among a handful of Black students chosen to integrate the previously all-White college – and set her heart on becoming a research mathematician.

In 1952 she turned up at the aeronautical laboratory in Hampton, Virginia, to ask for a job at the forerunner to NASA, the National Advisory Committee for Aeronautics. She had heard about a unit of Black women known as "computers" who performed calculations for aeronautical engineers working on supersonic flight and missiles.

A haughty White woman behind the front desk told her that "our quota for coloured mathematicians has already been filled this year". Still, Johnson insisted on filling in an application form. She worked as a substitute teacher until she was offered a post a year later.

On her first day she was amazed to see rows of Black women seated at desks using mechanical calculators, the room alive with the sound of fingers on keyboards. She quickly discovered that male engineers concentrated on big-picture theories and expected women to explore the finer details.

She felt the agency was propelled by a sense of purpose that to an extent transcended the racial strife beyond its walls, though the lavatories and cafeteria were segregated until 1958. She used the lavatory nearest to her, regardless of its designation, and ate at her desk.

The engineers respected the ability of the Black "computers", who were required to have a high-level college degree. Their White counterparts were often less qualified; many were married to engineers. "All of us," she remembered, "were known as computers with skirts."

Office politics were delicate. Early in her career she noticed an engineer inevitably had made a miscalculation and politely asked if it was possible his formula might be inaccurate. His face turned cherry-red. "If the wind tunnels hadn't been running in the background, with their constant whoosh and roar, I might have heard a pin drop in the room," she wrote. But she remained on the team. "Quietly the quality of my contribution began to outweigh the arbitrary laws of racial segregation and the dictates that held back my gender."

Johnson was assigned to the Space Task Group when NASA was established in 1958. Though trusted to work on top-secret projects as an important team member, she was never invited to meetings by engineers. One day she asked to attend a briefing but was told, "the girls don't go". When she pressed her case, asking, "Is there a law against it?", her boss allowed her in.

In 1960 her name appeared on the cover of a NASA technical report, *Determination of azimuth angle at burnout for placing a satellite over a selected Earth position*. This marked the first time a woman in the flight research division received an authorship credit. Previously, only men were named on the front page of reports, regardless of who had contributed.

Working by hand, sometimes with a slide rule and a pencil – computers were increasingly available but liable to glitches and their accuracy was not yet fully trusted – she calculated the trajectory of the 1961 mission on which Alan Shepard became the first American in space.

After Apollo 11 she performed computations for a possible mission to Mars and worked on the Space Shuttle programme and on a satellite that monitored atmospheric conditions. She also tutored students and wrote numerous research reports before retiring in 1986.

Near the end of a life largely lived backstage, which suited her unassuming, collegial personality, her achievements garnered widespread attention. In 2015, when she was 97, President Obama presented her with the presidential medal of freedom, the country's highest civilian award

A 2016 book, *Hidden Figures* by Margot Lee Shetterly, told the stories of Johnson and two colleagues, Dorothy Vaughan and Mary Jackson. It inspired a film of the same title which starred Taraji P Henson as Johnson. The film, which Johnson described with her usual precision as "75 per cent accurate", was nominated for three Academy awards, including best picture. Though it won none at the ceremony in 2017, Johnson made an appearance on stage with cast members and was given a standing ovation.

A bespectacled "Inspiring Women" Barbie doll in her likeness was produced as a tribute, and in 2017 NASA opened a computational research facility named in her honour. At last, she was, as the agency stated upon her death, "a figure hidden no more".

Katherine Johnson, NASA mathematician, was born on August 26, 1918. She died on February 24, 2020, aged 101

Katherine Johnson

SIR KEN DODD

Celebrated and singular comic whose inspired and relentless lunacy was honed over a career lasting 64 years

One of Ken Dodd's favourite books was Sigmund Freud's 1905 treatise *Wit and Its Relation to the Unconscious*. He read it as part of his professional research and characteristically he got a gag out of it. "I was the unconscious one."

Yet Dodd knew that making people laugh was a serious matter and few comedians have spent so much time analysing the theory behind tickling what he called our "chuckle muscles".

An assiduous student of the psychology of humour, when he performed in Oxford he visited the Bodleian Library to study rare books on the subject. "Every time I went to a different town I'd go to the library and devour whatever books they had on laughter, humour and comedians," he recalled.

Eventually he had little need to visit public libraries, for he built his own book-lined study that housed more than 50,000 volumes at his Knotty Ash home in Merseyside. There he pored over the philosophical theories of Freud, Bergson, Schopenhauer and Wittgenstein, although he liked to point out that none of them had played the second house at the Glasgow Empire on a Saturday night.

Dodd could learnedly discuss Freud's theory that humour depends on a "psychic economy" that overcomes inhibitions, or talk at length about comedy's reliance on "the perception of incongruity", but mostly he just preferred to tell his jokes, thousands of them that poured out of him at breakneck speed in a seemingly manic stream of wordplay and witty one-liners.

"You're like a gladiator," he said of the stand-up comic's stagecraft. "You buckle on your sword and helmet and you take on the audience. I reckon you've got 30 seconds to win them over. After the 'hello' gags come the topicals, then the surreal stuff. Eventually you can go wherever you want and say whatever comes into your head."

What came into Dodd's head was sometimes eccentric, frequently incongruous and often hilarious. To catchphrases such as "how tickled I am" and "by Jove, missus" he added his own bizarre lexicon – "plumptiousness", "discomknockerated", "tattifilarious" – and the absurdist word pictures he painted were masterpieces of inspired lunacy, perhaps only rivalled by Spike Milligan.

He would invite sympathy for men's legs "standing around alone and in the dark all day". Then he might confide, "If my mother knew

I was doing this she would be ashamed – she thinks I'm in prison." Or confess: "I have kleptomania. But when it gets bad, I take something for it."

His timing and delivery could make even the most hackneyed puns seem funny. "Did you hear about the shrimp that went to the prawn's cocktail party? He pulled a mussel," should have raised a groan from anyone over the age of ten. Yet the way Dodd told it brought the house down.

"There's no such thing as an old joke, just jokes that people have heard before," he said. He claimed that in more than 60 years as a professional entertainer he had never done the same show twice. Yet his best gags were like old friends. In later years he would thank his audiences for being "so patient waiting for the new joke".

With his wild, popping eyes, buck teeth and electric-shock hair standing out like a fright wig – "the face that launched a thousand quips" – he would brandish his "tickling stick" and ask a gasping woman in the audience if she had ever been tickled "under the circumstances".

Dodd was cheeky, with a hint of a Donald McGill seaside postcard, but never overtly lewd. He sometimes warned his audience that he was going to talk dirty and then shouted, "Sooty cobwebs!"

His "tickling stick" was cast in bronze as an appendage to the statue of him at Liverpool Lime Street station, about 20 minutes from Knotty Ash, the suburb where he lived all his life and became famous as the mythological home of the "Diddy Men", his Lewis Carroll-like invention of a race of 3ft-high manikins who inhabited a world of jam butty mines, gravy wells and broken biscuit repair works.

If his patter gave the impression of a chaotic brainstorm, in reality his preparation was meticulous. He kept hundreds of notebooks in which every joke he told was tabulated according to the laugh it received. "B" was for belly and "D" for dud, and he even compared how each gag had gone down with different audiences around the country, making up what he called a "giggle map of Great Britain".

He colour-coded his jokes on "a rainbow of laughter". At the top was white laughter, inspired by "the sheer joy of being alive". Yellow laughter was the currency of clowns and slapstick, and red the laughter of romance and love. "Then at the very bottom are the dark colours of satire and cynicism," he said. "They're good laughs, but at the same time you are dealing with mysterious dark forces."

He used it sparingly, but when he wanted he could be sharply satirical. "Isn't this marvellous, Mrs Thatcher? I'm talking and you're listening," he quipped from the stage of the London Palladium when the Conservative prime minister was sitting in the audience.

He was a natural on television and his shows ran throughout the 1960s and 1970s. He was often given his own Christmas Day special and was also a regular on *The Good Old Days*. It was broadcast from the City Varieties in Leeds and he was in his element in its re-creation of the atmosphere of the Victorian music hall.

Surprisingly, given the visual nature of much of his humour, he was also successful on radio and his shows ran for many years on Radio 2.

Yet his first love remained treading the boards and he was still touring at the age of 90 and was known to clock up 50,000 miles a year to appear around the country. In 1974 he earned a place in the *Guinness Book of Records* for the world's longest uninterrupted joke-telling session: 1,500 jokes in three and a half hours at a Liverpool theatre, working out at 7.14 "tpm" (titters per minute).

His marathon shows could run for five hours and even in old age he regularly broke the midnight curfew. Once Dodd started, he could not stop, a trait that did not always go down well with producers or theatre technicians, who complained that they were missing their last pint and the train home.

It delighted his audiences, however, and it became a tradition that as the witching hour approached, he would tell them: "Do you give in? Don't worry. I know where you all live and I'll follow you home and shout jokes through your letter box." His love of performing was such that his friend Bob Monkhouse once said that everything that happened off stage in Dodd's life was merely an interval.

Like many comedians dating back to Pagliacci, his carefree and jokey exterior concealed a complicated inner man. For 22 years he was engaged to Anita Boutin, a former nurse who devoted herself to his professional and personal welfare. He was heartbroken when she died of a brain tumour in 1977 at the age of 43, but he never convincingly explained why they did not marry. When he was asked by Anthony

Clare during a grilling on BBC Radio 4's *In the Psychiatrist's Chair*, the best he could come up with was that he had been "too busy".

He was subsequently involved in a long-term relationship with Anne Jones, a former Bluebell dancer who appeared in his shows and acted as his manager. They lived together in an 18th-century rambling mansion in Knotty Ash, where they married on March 9, 2018, two days before his death. She played the organ every Sunday in the church where as a boy he had sung in the choir, "until they found out where the noise was coming from". He remained a regular church-goer.

Although by temperament a private man, he was well liked by fellow comics and several of them, including Eric Sykes and Roy Hudd, appeared as character witnesses during the darkest episode of his life when he appeared at Liverpool Crown Court in 1989 charged with income-tax fraud.

He was accused of making "cash and carry" flights to the Isle of Man and Jersey, depositing money into 20 secret accounts and not paying the children from stage schools who played the Diddy Men in his shows.

He hated the personal revelations that emerged in his trial. Part of his defence was that the stress of attempting to become a father had led to his "misunderstanding" of his tax position and he visibly squirmed when Jones was cross-examined about the years they had unsuccessfully spent trying for a baby. In his shows he often sang a duet with his ventriloquist's dummy; it was as if he was singing a lullaby to the child he never had.

The court also heard that £336,000 had been found in cash, stashed in suitcases in his attic. Rather than an attempt to avoid tax, it was an excessive example of "putting something aside for a rainy day", a legacy of his father gambling much of the family income away and his mother battling to make ends meet. "What does a hundred thousand pounds in a suitcase feel like?" the judge asked him. "The notes are very light, m'lord," he replied.

After a three-week trial he was acquitted. The turning point in the case was widely held to have come when George Carman QC, defending him, told the jury, "Some accountants are comedians – but comedians are never accountants."

Dodd capitalised on the headlines his trial had brought with an eight-month run at the London Palladium and wove material mocking the tax authorities into his act, introducing himself as "Kenneth Arthur Dodd: singer, photographic playboy and failed accountant."

He was born in 1927 in Knotty Ash, which sounded like one of his surreal inventions but was a close-knit village, later suburb, on the outskirts of Liverpool. His parents, Arthur and Sarah Dodd, ran a coal merchant business and were keen amateur musicians, who performed in the pubs and clubs of Liverpool. He caught the entertainment bug early when he was given a Punch and Judy set as a child. A little later he acquired a ventriloquist's dummy and an instruction manual after responding to an advertisement in a comic that read: "Fool your teachers, amaze your friends – send 6d in stamps!" He named the dummy "Charlie Brown" and gave his first performance at the age of eight at the local orphanage. His father wrote the script and his fee was half a crown.

Even in childhood his comic eccentricities set him apart from his peers. He would walk backwards all the way home from school to see if it could be done. He then tried riding his bicycle with his eyes shut for the same reason. He hit a kerb and pitched over the handlebars, resulting in his protruding teeth, an invaluable comic asset that he claimed he insured for £10,000.

He won a scholarship to grammar school, where his headmaster instilled a lifelong intellectual curiosity by telling him: "You have not come here to be educated – you have come here to have your mind opened." The Second World War was being fought, however, and he left school at 14, first to help his father with his coal round and then in peacetime as a travelling salesman "on the knocker", going from door to door.

At the same time he appeared in local stage shows and dreamt of becoming an opera singer. His mother encouraged him to develop a burlesque act and he took to performing as "Professor Yaffle Chuckabutty, Operatic Tenor and Sausage Knotter", with a painted-on moustache and a battered old euphonium, which he couldn't play, but used as a prop "to keep my hands still".

His professional debut came in 1954 on the variety bill at the Empire Theatre, Nottingham, his name "just a little bit bigger than the printer's at the bottom of the bill".

At 26 years old he was a late starter, but the font size of his name grew rapidly on the northern variety circuit and by 1958 he was topping the bill in the summer season at Blackpool Opera House. His television debut came the next year and his first appearance at the London Palladium in 1965, when he stayed for 42 weeks. The record-breaking run was fuelled by his million-selling hit, *Tears*, which knocked the Rolling Stones's *(I Can't Get No) Satisfaction* from the top of the UK charts and stayed at No 1 for six weeks.

In another life he might have had a career as what he referred to as a "legitimate" actor. The playwright John Osborne called him "an incredible phenomenon of human invention and overwhelming energy" and once took the cast of a play he was directing at the Royal Court to see Dodd perform and learn from his stagecraft.

He played Malvolio in a production of Shakespeare's *Twelfth Night* at the Liverpool Playhouse in 1971 and, 25 years later, he appeared as Yorick in a flashback scene in Kenneth Branagh's film of *Hamlet*. Although he had no lines to speak, he was perfectly cast as the jester described by the Prince of Denmark as "a man of infinite jest".

His jesting earned him a knighthood for tickling the chuckle muscles of the nation. "Anger and despair and depression are the enemy of the joker," he said. "My job is to try and dispel those thoughts."

Sir Ken Dodd OBE, comedian and singer, was born on November 8, 1927. He died on March 11, 2018, aged 90

ROBIN DALTON

*Socialite, memoirist and spy who seldom said no when suitors proposed
and went on to become a literary agent and film producer*

"The reason I've had a good life," Robin Dalton told an interviewer
in 2017, "is that I never say no to anything."

She did not say no to the US and British servicemen who courted
her in her native Sydney during the Second World War. She certainly
did not say no to partying with the belle monde in post-war London,
and became a friend of John F Kennedy in the process. She seldom
said no when suitors proposed to her and was on occasion engaged to
more than one at once. Three of them she actually married.

When asked to spy for Thailand in the 1950s she once again
consented. And so it went on. In later life she forged a career for herself
as one of London's leading literary agents, with a dazzling list of
clients, before becoming (in her late sixties) a successful film producer
working with numerous big-name actors and directors.

A socialite blessed with prodigious energy, intelligence and zest
for life, Dalton lived a life rich enough comfortably to fill three
memoirs, and was still going strong in her nineties. Asked by Diana

Athill, her friend and fellow nonagenarian, whether she had trouble sleeping, she replied: "I rather enjoy not being able to sleep because I enjoy trying to remember all the people I've been to bed with."

Robin Ann Eakin was born in Sydney in 1920 and raised in a remarkable household in the city's bohemian district of Kings Cross.

Her father, a Presbyterian from Northern Ireland, was a doctor whose wealthier patients subsidised his treatment of prostitutes and criminals. Her mother was a Polish-Australian Jew who smoked 100 cigarettes a day and regularly invited strangers to stay. Dalton's father did not speak to his mother-in-law for 35 years despite living in the same house, telling his daughter: "I could not take my trousers off without turning round and finding your grandmother watching me."

Also inhabiting the house was a bevy of eccentric great aunts, fondly recalled in Dalton's 1965 memoir *Aunts Up the Cross*. "My Great Aunt Juliet was knocked over and killed by a bus when she was 85. The bus was travelling very slowly in the right direction and could hardly have been missed by anyone except Aunt Juliet," the book began.

An only child, Dalton was indulged and spoiled by the entire household, and grew up precocious. She wrote a fictitious book about her relations at the age of eight, had read most of Thomas Hardy by 12, and at 18 married John Spencer, an alcoholic barrister 13 years her senior who was serving in the army at the start of the Second World War.

The marriage lasted five months. Spencer routinely abused her, once tried to shoot her through the bathroom wall and hired a private detective to track her assignations with other men. He accused her of adultery. The divorce caused a scandal. "I knocked the war off the front page," Dalton quipped.

Unabashed, she became a secretary to an American supply chain commander for the Pacific region. "We went straight from working at US supply depots or driving a truck by day to the arms of pilots or sailors on leave by night," she wrote. "In five months of marriage I didn't learn what an orgasm was – it took the British Navy," she recalled. "I gathered two American fiancés, one engagement ring and was the cause of one divorce."

Dalton then fell for a British naval officer, David Mountbatten, the third Marquess of Milford Haven and great-great-grandson of Queen

Victoria. Their families disapproved of the match, so she employed subterfuge to persuade her father to let her go to Britain. She accepted a marriage proposal from a Scottish paratrooper of whom her father did approve, flew to London on one of the first post-war flights out of Australia, then shamelessly ditched her fiance and rejoined the marquess.

Despite the rationing and rubble, Dalton loved the capital. Supplementing her parental allowance with some freelance journalism, she mixed with artists, aristocrats and "quite a few kings, ex-kings and almost-kings".

The marquess was best man when his cousin, Philip Mountbatten, married Princess Elizabeth in 1947. Dalton was not invited to the ceremony, but she procured the first Decola (a self-loading record player) for him to give the royal couple as a wedding present.

More and diverse lovers followed – a dashing Swede, a gay ballet dancer. "There was never a time when I was not, actively, in love," she once said of her life. "I don't remember any of it being unrequited. One floated on a cloud of love affairs, more or less effortlessly gliding from one to another." Then she met Emmet Dalton, a handsome Irish doctor whom she married in 1953 and with whom she had two children – Lisa, now an artist, and Seamus, a doctor who works in Australia.

During their honeymoon in Cornwall she was asked by one of her "almost king" friends, Prince Chula of Thailand, to undertake anti-communist espionage work for his government while working in the guise of a press attaché at its London embassy. She learnt Thai at the School of Oriental and African Studies, toured the diplomatic cocktail circuit to glean information, and periodically visited Bangkok. "What went on taught me that every single crazy thing you see in a spy film or book is true," she said.

Her life as a spy ended abruptly when her second husband – the man whom she always described as the greatest love of her life – died from a heart condition at the age of 33, leaving her alone with two young children and no means of support. Friends rallied round. Chula offered to pay for Lisa's education, and Sir Steven Runciman, the historian, for Seamus's. Kennedy sent Lisa a beautiful coat, allegedly with banknotes stuffed in the pockets. Dalton moved with her children to a friend's dilapidated castle in Italy, then back to Australia, before returning to London where Runciman gave her the last 18 years of his lease on a huge house in St John's Wood.

Dalton set herself up as a literary agent in Covent Garden, and flourished. She acquired the likes of Joan Collins, Margaret Drabble, Arthur Miller, Iris Murdoch, Edna O'Brien, John Osborne, Ruth Prawer Jhabvala, Sonia Orwell (George's widow) and Tennessee Williams as clients.

She held parties for clients and publishers in her St John's Wood home and "they nearly all became my best friends", she said. "The secret of being a successful, though not necessarily good, literary agent is to have lots of energy and very few clients. You give them all your time and they think you're fantastic."

Another client was William Fairchild, an author and screenwriter with whom Dalton lived for nearly 30 years before they married in 1992. They were frequent visitors to Biarritz, where their friends included the actors Michael Blakemore, Tim Pigott-Smith and Michael Frayn and the broadcaster Clive James.

Dalton's switch to films came in the mid-1980s. Unable to sell the film rights for one of her client's books, *Madame Sousatzka* by Bernice Rubens, she thought: "I'm bloody well going to buy this myself." She did so, and produced the award-winning film with John Schlesinger as director and Shirley MacLaine, Peggy Ashcroft and Twiggy in starring roles.

Other films included *Emma's War* (1987) starring Miranda Otto and Lee Remick, *Country Life* (1994) starring Sam Neill, and Peter Carey's *Oscar and Lucinda* (1997) starring Cate Blanchett and Ralph Fiennes. She was later appointed a Member of the Order of Australia for "significant service to the film industry as a producer, literary agent and author, and as a mentor to emerging actors and writers".

Fairchild died in 2000. Neither that nor her advancing age slowed Dalton down, though she did rediscover her mother's Jewish faith. She wrote two more (albeit slim) books in her nineties. One was a memoir, *One Leg Over*, whose title allegedly referred to the difficulty of getting out of a bath when old. The other, *'Dead' is a 4-Letter Word*, poked fun at the concept of death and expressed the hope that she would have a "jolly" one.

"If you believe in reincarnation, I must have been pretty good in my last life," she said. "I'm terrified of what the next one will be. Haven't been so good in this one."

Robin Dalton, literary agent and spy, was born on December 22, 1920. She died of a stroke on July 8, 2022, aged 101

PADDY MACKLIN

Eccentric Cornish sailor whose free spirit led him to circumnavigate the world solo with little more than a school atlas, food and whisky

Paddy Macklin rarely emerged for breakfast without first smoking a joint. Yet on December 17, 2009, he set out from Falmouth, in Cornwall, determined to sail single-handedly and nonstop around the world in Tessa, his 27ft wooden, engineless yacht.

He had food for 600 days, a supply of whisky and other essentials, but no corporate support or high-tech gadgets, not even an emergency position-indicating beacon. "I wanted to recapture the spirit of true amateurism in sailing," he declared. His goal was to beat the 312-day record set by Sir Robin Knox-Johnston in 1969.

True to his calling Macklin navigated using a "perfectly good" 1950s Philip's school atlas. He declined to check the weather forecast and within days had hit a storm in the Bay of Biscay, where he was "thrown around like a rock in a washing machine". When he failed to contact his family by satellite phone, his one concession to modernity, they alerted the coastguard who were also unable to reach him. A Spanish aircraft was dispatched to fly over his last-known position but found nothing.

After hearing his name on BBC radio Macklin called his sister Miranda, explaining that he had not wanted the satellite phone to get wet. "He didn't realise we were all so worried," she said. "I have given him an almighty telling-off and told him never to do this to us again."

He had an even closer shave when a freighter almost ran him down near the Canary Islands, cutting across his bow less than 50ft away. "It wasn't actually that frightening because I was fast asleep," he said. "I eventually woke up and there were all these lights above me. And then he was gone."

A second big-ship encounter occurred in the South Atlantic, far from any shipping lanes, while Macklin was naked on deck as his freshly laundered clothes dried in the sun. He saw the culprit bearing down on him, grabbed some trousers and tried in vain to hail the offender. "I shone a searchlight on his bridge window, but got no response," he said, adding that he was only saved by making a dramatic change of course. "It was as if he really wanted to run me down."

Rounding the Cape of Good Hope he continued towards Australia, battling against high winds and heavy seas. "This was, after all, midwinter in the Roaring Forties, so nights were extremely long and days very short," he wrote in *Captain Bungle's Odyssey* (2014), a self-deprecatingly titled but gripping account of his voyage.

One night he encountered a ferocious storm. "The seas had become monstrous mountains 40-60ft high, huge tumbling breaks collapsing down their fronts," he wrote. As the blackness closed in, he wedged himself across the cabin, wrapped in bedding. "Sleep was out of the question. I just lay there and waited." There was no chance of rescue nor would he call for help, saying that he was "prepared to drown like a gentleman".

The "growling thrump" of the huge breaks meant that Tessa would inevitably go over. "The first knockdown was of course the most shocking," he said. "There was an almighty roar like an express train, then an explosive crash as the break hit the side of the boat. In a split second, Tessa was on her side, with the mast horizontal. Everything in the cabin that could fly flew fast as we were smashed sideways at high speed."

A series of rollovers followed that "were almost benign by comparison as they were relatively quiet". There was even a double rollover. "As Tessa righted herself . . . my first reaction was to shine the torch through the dome to check the mast," he wrote. "Phew. Still there. Losing the mast was my greatest fear, and although I could see other damage, mast and rig were still intact."

The next morning Macklin found that his solar panel was shattered into tiny pieces, equipment was strewn around the cabin and, worst of all, his food supplies were contaminated by seawater. "I finished trying to restore the cabin to a semblance of order, made a cup of tea, smoked a cigarette and wondered what to do," he recalled, noting that another storm would be along soon. "Apart from the fact that I was battered and exhausted, with toes like fat chipolatas, I was close to suffering from frostbite."

He contemplated putting into Tasmania, 450 miles away, but it dawned on him that he could reach New Zealand, where he had friends with a good slipway and a pressure washer. "After all, what was another 1,700 miles across the Tasman Sea in winter between old friends? Decision made."

Although Macklin's goal of completing a nonstop voyage around the world had now been jettisoned, he was determined to finish the journey. After four months' repair and recuperation he set sail again, heading round the tip of South America and across the Atlantic Ocean, returning to Falmouth and a champagne reception on May 12, 2011.

Along the way he had lost several teeth, broken a handful of ribs and suffered from severe loneliness. However, he had read a pile of books and smoked or otherwise consumed a sizeable quantity of recreational drugs. "I like being stoned and I miss being stoned," he said when explaining how he ran out just before entering Drake's Passage. "I mean, in Britain it's no longer a question of who does, but who doesn't. It's no big deal."

Patrick Noel Macklin was born in 1957. He was named after the travel writer Patrick Leigh Fermor, a friend of his mother, Shelagh Cooper (née Mulligan), who took part in the Tulip Rally with Pat Moss, Sir Stirling Moss's sister. His father was Lance Macklin (obituary, September 4, 2002), a brilliant racing driver who was involved in the sport's worst accident at Le Mans in 1955 in which 80 people were killed. "I think he would have been proud of what I did," Macklin said. "In fact, I had a little jar with some of his ashes, which I put overboard after Cape Horn."

There were other intrepid relations including his grandfather, Sir Noel Macklin, who designed the Invicta sports car in 1925 and gunboats in the war. His cousin Cristina was married to Taki Theodoracopulos, the Greek journalist who wrote admiringly about Macklin's odyssey in *The Spectator*: "A real Sir Galahad, like his dad, in that old-fashioned eccentric way of Englishmen before they became slaves and took orders from Brussels."

Macklin's parents divorced in 1963 and his father married Gill McComish, a New Zealander, and moved his children to her homeland. Paddy, who had been expelled from several English schools, failed to settle and after a couple of years was sent back to England and to a prep school that was "like a prison".

He continued to misbehave at Lancing College. On one occasion he was summoned to the headmaster's office but at the appointed hour he was nowhere to be seen and instead a stone came crashing through the window. "I couldn't wait to become a hippy," he explained.

Taking up plastering and decorating meant that whenever he saved a bit of cash he could travel, returning to work only when the money ran out. In what he called his "Trainspotting years" he lived in a squat in Clapham and developed a heroin habit. A great uncle bequeathed him a flat that he sold. He moved close to the sea, bought a yacht and taught himself to sail, on one occasion reaching North America. One day he read about a sailor who tried to beat Knox-Johnston's record but lost his mast off the coast of South Africa. Immediately he resolved that the record was his for the taking.

After returning from his odyssey the increasingly crapulous Macklin decided to continue with his ocean voyages, setting his eye on the North West Passage. But reality struck and he resumed plastering and decorating while living on the boat, where his days started increasingly slowly. He was unmarried and is survived by his mother and his sister.

He had one more brief moment of fame: after her divorce, his mother had married Sir Anthony Montague Brown, Winston Churchill's former private secretary, who in 2016 was confirmed as the father of the Archbishop of Canterbury, Justin Welby. Macklin had suspected as much and in 2013, when Welby's appointment was announced, broached the subject with Montague Brown, who was then in a care home. He was asked to arrange an introduction, but Montague Brown died before meeting the archbishop. "Let me put it this way: le coq was très sportif," he told *The Sunday Times* of his stepfather.

Looking back, Macklin was asked to reflect on what he had got out of his 17-month round-the-world trip. "Now that I'm a Cape Hornier, I can have an earring and toast the Queen with one foot on the table," he joked, adding more seriously that the biggest lesson he learnt was never to trust the lookouts on commercial shipping.

Paddy Macklin, sailor, was born on September 18, 1957. He died of cirrhosis of the liver on January 31, 2023, aged 65

MAJOR SIR MICHAEL PARKER

Pageant master extraordinaire, pyromaniac and 'accidental showman'
who was frequently obliged to apologise to the Queen

Queen Elizabeth II's Silver Jubilee was not Michael Parker's finest hour. The plan was to have a nationwide chain of 150 beacons, with the first, in Windsor Great Park, being lit by the Queen. It was 60ft high and so vast it had empty spaces inside it, into which Parker had stuffed all manner of pyrotechnics to make sure it lit in spectacular fashion. A Royal Signals major was on hand to press a detonator, once the Queen had ceremonially lit the "fuse" that would, live on television, wend its fizzing way along the ground towards the beacon.

Parker had not anticipated that a 20,000-strong crowd would turn up to watch. The throng was so great, the Queen's route to the beacon was blocked for an hour, by which time the Olympic torch that a boy scout was supposed to hand to the Queen had gone out – and he had started crying. The torch was hastily refuelled, but when the Queen lowered it to the fuse, the waiting major prematurely pressed the button and the bonfire, 60 yards away, burst into flames. The Queen watched the fuse meander towards the already burning beacon, turned to Parker, and said: "Can't think why you bothered to ask me."

"At that stage," Parker recalled in his drawling, officer's voice, "I had to say 'Your Majesty, everything that could possibly go wrong is going wrong' and then she smiled, turned to me and said 'Oh good, what fun'."

Parker, who produced pageants and performances for royalty and the nation for almost half a century, would delight in telling such stories of mishap and mayhem. Indeed he titled his memoir *It's All Going Terribly Wrong: The Accidental Showman*. In them he described the 320 epic events he produced over his career, with casts of thousands, including 26 Royal Tournaments, the Queen Mother's 100th birthday, and the VE and VJ Day celebrations. In the foreword, Sir Cameron Mackintosh wrote: "America may have given us PT Barnum and Florenz Ziegfeld, but Michael Parker in full military flood makes Andrew Lloyd Webber and me feel like wallflowers."

When celebrating the wedding of the Prince of Wales with fireworks in Hyde Park in 1981, the King's Troop Royal Horse Artillery drove their guns over the control cables, breaking many, so the pyrotechnics exploded in random order. This was probably the first occasion when a journalist reported that Parker had to say "sorry" to the Queen.

Although he would characterise himself as "the man most frequently obliged to apologise to the Queen", he was such a perfectionist that, most of the time, the odds were that only the monarch and he had noticed whatever misadventure had marred the occasion. No matter the splendour of the audience or the scale of the event, nothing appeared to daunt him; he would just murmur: "If it's not difficult, it's not worth doing."

No martyr to shyness, Parker's theatrical flair first came to notice when, as a subaltern in the Queen's Own Hussars, he staged a Samuel Beckett play in a disused aircraft hanger in Detmold, Germany. The sets he designed were so elaborate they could not possibly have withstood handling by military scene shifters. He overcame this difficulty by constructing a circular stage in four segments and, as rotation was out of the question on such a primitive site, the audience moved their chairs round to greet each act in turn.

Occasions on stage quickly became too small for his burgeoning imagination and gave no scope for the favourite features of his repertoire – fire and pyrotechnics. He was soon in great demand and an early high point was a portrayal of the destruction of the Spanish Armada, at midnight, on a small lake in the garden of an officers' mess in Germany. The night sky was lit for miles around and the high and would-be mighty of the British Army of the Rhine greatly enjoyed it. Dawn revealed that not all had gone exactly to plan. Most of the small canvas assault craft used as hulls for the men o' war had burnt to the waterline.

Regimental funds were hastily tapped to provide replacements in case a crossing of the Weser, in either direction, might be required.

Parker nevertheless went on to produce the Berlin Military Tattoo several times and he remained associated with the event until the last one in 1992. His success there led to his becoming producer of the Royal Tournament from 1974 until the final performance in 1999 and of many other events, at home and abroad, that called for his talent for organising large numbers of people to do something to which they were completely unaccustomed in a short time.

When confronted by an implacably difficult personality he would say: "All right, we'll compromise, we'll do it my way." Somehow, this formula always worked. How else could a hundred sailors be persuaded to don straw hats and dance the hornpipe at the Royal Tournament, or for that matter a bagpipe player do a "death slide" from 100ft?

Never reluctant to share his views, Parker was critical of the Household Division for staging events on Horse Guards Parade, as he put it, "the wrong way round" with the sovereign appearing for her birthday parade from the back. He argued that the white façade of Horse Guards provided the perfect background and – with their backs to it – the Guards would face Her Majesty to greet her with a royal salute.

Although unsuccessful over the Queen's birthday parade, he realised his dream to mark the 100th birthday of the Queen Mother in 2000 – and proved his point even if the pageant did come close to chaos when camels, seeing sand that had been laid down for them to walk over on Birdcage Walk, chose to lie down on it instead. The elephant Parker was riding, meanwhile, reared up when the Red Arrows flew overhead. "When they did their whoosh past, Maureen my elephant said 'f*** this' and went up on her hind legs," he recalled. "I only just managed to cling on."

When Her Majesty's much trumpeted giant birthday cake failed to inflate, at the very last moment, Parker's decision to allow the child performers to go ahead – without the cake – demonstrated his true flair. The children rose to the occasion with artistic passion, producing the cake in the imagination of the audience.

His mission, he declared, was always to "ginger up" events that would otherwise be "dreary", even if that meant they ended up "a complete Horlicks". That might include massed harps, the recreation of the siege of Moscow (involving walls of flame, of course), and commemorating St Patrick's Day at the Irish Guards barracks by hiring snakes which duly escaped – as did a tarantula he had hired for another military event, leading to soldiers running around in panic.

Michael John Parker was the son of Vera Wilkins (née Parker) and Sydney Wilkins, an army captain. His home life was "miserable" and he changed his name to Parker by deed poll after his parents' separation. He was educated at Hereford Cathedral School and RMA Sandhurst, from where he was commissioned into the Queen's Own Hussars in 1961. "The army became my first real family," he reflected. His affection for military life never faltered, for his regiment in particular, but he was unable to resist the less serious side. One of his publications was The Awful Troop Leaders' Gunnery Crib.

After leaving the regular army in 1971 – explaining that he had no ambition to become a general "because they are all old and smelly" – he continued an attachment to his regiment in the Territorial Army.

He was a perfectionist at home as well as in his work. A bon viveur and an accomplished cook, his guests knew to expect fine food and wine. His idealist approach to interior decorating and gardening led to his designing and painting his own wallpaper, and allowing in his garden only blue and yellow flowers – the regimental colours of the Queen's Own Hussars.

Cheerfully describing himself as a "pyromaniac", he seemed to be at his happiest when carrying a jerry can full of kerosene. "Controlled fire is very exciting," he would say. His most ambitious plan, to turn the Thames into a "river of fire" to mark the millennium, was, however, thwarted. "I had planned to use 28 barges; in the end they used eight or nine, and turned it into a river of splodges."

For a long time, much as he enjoyed the company of women, he remained "too busy to marry", working into the night, painting sets and inventing wild stunts involving fireworks because "I just love blowing things up".

He eventually did marry in 2005. Emma Gilroy had been his long-serving PA, the two having met at an event at the Royal Albert Hall in 1991. When asked what living with such a force of nature was like, Lady Parker replied: "No two days were the same."

Major Sir Michael Parker KCVO, CBE, producer of royal and national spectaculars, was born on September 21, 1941. He died from a heart condition on November 28, 2022, aged 81

IAN HAMILTON

---•---

Scottish lawyer whose gang of four sensationally stole the Stone of Destiny from under the coronation throne in Westminster Abbey

In 1296, the Stone of Destiny was looted from Scone Abbey, near Perth, by English forces led by Edward I. It was taken to Westminster Abbey and fitted inside the wooden throne upon which most subsequent English and British monarchs have been crowned. Despite promises that it would be returned, including in the 1328 Treaty of Northampton, the stone lay undisturbed for six and a half centuries until four Scottish students, led by Ian Hamilton, decided to bring it back.

At about 6am on Christmas Day 1950, Hamilton and his friends Alan Stuart, Kay Matheson and Gavin Vernon used a crowbar to break into the abbey. They retrieved the stone from inside the coronation chair, only for it to crash to the floor and break in two. While loading the chunks into their borrowed Ford Anglia, they were approached by a policeman who allowed them to carry on after Hamilton and Matheson fell into an embrace, pretending to be lovers.

A manhunt was soon under way, with roadblocks across the

Cheviot Hills closing the Scottish border for the first time in centuries. While the English police expressed a keen interest in every northbound car, their Scottish counterparts took a different approach. "Aye," one said, "sure we're looking for them, but no' so damned hard that we'll find them." Hamilton had in fact driven southeastwards and buried the stone in a wood near Rochester in Kent. He then travelled to his parents' home in Scotland. "I've lost my watch – in Westminster Abbey," was his opening line. "Was it you?" exclaimed his mother in delight. He later called into a central London police station to ask if the watch had been retrieved, but was given short shrift. He hoped that the Earl of Mansfield, owner of Scone Palace, would take the stone. As he was ushered in, Mansfield said: "Don't tell me your name, it is better that I shouldn't know it."

After hearing him out, the peer announced that regrettably he could not get involved. Hamilton begged him not to reveal his description to the police. "Good heavens," snapped his lordship. "Do you think I am an Argyll to betray a fellow Scotsman? I shall give them no description."

A few weeks later Hamilton and his colleagues retrieved the 152kg (336lb) stone and drove it to Scotland. As they crossed the border, "we pulled back the coat that covered the stone, and each poured out a little of the wine of the country on to it, signifying its return to the Celtic people". He arranged for it to be repaired by a Glasgow builder called Bertie Gray but, fearing a change in public opinion, then had it wrapped in a saltire and left in the ruins of Arbroath Abbey, where the 1320 declaration had been signed asking the Pope to recognise Scottish independence.

It was returned to Westminster Abbey in February 1952. No charges were brought against the four Scots for fear of making them martyrs, though Sir Hartley Shawcross, the attorney-general, told MPs: "The clandestine removal of the stone from Westminster Abbey, and the manifest disregard for the sanctity of the abbey, were vulgar acts of vandalism which have caused great distress and offence both in England and Scotland." Nevertheless, Hamilton, Stuart (obituary, June 24, 2019), Matheson (obituary July 12, 2013) and Vernon (obituary April 2, 2004) had put their cause on the political agenda.

In 1996 John Major, the prime minister, said the stone was to be returned to Scotland on St Andrew's Day, though it would still be used in London for coronations. Hamilton was unimpressed, declaring it a "cheap election trick". The stone was placed in Edinburgh Castle and, after being moved to Westminster Abbey for the coronation of Charles III, it was agreed it should head to a museum in Perth.

Ian Robertson Hamilton was born in Paisley, west of Glasgow, in 1925, the son of Martha (née Robertson), who recounted Scottish folklore tales to her son, and John Hamilton, a tailor who "measured his customers and pinned patterns and bits of cloth to them until he had built up a suit as enduring as a Clyde-built ship". He was from a long line of agitators: a criminal ancestor demanded to be hanged on a silk rope rather than a hemp one, while the military career of his grandmother's great-uncle Tom almost came to an end when he called publicly for his commanding officer to be prosecuted for cowardice.

On Sundays, Hamilton listened to sermons at the kirk. "Gradually, it dawned on me that they were a load of rubbish," he wrote, adding: "Fornication is fun, despite what ministers say." He was educated at the John Neilson Institute, a fee-paying school in Paisley that "kept me from meeting poorer children". During a wartime visit by George VI he was instructed to join fellow pupils cheering along the route but instead "got on my bike and went home". His absence was noticed and he was hauled up before the entire school.

Wanting to fly, he tried to join the RAF in 1943 but was too young. He finally signed up in 1945, serving as a flight mechanic and justifying his presence by explaining that "England is my favourite foreign country". He read law at the University of Glasgow at a time of growing dissatisfaction, with two million Scots signing the Scottish Covenant petition demanding home rule.

A year after publishing *No Stone Unturned* (1952), one of several books about the Stone of Destiny incident, he was admitted to the bar. However, he refused to swear allegiance to Queen Elizabeth II, insisting that she was merely Queen Elizabeth and the use of the regnal number was in breach of the 1707 Act of Union because Elizabeth I had been queen of England and not Scotland.

A court case in which he was joined by John MacCormick, rector of the University of Glasgow, ruled against them, saying the monarch's title was the sole prerogative of the sovereign. Winston Churchill weighed in, suggesting the sovereign should use whichever of the Scottish or English number was higher, though when Hamilton took silk in 1980 he simply swore allegiance to Queen Elizabeth.

After a "misspent youth" that included "a holiday in Holland as the guest of a glorious woman, the first of many with whom I have been endlessly in love", he met Sheila Fenwick, a domestic science teacher from Sunderland. They married in 1954 and had three children. The marriage was dissolved because "paradoxically, but not perhaps surprisingly, Sheila got fed up with my antics".

In 1973, while on a canoeing trip across Scotland, he capsized on the Falls of Lora, near Oban. Swimming ashore, he was met by Jeanette Stewart, whose family were hoteliers in Argyll. They married the following year and she also survives him with their son, Stewart, who works in the film industry.

Meanwhile, Hamilton had set up Castle Wynd Printers, publishing four paperback volumes of poetry by Hugh MacDiarmid, a key nationalist figure who confessed to having contemplated stealing the stone himself. Over the years Hamilton was also a bus driver, market gardener, playwright and curator at JM Barrie's birthplace in Kirriemuir, Angus.

In a case of gamekeeper-turned-poacher, he was appointed a crown prosecutor in Scotland in 1964. Yet before long he had become a state advocate to the Zambian government. He retired from legal practice in 1967 to work for the National Trust in Scotland and to farm in Argyll, but after seven years returned to the law. Dismayed at the outcome of the 1979 Scottish devolution referendum, he emigrated to Canada. Eighteen months later he was back in Scotland, declaring that Canada was "too boring".

As a member of the SNP he continued to rage against what he saw as English nationalists' rule over Scotland, writing in *The Sun* in 1993 to call "for a campaign of civil disobedience against the Westminster government".

Some years later Hamilton had a cameo role in *Stone of Destiny* (2008), a charming film about the famous affair in which he was played by Charlie Cox. "It was an absolutely splendid adventure," he said, insisting that he had no regrets about his role in the audacious heist. He also enjoyed quoting an ancient Gaelic saying about the stone, which in English reads: "Unless the fates shall faithless prove and prophet's voice be vain; Where e'er this sacred stone is found, the Scottish race shall reign."

Ian Hamilton KC, lawyer and campaigner, was born on September 13, 1925. He died on October 3, 2022, aged 97

DAME VIVIENNE WESTWOOD

———————●———————

Eccentric and iconoclastic British fashion designer who helped to start a
punk revolution and changed the way women dress

Vivienne Westwood did not feel pretty as a child, but while roaming a wood near her family home in Derbyshire she dreamt of becoming a beautiful tree fairy.

"I daydreamed that I would be walking in this wood and I would have this little house under these tree roots. I would have this fantastic dress and just come upon one or two little boys that I knew and they would just really be impressed by this dress. I always had this idea that some day I could make myself better."

She did. As fashion designer, revolutionary, iconoclast and emblem of English eccentricity she essayed a career that started by creating the look of the punk subculture of the mid-Seventies and ended with her moving into the fashion mainstream.

She may have come to fashion design at the comparatively late age of 33 but made an immediate and shocking impact as one of the chief progenitors of punk fashion.

To realise her original vision of "a rock'n'roller who was also an urban guerrilla", Westwood produced an aesthetic of ripped "bondage" trousers held together by safety pins, "Tits T-shirts", spiked dog collars, moth-eaten mohair jumpers and swastikas. As Westwood put it in a polite and considered voice that never lost its Derbyshire inflection, "We were just saying to the older generation we don't accept your taboos and your values and you're all fascists."

Thus attired, the band the Sex Pistols and their inner circle were in effect Westwood's first fashion show as they spread anarchy in the UK, snarling, pogoing, gobbing and generally disporting themselves to the outrage of Middle England. Disenfranchised youths wore her designs or made their own versions in homage.

Westwood was politically motivated from the start. "It was the idea that the world was so mismanaged that we hated the older generation because they weren't doing anything about it."

In the Seventies, at the height of her notoriety, Westwood took her creative direction from her then romantic and business partner, Malcolm McLaren (obituary, April 9, 2010), manager of the Sex Pistols. Yet when McLaren abandoned her and their business to pursue the anarchist subcultures of New York, Westwood came into her own, developing her skills as a seamstress to become a world leader in fashion. Even then Westwood never stopped feeling like an outsider.

A voracious reader and lover of history, the liberated Westwood became increasingly preoccupied with refashioning past cultures in modern times, exemplified by the Victorian corset and crinoline. It was not to be worn as an undergarment but as outerwear, translating it from a symbol of female repression to its antipode.

In an age when female fashion empowerment was exemplified by the shoulder pads worn by Joan Collins in *Dynasty*, Westwood liberated the corset as part of the dress that became known as the "mini-crini" in 1985. The corset was combined with a miniature and far sexier version of the Victorian structured petticoat.

Jasper Conran said: "Vivienne's effect on other designers has been rather like a laxative: Vivienne does and others follow." From Westwood's corset came Jean Paul Gaultier's black satin conical bra for Madonna's Blond Ambition tour and the now-ubiquitous crop top.

She went on to develop a more recognisably British style, incorporating traditional indigenous fabrics into her repertoire, such as tweeds, tartans and Argyll knitwear in witty reimaginings.

The idea for her celebrated Harris tweed collection in the autumn of 1987 was inspired by "a little girl I saw on the Tube one day. She couldn't have been more than 14. She had a little plaited bun, a Harris tweed jacket and a bag with a pair of ballet shoes in it. She looked so cool and composed standing there," said Westwood, who herself was instantly recognisable for her apricot-coloured wispy curls piled atop a whitened face while wearing her avant-garde creations.

Under the umbrella of her eponymous brand, she developed the semi-couture line Gold Label, a ready-to-wear line Red Label, Vivienne Westwood Man and the diffusion line Anglomania. When the model Naomi Campbell toppled over in a pair of purple mock-croc platforms at a Westwood show in 1993, the fact that it greatly boosted the model's career and Westwood's renegade brand spoke volumes.

"I think women can be icons of beauty, hourglasses of femininity teetering along on high heels and everything," Westwood said.

Westwood's special brand of patriotic iconoclasm earned her the sobriquet "the alternative Queen Mother". She revelled in the irony when she visited Buckingham Palace in 1992 to be appointed OBE. She caused a sensation when posing for the paparazzi outside the gates of the palace as she spun around in her skirt without underwear.

"I wished to show off my outfit by twirling the skirt. It did not occur to me that, as the photographers were practically on their knees, the result would be more glamorous than I expected," she recalled. "I have heard that the picture amused the Queen." She was advanced to a damehood in 2006.

Vivienne Isabel Swire was born in Tintwistle near Glossop, Derbyshire, in 1941, the eldest of three children to Gordon Swire, who was descended from a long line of shoemakers, and Dora (née Ball). Her parents ran a greengrocer and post office in the town.

The child would spend long hours reading by the warmth of the range as her mother cooked while exclaiming of her daughter to no one in particular: "Oh, she's in her glory."

It was an idyllic childhood in the Peak District in which her happiest times were spent climbing and jumping out of trees.

"I wanted to be a hero and saw no reason why I couldn't be one," she recalled. Vivienne first learnt to be a seamstress at the knee of her mother, who made clothes for the family. Bright enough to attend Glossop Grammar School, she was making tailored suits by 16.

A year later, Vivienne's parents moved to Harrow, northwest London, to become postmasters. Westwood was unhappy at her new London school because she felt self-conscious about her Derbyshire accent. Tall and striking with long, dark hair, she had a very particular but conventional dressing style.

After school, she embarked on a silversmithing course, but it was short-lived because she was more interested in earning a wage. She learnt to type and found work as a secretary.

The green-eyed Westwood's favourite pastime was rock'n'roll dancing, for which she made her own dresses and padded her bras to ape the glamorous and voluptuous look sported by stars of the late Fifties such as Marilyn Monroe and Sophia Loren. In later years, Westwood's clothes would make women look sexy and curvaceous. "Fashion is about sex," she said.

It was while jiving in late 1961 that she met Derek Westwood, an accomplished dancer and tool shop apprentice. In 1962 the pair were married and they moved to a house on the same street as her parents. A year later she gave birth to Ben Westwood (today a soft-porn photographer) and took on a teaching position at a primary school in Willesden, where she felt a kindred spirit with the "naughty ones", who were often from the poorest families, and would take them on camping weekends.

Her husband was devoted to her but a life driven by convention left Westwood feeling claustrophobic and unfulfilled. In 1965 she left Derek despite his pleadings because "I was not learning from staying with him". A few months later, she moved into a squat with her brother and met a student called Malcolm McLaren, who was also living there.

He was 19 and known to his contemporaries as "Talcy-Malcy" on account of the talcum powder he applied to his head in an attempt to disguise his red hair. She struck up an unlikely friendship with McLaren that led to her taking his virginity.

Westwood became pregnant in early 1967. McLaren obtained money from his grandmother to procure what would still have been an illegal abortion, but on the way there Westwood had a change of heart and spent the money on a coat from Bond Street. She and

McLaren set up home in south London.

McLaren was angry with the world and his lot in life, having been abandoned by his parents at an early age. He enrolled at art school, evangelical about art's political power and obsessed with cult fashions. A natural svengali, he encouraged her to supplement their meagre income, a composite of state benefits and student grants, by designing jewellery and selling it on a stall in Portobello Road market.

"I latched on to Malcolm as someone who opened doors for me," she recalled. "I mean, he seemed to know everything I needed at the time."

He also advised her to abandon her "dolly-bird" look and don the uniform that was to remain a recurring Westwood motif. Five years later, again on his advice, Westwood took a razor to her hair, dyed it flame-red and created a style that would not only be popularised by David Bowie but would also become the hallmark of punk.

In November 1967 Westwood gave birth to Joseph Ferdinand Corré (co-founder of Agent Provocateur in 1994). McLaren did not take easily to fatherhood and refused either to be present at the birth or for the child to later call him "Dad".

For the next decade, father and mother were intermittently together. Money was so scarce that at times Westwood was forced to scavenge Clapham Common for food and pack the children off to boarding schools with no intention of paying the bills. When her sons were aged 13 and 9, she ordered them to cycle to Devon to visit their grandparents, sleeping in a tent on the way. When Ben arrived home on Mother's Day and gave her some daffodils, Westwood threw them away in front of him and told him that Mother's Day was a load of "bollocks".

By 1971, after McLaren had graduated from art school, they scraped together enough cash to take over the shop floor of 430 Kings Road in what was then still an affordable and bohemian Chelsea.

The Westwood-McLaren partnership first traded under the name Let It Rock and sold an eclectic mix of Fifties vinyl, memorabilia and clothing that had either taken their fancy from market rummaging or that Westwood had copied and run up on her sewing machine. Signature pieces were drainpipe trousers and brothel-creeper shoes. Despite it being the heyday of the hippy chic popularised by Ossie

Clark, this was a shrine bravely devoted to a world of bubble-gum popping youth fashions and musical tastes of the late 1950s. The shop found an instant niche, and by 1973 it had become cool enough to supply the wardrobe for Ringo Starr in *That'll Be the Day*.

The shop would have four reincarnations: in 1972 it was renamed (in tribute to James Dean) Too Fast to Live, Too Young to Die, then Sex, in 1974, to taunt a prudish public with its sale of fetish gear. Westwood, dressed in the garb that adorned the rails, would police the shop like a dominatrix, ordering customers to leave if they so much as raised an eyebrow at what was on sale. Her equally unconventional shop assistant was Jordan Mooney (obituary, page 260).

In 1976 the shop became Seditionaries in response to her and McLaren being sued for sedition for the anti-royalist designs that featured the Queen's face. In 1981 the shop was finally renamed Worlds End – a name that remains today.

In 1976 McLaren had taken on the management of the Sex Pistols. While the group were brilliant publicists for the shop, his interest in them indicated his mind was straying from his ventures with Westwood.

His absence gave her an opportunity to take centre stage. She put their teenage son, Joe, in charge of her fledgling fashion business and in 1981 she created her first collection for the autumn/winter of London Fashion Week. Westwood had always slaked her thirst for knowledge by lapping up art and literature, and she called the collection Pirate in reference to her buccaneering through history to plunder inspiration from dandy highwaymen, French revolutionaries and the traditional costumes of Native Americans. The collection would greatly influence young British designers including John Galliano and Alexander McQueen and help to fire up a movement that would put British fashion on the global map.

The collection inspired the look of New Romantic bands such as Spandau Ballet and Adam and the Ants. She had a show the next year in Paris, the first British designer to do so since Mary Quant in 1963. Lady McAlpine, whose husband was a Conservative Party treasurer, was an early patron and earned particular compliments from Margaret Thatcher when she turned up in Downing Street in a Westwood creation.

Buoyed by her growing profile, Westwood opened a second shop called Nostalgia of Mud on St Christopher's Place near Bond Street. However, her early fame did not lead to financial success and Westwood was struggling with bills: she was often forced to pay her employees in clothes.

By 1984 the business was on the brink of bankruptcy as the second shop was forced to close and McLaren finally left to pursue his musical interests in New York. They had been a couple off and on for nearly 20 years and McLaren had often been verbally and physically abusive. He did not give her the credit she deserved for creating the look of punk, referring to her as "my seamstress". He had, however, given her a parting gift of encouraging her to start a fashion business in her name in their last years together.

At about this time Westwood met Carlo D'Amario, an Italian businessman who had been impressed by her work and amazed by her lack of cash. He saw in Westwood a business opportunity, bought 30 per cent of the company and became managing director. He also became her lover.

By 1984 the romantic union between Westwood and D'Amario had ended, although he continued in his position at the helm of an ever-expanding and now international brand. In 1990 Westwood had been appointed professor of fashion at the Vienna Academy of Applied Arts.

It was an important appointment not only because it vindicated her creative achievement, something that Britain only later did through two exhibitions of her work – first in 2000 at the Museum of London and then in a retrospective at the V&A in 2004 – but because it was through this that she met her future husband, Andreas Kronthaler. Westwood, who had been largely single since the final break-up with McLaren nearly a decade before, married the student 25 years her junior in 1993.

For all the opulence of her clothes, Westwood lived an unpretentious life outside fashion that was remarkable for its lack of extravagance. Despite owning the considerable part of a business that had a multimillion-pound annual turnover, she lived with Kronthaler for several years in a former council flat in Clapham because it was convenient for cycling to and from her studios in Battersea. She did not own a mobile phone or read newspapers, and cadged other people's cigarettes. She could quote Bertrand Russell effortlessly.

Westwood did not retire. By 2015 she was reported to have 12 retail outlets in the UK and 63 worldwide and had plans to open big outlets in Manhattan and Paris. Some commentators wondered how she could square her environmental and "anti-fast fashion" credentials when she was increasingly growing her global empire and moving into more affordable retail. When she appeared in a feature-length documentary about her life and work, *Vivienne Westwood: Punk, Icon, Activist*, in 2018, she was noticeably more prickly than her hitherto charming persona, but the film demonstrated her enduring appeal. Her estimated personal wealth was $185 million and in recent years she was the largest donor to the Green Party.

Westwood said using her platform to campaign for the causes she cared about was part of the same thread that had motivated her and McLaren to shock Britain in the Seventies. "What I'm doing now is still punk," she said. "It's still about shouting about injustice and making people think, even if it's uncomfortable. I'll always be a punk in that sense."

Dame Vivienne Westwood, fashion designer, was born on April 8, 1941. She died on December 29, 2022, aged 81

ACKNOWLEDGEMENTS

In no particular order, because *Times* obituaries are unsigned, I would like to thank the following writers: Tom Dart, Tim Bullamore, Nigel Williamson, Allan Mallinson, Damian Arnold, James Owen, Martin Fletcher, Ivo Tennant, Tom Whipple, Valerie Grove, Walter Ellis, Chris Bowlby, Bill Kay, Bess Twiston-Davies, Dennis Kavanagh and Anna Temkin, who is also the deputy obits editor of *The Times*. I am also grateful to Sara Rumens, the features picture editor for *The Times*, and the editorial team at HarperCollins: Evangeline Sellers, Harley Griffiths, Kevin Robbins and Rachel Weaver. Because obits are sometimes part prepared in advance, as works in progress, I would also like to thank my predecessors as obits editor of *The Times*, Ian Brunskill and Simon Pearson. Finally I would like to thank John Witherow for giving me this strange yet endlessly fascinating job.

Nigel Farndale

PHOTO CREDITS

Copyright for some photographs in this volume belongs to the family of the photograph's subject. HarperCollins would like to thank all those who have given permission for their photographs to appear in this volume. Every effort has been made to contact all individuals whose photographs are contained within this volume; if anyone has been overlooked, please contact HarperCollins.

Front cover: Jillian Edelstein, Camera Press London

Back cover (left to right): James Gifford-Mead / Alamy Stock Photo, Ian Bradshaw / Shutterstock, David Levenson / Shutterstock

Sidney Alford, Roland Alford

Keith van Anderson, courtesy of the family

April Ashley, Sidney Beadwell / Times Newspapers

Diana Athill, David Bebber / Times Newspapers

Naim Attallah, Times Newspapers

Eve Babitz, Paul Harris / Getty Images

Marquess of Bath, courtesy of the family

Igor and Grichka Bogdanoff, Niviere / Sipa / Shutterstock

Christopher Booker, Warhurst / Daily Mail/Shutterstock

Charles Burnett III, PA Images / Alamy Stock Photo

Raymond Butt, courtesy of the family

Paul Callan, Wharton / Times Newspapers

Professor James Campbell, courtesy of the family

Beatrice de Cardi, Gerrard 'Bill' Warhurst / Times Newspapers

Rupert Chetwynd, Aaron Chetwynd

Lady Chitty, Gill Allen / Times Newspapers

Stuart Christie, Nick Bradshaw / Times Newspapers

Richard Cole, Evening Standard / Stringer

Nancie Colling, Bowls International

James Crowden, Local World Newspapers

Robin Dalton, Chris Barham / ANL / Shutterstock

Wilfred De'Ath, Albanpix / Shutterstock

Lord Denham, Michael Ward / Times Newspapers

Ken Dodd, John Curtis / Shutterstock

Betty Dodson, Getty Images Entertainment

Lee Everett, Monty Fresco / ANL / Shutterstock

Peter Farrer, courtesy of the family

Fenella Fielding, ANL / Shutterstock

Baron Clement von Franckenstein, WENN Rights Ltd / Alamy Stock Photo

Zsa Zsa Gábor, John Dee / Shutterstock

Princess Emma Galitzine, ANL / Shutterstock

Fred Hamblin, Linda Turner

Ian Hamilton, The Times / News Licensing, Keystone / Stringer

Sir Jeremiah Harman, courtesy of the family

Hannah Hauxwell, ITV / Shutterstock

Celia Hensman, James Runcie

Ruaraidh Hilleary, courtesy of the family

Baroness Howe of Idlicote, PA Images / Alamy Stock Photo

Nexhmije Hoxha, Wikimedia Commons

Dickie Jeeps, PA Images / Alamy Stock Photo

Katherine Johnson, AP / Shutterstock

Rev David Johnson, courtesy of the family

Stephen Joyce, Science History Images / Alamy Stock Photo

Irving Kanarek, Bettmann / Getty Images

Ted Knight, Daily Mail / Shutterstock

Greg Lake, Dave Gerrard / Times Newspapers

Sam Leach, courtesy of the family

Gordon Liddy, ITV / Shutterstock

John Lucas, courtesy of the family

Richard Luckett, courtesy of the family

Paddy Macklin, Sabine Kelly / Captain Bungle's Odyssey by Paddy Macklin

Theodora di Marco, courtesy of the family

'Magic Alex' Mardas, Trinity Mirror / Mirrorpix / Alamy Stock Photo

John McAfee, Larry Marano / Shutterstock

Jordan Mooney, Ray Stevenson

Jan Morris, David Levenson / Shutterstock

Nicholas Mosley, Duncan Baxter / Times Newspapers

Keith Murdoch, Michael Brennan / Evening News / Shutterstock

James Wharram, courtesy of the family

Ardeshir Zahedi, CHARLES W HARRITY / AP / Shutterstock

Maurizio 'Zanza' Zanfanti, Pasquale Bova / Ropi / ROPI via ZUMA Press / Shutterstock